KEEPING PACE

KEEPING PACE
U.S. Policies and Global Economic Change

Edited by
JOHN YOCHELSON

A Center for Strategic and International Studies Book

BALLINGER PUBLISHING COMPANY
Cambridge, Massachusetts
A Subsidiary of Harper & Row, Publishers, Inc.

International Standard Book Number: 0-88730-252-1

Library of Congress Catalog Card Number: 88-10585

Printed in the United States of America

Library of Congress Cataloging-in-Publication Data

Keeping pace : U.S. policies and global economic change / edited by
 John Yochelson.
      p. cm.
   "A Center for Strategic and International Studies book."
   Includes index.
   ISBN 0-88730-252-1
   1. United States—Foreign economic relations. 2. Technological
innovations. 3. Economic development. 4. International finance.
5. International trade. I. Yochelson, John N.
HF1455.K424 1988
337.73—dc19   88-10585
                                                        CIP

CONTENTS

FOREWORD

The world economy of the 1990s will scarcely resemble the one in which this nation's current leaders have grown up. Most of those who will hold key responsibilities during the next decade, in both the public and the private sectors, were educated at a time when U.S. eocnomic and technological preeminence was taken for granted.

Now, largley as a result of the successes of U.S. policy since 1945, a number of the once unshakeable assumptions regarding America's position in the world economy are open to question. Even though the U.S. economy remains the world's most powerful, rapid gains elsewhere have significantly closed the gap. The U.S. lead in technological innovation has been narrowed and in some fields surpassed, and the dollar's future as the world's dominant currency looks less certain than it did a decade ago. Still, the United States is called upon to provide the vision and political energy to sustain global prosperity.

The challenges facing America's leaders in the years ahead are formidable. The revolution in information technology has not only integrated world markets but has sharply reduced decisionmaking time. Economic power promises to shift increasingly to the industries and nations that succeed in applying new technologies. The sharpening of competitive pressure has strained the multilateral institutions that have provided a foundation for U.S. international policies.

These challenges prompted the Center for Strategic and International Studies to organize a study group to examine the forces of

ix

change at work in the world economy and their implications for U.S. leadership. I had the pleasure of chairing this study group, whose deliberations began in Stowe, Vermont, during the summer of 1986 and have continued until the present.

The bipartisan CSIS study group brought together outstanding representatives from industry, labor, government, and the policy research community. We divided into three task forces: Robert Frederick, then-president of RCA, chaired a group on West-West relations; a task force on North-South issues was led by former Deputy U.S. Trade Representative William Walker and Westinghouse chairman John Marous; and Frank Carlucci, then-president of Sears World Trade, chaired our group on policy toward the Soviet bloc and China.

This book assembles the excellent working papers that served as a basis for discussion in our task forces meetings and plenary sessions. Some of these papers reflect sharply differing views over the definition and pursuit of U.S. interests, but all attempt to come to grips with the fundamental questions that must be addressed if the United States is to adjust to a new technological era while maintaining global leadership.

These papers, and the policy recommendations that will eventually flow from them, will be shared with the counterpart groups in Canada, Europe, and Japan that make up the Quadrangular Forum—a private collaborative effort that assesses the major challenges facing the industrial democracies. Our results will also be shared with the next U.S. administration.

The Center and the director of this project, John Yochelson, deserve the thanks of all of us for this timely and important effort.

—William E. Brock
Former Secretary of Labor and
U.S. Trade Representative

ACKNOWLEDGMENTS

This volume reflects not only the leadership of Senator William Brock and the insights of a superb group of contributors but the professionalism of outstanding colleagues at the Center for Strategic and International Studies.

Margaret Trimble, principal research assistant for this project, did an extraordinary job working with the authors and their manuscripts. Her diligence, energy, and creativity were indispensable. Her successor, Richard Schwartz, performed at the same high level in the final stages of this project.

INTRODUCTION

Although corporate America has been heavily criticized in recent years for its excessive focus on the short term, the pull of the immediate is accepted as all but inevitable in official U.S. economic policymaking. The pressures that limit policy horizons in Washington are clearly formidable. They stem from the two-year cycle of national elections, the diffusion of power in Congress as well as the executive branch, and the perennial crowding of agendas at the senior levels. The pull of the immediate is further reinforced by the sheer pace of economic change both domestically and internationally. A policy setting marked by sweeping innovation and unprecedented mobility of resources scarcely promotes the development of a long view.

The gearing of U.S. policy to the short term may be unavoidable, but its costs are nonetheless real. Three, in particular, stand out. First, the slant toward the short term fosters stop-and-go policies. Instability and unpredictability in the public sector inhibit and distort long-range business planning, reducing overall economic performance. Rapid shifts in U.S. priorities with respect to growth, inflation, and exchange rates during the 1970s provide a vivid case in point.

Second, short-term policies are ill suited to respond to the enduring, structural economic challenges faced by the United States. The kinds of challenges that arise from the application of new technology to the workplace, the internationalization of manufacturing, and the emergence of the newly industrializing countries will not yield to quick fixes.

Third, the U.S. policy process inhibits the development of a long-term vision of the U.S. role in the global economy. The transformations that have taken place in the postwar global economic order require such farsighted design to guide day-to-day decisions. In terms of leadership, a long-term vision is necessary to foster needed international support and cooperation.

This volume seeks to contribute to the shaping of a systematic view of interests and strategy in the international economic arena in the coming decade. Each chapter is, in the jargon of Washington, a "think piece" that analyzes a basic set of issues and assesses its policy implications. The chapters grouped in Part I examine the far-reaching impact of technological change on U.S. interests across the board. Part II focuses on the U.S. approach to global economic development. Part III looks at a series of underlying challenges to the international financial framework and the structure of the multilateral trading system.

In Part I, Harald B. Malmgren's opening chapter lays out a powerful argument that the world economy is being transformed by a technological revolution comparable to the industrial revolution of the eighteenth century. The driving forces of change are extraordinary advances in the creation of new materials, information technology, new manufacturing processes, transportation, and biotechnology. These advances are compressing time for decisionmaking; breaking linkages between labor, raw materials, and industrial output; blurring distinctions between commercial and defense technologies; and making possible the development and marketing of goods and services on a truly global basis.

The key challenge posed to the United States in this new technological era, according to Malmgren, is not loss of competitiveness but loss of autonomy. The forces at work are bound to erode the national sovereignty of all nations, even the world's preeminent economic power. He states:

> The pace of technological change and of the responses by private enterprises is overrunning the ability of governments to guide or manage structural adjustments. Existing regulatory regimes are rapidly being made obsolete, and traditional concepts of competition based on national markets are being made irrelevant by growing transborder competition spurred by the accelerated diffusion of technology on a global basis.

Malmgren argues that U.S. interests in this setting will best be served by a posture of maximal openness and receptivity to global economic transformation. On the domestic side, this requires stable macroeconomic policies to underpin growth and a priority effort in public education to prepare the United States politically, psychologically, and scientifically for the changes that are underway. Internationally, the United States must resist the cycle of defensiveness that is overtaking all of the advanced industrial economies as well as many of those in the developing world. Policies that seek U.S. competitive advantage at the expense of others will ultimately damage national economic interests, reduce growth in the world economy, and put the United States at odds with its most important allies.

Pat Choate and Juyne Linger make a strikingly different assessment. While concurring that a new technological era is at hand, they see a pervasive pattern of U.S. slippage and vulnerability. The United States is losing its edge in penetration of global markets, commercial applications of technology, and the process of innovation itself.

Choate and Linger attribute U.S. decline partly to domestic factors. U.S. industry failed to grasp the full extent of the international challenge that began to develop in the 1970s. Its record in commercializing and applying new technologies has been deficient. U.S. performance has been further handicapped by tax laws, an antitrust code, and technology transfer regulations that fail to take account of global competitive realities. At the same time, Choate and Linger hold the U.S. government even more accountable for underreacting to developments overseas that have damaged the U.S. position: restrictions to U.S. access of foreign markets, heavy subsidies to foreign competitors, violations of U.S. patent and other intellectual property rights, and a policy of scientific exchange that has left the U.S. scientific establishment readily accessible to others without providing reciprocal openness to U.S. researchers.

Against this background, Choate and Linger advocate much greater assertiveness in U.S. policy. Domestically, they argue for a concerted effort to strengthen the nation's technological base through wide-ranging measures to improve the allocation of capital, upgrade the labor force, and spur not only the research and development of new technologies but their commercial application as well. Internationally, they call for full-scale use of U.S. leverage—including restricted access to the U.S. market—to enable U.S. industry to compete on equal terms.

The contrasting perspectives of Malmgren and of Choate and Linger pose a fundamental question. How should the United States address the technology-driven issues that will continue to dominate the international agenda for the foreseeable future? For Choate and Linger, "the key point is that technology is a major national economic asset" to be aggressively nurtured. For Malmgren, technology is an increasingly shared asset to be developed cooperatively.

The discussion of East-West technology transfer by Stephen A. Merrill tilts, in the final analysis, toward Malmgren's thesis. Merrill suggests that the ebb and flow of pressures for restriction of sensitive technology to the Soviet bloc were once governed mainly by the state of East-West political relations. Now, however, such pressures are likely to be far less influenced by Soviet behavior than by "revolutionary technological and economic changes confined almost entirely to the West."

Merrill identifies several new technological realities that will affect U.S. policy toward technology transfer over the next decade: (1) the increasing availability of advanced, militarily sensitive technologies from non-U.S. sources—not just Japan and Western Europe but also the newly industrializing countries; (2) the increasing scope of commercial technologies that have military applications; (3) the growing dependence of the U.S. defense establishment on foreign components and allied collaboration in leading-edge research and development. These new realities create crosscutting pressures. On the one hand, the increased scope and availability of strategically significant technologies make compelling incentives to control their flow to the Soviets. On the other hand, these same factors, together with the web of technological interdependence in the West, reduce the capacity of the United States to impose controls unilaterally without incurring increasingly high commercial and political costs. The perception of these rising costs has triggered an effort to ease restrictions put in place by the Reagan administration. Looking ahead, Merrill does not see the imposition of unilateral sanctions as a viable alternative but rather urges U.S. policymakers to reach out to an increasing number of Western and newly industrializing trading partners to create a control "common market" of militarily sensitive technologies.

Robert R. Bruce, in his discussion of telecommunications, illustrates dramatically how national governments have been overwhelmed by the pace of technological change. Bruce points out that the process of deregulation in telecommunications, both domestically and internationally, has been only one source of pressure. The profusion of information-based services being developed has further contributed to a tangle of unresolved problems ranging from basic definitions through the provision of market access. Despite the impact of the Reagan administration in setting an international agenda of privatization in telecommunications, Bruce maintains that U.S. policymakers have major responsibilities to help U.S. firms participate in overseas markets where national governments still exercise commanding influence. Simply to rely on U.S. technological leadership and the play of market forces will not suffice. Rather, the

United States has no choice but to engage in complex bilateral and multilateral negotiations in this sector of comparative U.S. advantage. Bruce draws the provocative conclusion that the mismatch between technological change and governmental response has damaged U.S. commercial interests because Washington has been unable to support them effectively on a global basis.

In Part II, Ernest H. Preeg and Alan J. Stoga offer penetrating but different appraisals of U.S. prospects vis-à-vis the developing countries. They concur on the central point that no single shorthand reference, such as "the Third World" or "South" captures the growing diversity of the developing countries. The differential in their economic performance as well as their importance to the United States have been reflected in U.S. policy. Preeg and Stoga agree further that Washington must confront development challenges from an economically constrained position. The federal budget deficit has reduced prospects for both bilateral and multilateral assistance. The interlocking of U.S. financial exposure to the developing world and debtor country dependence on U.S. export markets promise to limit the margin of U.S. maneuverability all the more.

Preeg nonetheless sketches a comparatively hopeful scenario based on the implementation of policies now in place, while Stoga concludes that a complete reassessment of U.S. strategy is needed including consideration of second and third best options. Preeg identifies a number of underlying trends in the developing world that augur well for U.S. policy. He sees a positive side to the austerity that has been imposed on middle-income debtors since the early 1980s: namely, their being forced into a more efficient, market-oriented allocation of resources that provides a solid foundation for future growth. Preeg also sees the breakup of the developing countries as a single negotiating block as a welcome sign of pragmatism, which enhances the likelihood of successfully integrating middle-income nations into the GATT and IMF structures. Looking ahead, Preeg sees two additional underlying factors that will draw many developing countries closer to the West—the impact of the information technology revolution and the displacement of authoritarian regimes by market-oriented democracies. Against this background, Preeg contends that there is a window of opportunity to work out of the international debt-austerity cycle along lines proposed by U.S. Secretary of the Treasury James Baker in 1985. Success will require much creative diplomacy and modest increases in resources but no new vision.

Stoga draws a much gloomier balance sheet. While granting that the international financial system has successfully muddled through since the debt crisis of 1982, Stoga points to high costs on all sides.

The debtors have suffered stunning losses in growth and per capita income that, over the long term threaten the recent transition toward democracy. The United States not only has lost overseas markets as a result of debtor country austerity but also has absorbed the brunt of the indebted nations' drive to service their obligations by increasing export earnings. This, in turn, has contributed to the rising tide of U.S. protectionism and corresponding disenchantment with the overall U.S. role in the world economy. Notwithstanding the recent improvement in U.S. commercial bank balance sheets, Stoga sees little prospect for implementing the Baker proposal to stimulate growth through fresh capital flows to the developing world.

In this setting, according to Stoga, the United States has no choice but to rethink its position. A U.S.-led revitalization of the world economy through a multilateral trading system, the World Bank, and the IMF would be a best solution, but the United States seems to lack both the will and the means to recapture the role it played in the 1950s and 1960s. A strategy of shifting more global economic responsibilities to Japan and West Germany has been attempted by several recent administrations, but progress has been disappointingly slow. Failing these preferred options, the United States should give more weight to its bilateral ties with developing world countries of major economic and political importance—even at the risk that such bilateralism will further erode multilateral institutions.

What balance should the United States strike between its stake in the multilateral framework that has underpinned the world economy since 1945 and its stake in bilateral ties with key countries? This vital question, raised by Preeg and Stoga in the context of global economic development, applies equally to U.S. international economic strategy overall.

Irving S. Friedman, drawing on four decades of experience with the IMF and the World Bank, contends that these institutions should remain the linchpin of U.S. policy toward the developing world. The premise for U.S. leadership in both the Bank and the Fund remains valid: namely, that global prosperity best serves the interests of the United States. Friedman is decidedly optimistic with respect to the future of the IMF. Already, the Fund has assumed important new responsibilities in managing the international debt problem. Its objectives, policy orientation, and lending procedures are clearly understood and universally applied. The Fund has the capacity to play an enhanced role in stabilizing international exchange rates and providing additional global liquidity should it be called on to do so.

Friedman has a more guarded prognosis for the World Bank, which, in his eyes, lacks a sense of mission and unifying general philosophy. The recent shift of the Bank's focus from long-term project lending to short-term policy lending has proven difficult. Even though the Bank has always been headed by an American, the U.S. government has not provided as much direction as it has to the Fund. Such direction is necessary to fill current gaps in the Bank's performance.

Looking outside the international financial institutions, Cynthia Day Wallace asks how much the United States can rely on foreign direct investment to advance its interests in the developing world. Wallace notes that the slowdown of growth and virtual halt of commercial bank lending to many developing countries has renewed their interest in foreign direct investment. However, constraints on such investment are still widespread, and the scale of private-sector resources available remains limited. Wallace sees favorable prospects but no *deus ex machina.* Moreover, following the reasoning of Robert R. Bruce, she concludes that there is no viable substitute for an internationally negotiated regime to allow market forces to operate smoothly.

In Part III, Lawrence Veit argues against the need for U.S.-led structural revision of the international monetary framework. He examines the breadth of national interests in the stability of the exchange-rate system, its capacity to reflect changes in economic fundamentals, and in the value of the dollar itself during any given interval. Veit sees no practical alternative to the current system of floating rates, yet he contends that U.S. interests demand a conscious, activist policy toward the dollar. Although the forces that determine its value are wide-ranging and at best partially understood, Washington can still have a controlling impact through the macro-economic course it sets. In international matters, if not in trade, the United States retains wide latitude for action and should make use of it selectively.

Penelope Hartland-Thunberg sees severe structural deficiencies in the multilateral trading system that are being pointed up by China's application to join the GATT. While supporting the political rationale for bringing China more fully into the world economy, Hartland-Thunberg contends that the actual process of doing so raises two basic problems that have long been ignored or avoided: how to manage relations between market and centrally controlled economies; and how to adjust the responsibilities of the developing countries, which have thus far been relieved of GATT's most important obligations to provide open markets and reciprocal, nondiscriminatory treatment to trading partners. Despite its selective adoption of market-oriented policies, China remains a centrally directed economy with enormous potential to affect world markets in sectors in which it concentrates resources. Should China be admitted to the GATT with all of the prerogatives of a developing country, resulting economic disruptions could easily overshadow projected political gains.

The momentous issues posed by China's application, according to Hartland-Thunberg, should trigger a searching effort to readjust the GATT: first, by establishing more effective grounds than those now in place for dealing with nonmarket economies on bedrock questions of reciprocity, subsidies, and discrimination; second, by coming to grips with the problem of "graduating" developing countries to assume their full measure of responsibilities within the multilateral trading system. Hartland-Thunberg warns that adjustments of this magnitude may not be possible in a consensus-bound, one-nation one-vote organization. A redistribution of power within the GATT, giving more weight to those nations with a greater stake in trade, may be required.

Henry R. Nau sees an opportunity within the current GATT structure to accommodate the priority interests of the newly industrializing economies and the West. The United States and other OECD nations need developing world markets for the rich array of technology-based services they can provide. The NICs, in turn, need sustained access to Western markets in such politically sensitive industrial sectors as steel, textiles, and shoes if they are to generate the export earnings to sustain growth. It should be possible to negotiate a tradeoff along these lines in the current Uruguay round. Nau finds progress to date disappointingly slow, yet he attributes the lack of movement more to failings of political leadership than to structural flaws in the GATT itself.

Gary C. Hufbauer and Jeffrey J. Schott see little prospect that either multilateral or bilateral negotiating approaches will yield a dramatic improvement in the U.S. trade position between now and 1990. Even with the sharp decline of the dollar, Hufbauer and Schott forecast $100 billion plus merchandise trade deficits. In their view, the strongest surplus countries—Japan and West Germany—seem unwilling to relieve pressure on the U.S. market by serving as locomotives of global growth. The conclusion of a U.S.-Canada free-trade agreement notwithstanding, the contentious bilateral issues that dominate U.S. agendas with the European Community, Japan, and the NICs focus more on trade restriction than liberalization. The GATT round cannot be expected to produce concrete results on "traditional" trade problems (subsidies and import safeguards) or the "new issues" (services, investment, and intellectual property rights) for the next several years. At best, U.S. negotiators can only aim for preliminary agreements in the GATT to provide credibility for the negotiating process while seeking to contain protectionist pressures at home.

Robert L. Paarlberg reaches the provocative conclusion that U.S. international interests in agriculture will be advanced more quickly by restructuring domestic farm policies than by relying on protracted GATT negotiations. Paarlberg asserts that resistance to change is so great internationally that the United States cannot afford to hold itself hostage to a multilateral negotiating process in sectors where it retains significant advantages. Thus far, U.S. farm policies have helped support world prices by limiting production in wheat, corn, soybeans, and other cereals. If the United States liberalizes its own policies, it has the leverage in world markets to prompt adjustments by others.

It would be presumptuous to suggest that the contributions to this volume provide any more than a starting point to the development of international economic strategy. Beyond the insights they afford on specific issues, they indicate two essential guideposts:

First, the United States must face up to a demanding domestic agenda to sustain its capacity for international economic leadership. The federal government has a limited but essential role to play in this regard. Its most immediate requirement is to move the nation toward living within its means by producing a macroeconomic policy that reduces consumption, increases savings, and promotes growth. More broadly, domestic policies must be formulated to take account of the internationalization of the U.S. economy, whose exposure to outside forces has created demands for greater innovation, higher productivity, more mobility of resources, and a growing capacity to operate globally. A substantial consensus has emerged in recent years for the measures that are needed to improve the long-term performance of the U.S. economy. The bipartisan commitment needed to implement them is lacking.

Second, the widely shared defensiveness regarding the U.S. role in the world economy that has taken hold must be overcome. For many, the explosion of the trade deficit and of foreign indebtedness mark an adverse flow of global economic power that can only be checked if the United States makes full use of its ultimate leverage— access to its domestic market. The chapters in this volume suggest a more balanced interplay of global economic forces that, while posing some severe problems, has also left the United States with a number of gains and with more varied sources of influence than protectionist threats. Neither the economic balance sheet nor U.S. security objectives warrant the adoption of a neomercantilist view of U.S. interests. The rest of the world will take its cue from the tone as well as the substance of U.S. economic diplomacy. The call for U.S. leadership from other countries remains strong, and its prospects will be greatly enhanced by a forward-looking approach.

THE TECHNOLOGY CHALLENGE

1 INNOVATION AND THE GLOBAL ECONOMIC ENVIRONMENT

Harald B. Malmgren

Throughout the industrialized nations of the West there seems to be a growing sense of urgency about the need for new policies to strengthen national economies and improve competitiveness. Even in the United States there is an increasing preoccupation with flagging national competitiveness and a rapidly widening controversy about means to restore world economic leadership.

In policy debates, the role of technology has become a focal point virtually everywhere. Countless proposals are being made for boosting national technological advances to help industries meet intensified global competition.

Yet in spite of a near-universal interest in the role of technology, there is very little analysis of the actual impact of technological change on the world economy in public policy discussion. There is a widening sense of the need for faster structural change to adapt to the new realities of economic competition. But there is little recognition of the revolutionary character of emerging technologies and their potentially overpowering effects on governments and their national economic policies.

THE RISE OF PROTECTIONISM AND ECONOMIC NATIONALISM

New policies are being devised, but their orientation tends to be inward-looking and based on past experience. Thus, there is a growing tendency toward economic nationalism, based on traditional

3

conceptions of how to use trade policy to improve competitiveness: boosting exports, limiting imports, and artificially enhancing home-based production and jobs. The consequence is that mutually conflicting policies are being generated among the Western nations that threaten to fragment their economic and political interests. Multilateral economic cooperation is being undermined as nations attempt to find their own separate ways to harness and restrain the forces of change.

In relying on trade policies to improve competitiveness, governments are essentially attacking the symptoms of rapid change without addressing the causes. One need not resort to sophisticated economic analysis to reach the obvious conclusion that if every nation acts to limit imports and boost exports, the ultimate result will be global economic contraction.

A major example of these tendencies can be found in the United States, where the national debate on economic policy is becoming permeated with references to the need to improve competitiveness and to deal more effectively with the technological challenges of Japan and other nations. There is a degree of recognition that exchange rates and profligate domestic economic policies have hurt U.S. competitiveness. But much of the policy discussion is formulated in terms of criticizing the practices of other nations, placing blame for deterioration of U.S. competitiveness on the allegedly unfair policies and practices of foreign governments.

One response has been a political push for import restrictions and import-retarding remedial actions in key industrial sectors. There have been demands for trade-restrictive countermeasures against alleged industrial targeting policies of foreign governments. There are growing demands for greater protection of U.S. technology through much tougher actions against imports that allegedly infringe on U.S. patents, copyrights, trademarks, and licensing arrangements. Some officials and politicians are advocating a drive to build up the so-called defense industrial base within a framework of national security objectives, excluding foreign enterprises or discriminating against them in key industries.

Furthermore, there was in the early 1980s an extensive national debate in the United States concerning the possible need for industrial policies aimed at enhancing competitiveness in key sectors. There was considerable public attention to the suggestion that government should play a more active role in stimulating, assisting, and guiding industrial innovation and adaptation. Given the constraints on government spending imposed by the federal budget deficit, and a long-standing public skepticism about government effectiveness in guiding the economy, these industrial policy suggestions soon evolved into arguments for greater protection against imports.

These discriminatory and trade-limiting responses have not, of course, been the only proposals made. Reforms of antitrust policy to allow more cooperation among enterprises in research and development (R&D), tax policies to favor innovation, changes in patent policy for government-funded R&D, and other positive proposals have also been widely discussed. Already some policy changes along these lines have been made.

This perceived need to improve national competitiveness in the face of global economic challenges is evident throughout the West. For example, among the member nations of the European Communities (EC) there is a growing apprehension about what is perceived as a Japanese–U.S. technological challenge to Europe's future competitiveness and economic well-being. There is a widespread feeling that Europe is falling behind and becoming vulnerable to economic domination by external interests. A prevailing sentiment is that technological rejuvenation of European industry is urgently needed, and for this to happen, a way must be found to generate sufficient economies of scale and size of market to guarantee adequate returns to R&D for European companies. The solution most often presented is that the EC must really become a single, integrated marketplace as quickly as possible, and cooperation among EC companies across national boundaries must be vigorously encouraged. Governments, it is also argued, must join hands in supporting European-scale technological projects—projects that will enhance Europe's relative global trading position in advanced technologies.

But this West European obsession with economies of scale and size of home market overlooks completely the international technological successes of many business enterprises based in comparatively small European economies, such as Sweden, Finland, and Switzerland. In spite of the smallness of their home market bases, a significant number of companies in each of these countries have emerged as world-class industrial competitors alongside the giant Japanese and U.S. multinationals.

Moreover, the widespread apprehension about the Japanese and U.S. competitive challenges seems to have caused a European blindness to the rapid emergence of the comparatively small newly industrializing countries (NICs) as significant world competitors in many advanced technology sectors. South Korean industrial enterprises, for example, are rapidly becoming internationally competitive in advanced consumer electronics, semiconductors, and small computers, and South Korean technology in the production of steel and in shipbuilding is second to none. The scale of domestic markets in the NICs can hardly be said to be the foundation of their rapid advances in technological capabilities and world competitiveness.

In Japan, there has long been a feeling of vulnerability to external forces. Technological progress for many years has been perceived as the principal avenue to growth, world competitiveness, and diminished dependence on the vicissitudes of global political and economic developments. The economic shocks of the 1970s—oil prices, exchange-rate volatility, inflation, the emergence of Third World competitors—gave increased impetus to the development and the application of emerging technologies in Japan. Government policymakers devoted much attention to the encouragement of technological advances, in part through direct assistance to industry but mainly through facilitation of, and sometimes even forcing of, R&D cooperation and sharing of knowledge among independent commercial enterprises. The government, in turn, would periodically articulate its national "visions" of the direction and character of technological change, and the implications for the structure of the Japanese economy and its global competitiveness. These visions provided a framework for business planning and financial commitments.

In more recent years, Japanese commercial enterprises have gradually pulled away from government guidance of their R&D. Public policy has become more focused on the promotion of what are called next-generation or emerging technologies. Acquisition of existing technologies from other nations is less of a concern now than autonomous generation of new technologies. The focus of competition among Japanese enterprises is shifting from cost competitiveness in producing and selling off-the-shelf goods to competitiveness in the generation of entirely new products and new methods of production. On the one hand, this shift is being spurred by a growing desire to catch up with the United States. On the other hand, there is a growing fear of the progress being made by the NICs in closing the competitive gap and challenging Japanese enterprises in world markets in both traditional and technologically advanced manufactures. Increasingly, there seems to be a feeling in Japan that world technological competition is becoming a race, with victory going to the swiftest rather than the most efficient.

Even the NICs seem increasingly preoccupied with enhancing their technological potential, and their industrial and trade policies have in recent years been adapted to this preoccupation. The intense economic nationalism and protectionism that characterize Brazil's informatics policy is one of the most visible examples.

One important conclusion that can already be reached is that many of the measures being considered or being taken in the West to shield national markets from external pressures are aggravating the difficulties of structural adjustment to changing international competitiveness. Because technology is increasingly transferable across borders, restrictions on the exports of certain countries simply encourage expansion of production in other countries, particularly the NICs. The rapid emergence of new entrants increases world productive capacity and artificially stimulates even more intense competition.

Major exporters increasingly respond to perceived protectionism by stepping up their foreign direct investment, jumping national borders, and building new production facilities in the major importing countries. At first glance this seems to help create new jobs, but its longer-term effect may often be to create additional domestic competitive pressures and even excess capacity. Ironically, the new foreign-owned plants are relatively more able to withstand intensified competition because of their state-of-the-art production technologies. For example, there can be little doubt that the U.S. automotive industry will suffer from excess domestic production capacity in the next few years. This problem will be greatly aggravated by the large capacity of Japanese-owned automotive plants already in place or now being built inside the United States, mainly in response to fears of protectionism and U.S. pressures for job creation.

Such industrial responses to accelerate movement up the ladder of technological progress and to employ new technologies in plants built in foreign markets cannot readily be stemmed by protectionism or a revival of economic nationalism. Put simply, government efforts to shield key sectors and guide structural adjustment are being overrun by the force and pace of technological change.

TECHNOLOGICAL THRUSTS
AND STRUCTURAL CHANGE

Thus, it is no longer possible to devise effective economic policies without taking into account the underlying technological thrusts and their implications for the structure of national economies and the pattern of world trade, investment, and delivery of services.

There are a number of major technological forces now at work that will require fundamental structural adjustments on the part of national economies:

The development of new, man-made materials will increasingly compete with, and substitute for, traditional materials generated from natural resources. There has been a fundamental reversal in the direction of technological change in materials science. Traditionally, technology has been used to process materials found in the ground or growing from it. Recent advances in materials science and engineering are making it possible "to start with a need and then develop a material to meet it, atom by atom" (Clark and Fleming 1986: 41). These advances are widely characterized as constituting a "materials revolution."

These "new materials" now being developed in Japan, Western Europe, and the United States will have a profound effect on the economic value of natural resources. The new man-made materials will be generated by new industrial processes and even new industries.

In the 1980s there have been many public expressions of concern about a potential deindustrialization of U.S. industry as a result of a perceptible decline of traditional basic industries like steel and copper. Little public attention has been given to the potentially expansive role of emerging new industries that produce superpolymers, composites, fiber optics, fine ceramics, and so forth.

Even by itself, the materials revolution should force a refocusing of public policy away from the prospects for traditional industries and toward the emergence of entirely new industries and processes. For example, U.S. policymakers should be asking whether the relative economic importance of key natural resources will diminish, leaving some countries, such as the resource-dependent LDCs, much worse off and the United States better off. They should reexamine the supposed criticality to national security of domestic resources (and selected imported raw materials) in the new context in which the defense department gives its highest R&D priorities to the generation of substitute new materials (because of their greater capabilities in military applications).

Accelerating advances in the technology of computers, telecommunications, and information-processing provide enormous economies of scale in supplying services and transferring technology. The changes taking place in the area of information management are so far-reaching that they have been characterized as the "information revolution." Many scientists believe that this revolution is generating historic changes on a scale comparable to, or even greater than, the changes that took place during the Industrial Revolution. This revolution is not simply a matter of faster, more powerful memories and rapidly declining costs of processing information. Advances in telecommunications represent only a part of the revolution taking place.

Applied research is becoming faster as past knowledge becomes more readily available to researchers and experimentation is assisted by simulation and the bare beginnings of artificial intelligence (AI). Product life cycles are shortening. Process and product technologies are becoming instantly transferable through global computer-telecommunication links, widening dramatically the potential suppliers of goods and services in the world marketplace. Goods suppliers increasingly are able to provide accompanying engineering services, enabling much closer and more interactive producer–consumer relationships, thereby changing the nature of competition from selling previously designed machinery, equipment, and components to provision of design services, process technology, tailored equipment and components, redesign, and continuous engineering support. These developments sharply reduce the significance of geographic distance and dramatically shorten the response time needed to meet changing consumer demand.

Industrial processes are being reoriented within the framework of computer-integrated manufacturing (CIM) and flexible manufacturing systems (FMS). The emerging reorientation of industrial processes is based on multipurpose, reprogrammable equipment and systems combined with entirely new materials processing techniques. The changing character of production processes will provide opportunity for much greater flexibility, small lot production, minimal inventories, rapid market response, and product adaptation, while maintaining and even enhancing economies of scale in use of plant and equipment.

The greater reliance on CIM, and the improvements in production systems that are possible with CIM (such as robotics, automated transfer, industrial lasers, and new techniques for precision forming and shaping) will tend to reduce the importance of labor costs in competitiveness. There may be a substantial labor-displacing effect, which could have significant implications for competitiveness of enterprises in countries that rely on low labor costs for export competitiveness. (For example, the automation of sewing could greatly alter the world pattern of apparel production and trade, leaving massive job displacement in its wake in some of the LDCs as well as in the United States.)

CIM will inevitably result in shorter product life cycles as continuous adaptation and tailoring of products become easier. Competitiveness will increasingly depend on speed of response and character of product-related services.

Improvements in transportation, especially in the technology of aircraft, bring production centers and markets much closer in terms of time and relative cost. Lighter but stronger airframes and lighter, higher-performance aircraft engines will mean greater weight capacity, greater distance feasibility, and shorter landing and takeoff requirements, thereby intensifying competitiveness of air transport relative to other modes of transportation and giving even greater emphasis to speed of response to consumer requirements.

Rapid advances in life sciences are likely to alter demographic profiles and enhance human capabilities across all age brackets. The human resource development of nations will become increasingly important to the dynamics of growth and competitiveness. The share of services in total national employment is likely to continue to grow in virtually every nation, placing growing importance on the quality of the human resource base in maintaining and improving competitiveness. This growing dependence on the overall strength of the human resource base will give greater emphasis to reforms of education and the quality and distribution of services (health maintenance, life-sustaining services, and quality-of-life services). Thus, it must be anticipated that competitiveness will depend on more rapid and more tailored responses of suppliers to rapidly evolving and increasingly individualized demand.

Biotechnology developments may open the way for major advances in the production (and location of production) of food and improvements in such diverse areas as industrial processes, management of wastes, memory technology, and even in animal and human characteristics. The unknowns of biotechnology—the dangers as well as the potential benefits—are central to any assessment of future thrusts. Developments currently under way reveal only a glimmer of what these future thrusts might be. It can nonetheless already be said that developments in this field are likely to change greatly the nature of world food production and distribution, with major effects on agricultural and agribusiness technologies and competitiveness.

THE ACCELERATING PACE OF CHANGE

Throughout history technological change has brought about changes in the pattern of world economic activity. What is new is the acceleration of the pace of change, combined with the emerging capability of changing the character of nature's building blocks to open entirely new avenues of production—and even, potentially, new avenues of evolution.

In essence, an entirely new paradigm is unfolding. In this perspective, scientists who characterize the current changes as an information revolution or a materials revolution may be somewhat understating the profound significance of the wide array of technological advances now cumulatively coming to bear on national economies. This technological revolution is, in other words, likely to generate historical discontinuities—with past experience sometimes a poor guide for future policy decisions and commitments of human and financial resources.

The acceleration of change brings about a compression of time, from the point of view of decisionmakers. The economic behavior patterns that presently characterize the world economy and are embodied in institutional and political processes of decisionmaking, are very time sensitive. Time is taken to evaluate new ideas and assess their commercial potential. Producers seek, and plan on, adequate time to ensure that expected returns can be achieved from plant and equipment investments that implement new technologies. Competitive countermeasures take time to put in motion. Petitions for government assistance or action against foreign interests take time to consider. Legislative policy changes take a long time to develop. Government-to-government negotiations on salient problems take years.

Rapid economic change invariably means disruption to sectors and geographic regions—bringing about political pressures to alleviate the pains of adjustment. There are congenital tendencies in our economic institutions and political processes to slow things down, to seek breathing time, and to retard the pace of structural change through measures that shield disrupted enterprises or industrial sectors from global forces of change.

Against these built-in institutional tendencies to stretch out the time taken for change, the emerging technology thrusts are accelerating the pace of change. Information technology is shortening the time required to produce a new service, or a new good embodying an idea. It is shortening the time necessary for managers to respond to changing demand and supply characteristics of their markets. It is shortening the time lag in international diffusion of technology.

One of the consequences of a shortened economic time span is faster product obsolescence in world competition. As the market life cycle of many products shortens, there is a growing need for faster responses and faster adaptation of production systems without time-consuming investment in new plant and equipment. The time factor in competition—responding quickly and staying ahead through rapid innovation—is itself altering the way in which products and services are generated, forcing producers and suppliers to devise flexible, adaptable, reprogrammable production and delivery systems, and increasing both the incentive and the need to provide supporting services in conjunction with the sale of goods.

In such a competitive environment, R&D cannot be attributed to particular products; R&D becomes an ongoing process necessary to remain a viable, competitive entity. Measurement of performance, accounting standards, tax treatment—all such traditional concepts become obsolete. Only contemporaneous measurement of the performance of R&D makes sense. This means treating R&D as current nonattributable overhead costs, or, in public policy terms, treating the level of R&D spending as an underlying measure of the strength of a corporation, much like capital asset value.

STRUCTURAL IMPLICATIONS

What are the structural implications of these fundamental technology thrusts and the compression of time allowed to deal with them? First, it is likely that there will be significant shifts in relative competitiveness among industrial sectors and shifts in relative economic power among nations. These shifts may not always move continuously in a single direction. Building plants in other nations and securing components from foreign suppliers (outsourcing) may prevail for some periods, while domestic consolidation and centralization may prevail in other periods. For example, the U.S. automotive industry may for a time move toward global sourcing, but there are strong economies to be gained from consolidation when CIM and the novel characteristics of new materials become more widely relevant to automotive production. Emergence of new materials will have an effect not only on traditional resource-processing industries and countries; there will also be significant effects on production methods (obsolescence of machine tools and emergence of precision-forming, laser treatment, and other entirely different processes of cutting, bending, shaping, and refinishing based on CIM) and on the global management of remote production facilities (on-line programming by engineers in remote locations).

In assessing relative economic and political power of nations in coming years, it is apparent that countries that adapt quickly will tend to be stronger, and those that have difficulty adapting will tend to fall behind. The resilience and flexibility of an economy will therefore be vital determinants of relative power as technological change works through national economies. In this regard, relatively rigid, centrally managed economies like that of the Soviet Union will have great difficulty keeping pace. Indeed, even if the decentralization efforts of Chairman Gorbachev were to be widely implemented, it is difficult to foresee any circumstances in which the economy of the Soviet Union could adapt to the pace of change likely in the West. The United States, Japan, Canada, Western Europe, and the NICs will probably stretch their technological lead over all the centrally planned economies. Among the Western countries, some of the European nations could lag unless there is further loosening of the constraints on independent enterprises imposed by regulations and social policies. This leaves a question mark about the future of such economies as those of South Asia and China. Perhaps more historically significant is the very poor outlook for many of the developing countries that are heavily dependent on natural resources and are already in difficult circumstances.

Second, major transformation of national and global systems for delivery of services is under way, particularly through advances in information technology. Vast economies of scale globally are achievable through consolidation of a variety of services and delivery through computer-telecommunications networks (witness the emergence of so-called financial supermarkets). On the other hand, small, innovative entities can provide services globally through the same kinds of mechanisms in such varying fields as engineering, software support, medical diagnostics, and management information services. Once supporting services such as software development can be routinized, it will be possible to assign such services activities to remote locations (for example, assignment of technical support activities to underemployed technicians in South Asia).

Third, growing world competition from new entrants at home and abroad can be expected to be generated by the accelerated international diffusion of technology. Countries that remain "plugged in" to globally available services and technology information can keep pace with world markets, but countries that try to develop indigenous technologies through protectionist measures and exclusion of foreign technologies and communication will eventually find themselves falling back, "plugged out" from world competition. The nationalistic, restrictive informatics policy of the Brazilian government poses this long-term danger for Brazil's economy.

Fourth, the acceleration of change will tend to undermine or counteract government policy measures taken to limit or impede imports of particular products. The consequence of import-restraining measures may often be to accelerate the introduction of new, substitutable products and the establishment of new foreign and domestic sources of production, greatly intensifying competitive pressures. Thus, ironically, protectionist actions will tend to increase, rather than moderate, the very competitive pressures that initially gave rise to pleas for protection from firms and workers.

Fifth, there is likely to be change in the global pattern of demand for labor, but in yet uncertain ways. Transformation of manufacturing processes, through automation of sewing and bonding in production of apparel, for example, will tend to change fundamentally the industrial development path for many LDCs. Labor demand in some regions may fall, while rising in other regions characterized by new technologies of production in new facilities. Skill requirements may vary continuously throughout the life of individual workers, and their versatility may become more important than specific skills and experience in specific tasks.

Industrial and agricultural jobs will continue to shrink as a share of total employment, even if present levels of production are maintained in key sectors. The orientation of education will have to be altered, but the appropriate direction of change is still very unclear (for example, will there be a need for lifetime reeducation?).

Sixth, private enterprises will have to become far more knowledgeable about worldwide developments among both present and potential competitors. To limit risks from competitive surprises and to enhance the ability to synthesize a variety of technologies, enterprises may increasingly seek to devise cooperation arrangements among two or more industrial partners in various parts of the world. Engineers operating at different geographic points will increasingly work interactively through global telecommunications networks to develop new technologies cooperatively. These tendencies will increasingly obscure the national origins of particular technologies.

It is also likely that there will be a decreasing emphasis in some manufacturing enterprises on making things to sell and on direct investment in foreign production facilities, and growing emphasis on global provision of services (R&D, design, engineering, procurement, trading, finance, customer support, and so forth).

Competitiveness of private enterprises will tend to depend on the basic strategies of those enterprises. Planning for change, and adapting quickly to it, may become the most vital element in maintaining and enhancing competitiveness. This will often require increased emphasis on diversification and risk management through diversification of markets (geographically and among demand segments), products, production location, production methods, financial arrangements, and R&D.

POLICY RESPONSES

The pace of technological change and of the responses by private enterprises is overrunning the ability of governments to guide or manage structural adjustments. Existing regulatory regimes are rapidly being made obsolete, and traditional concepts of competition based on national markets are being made irrelevant by growing transborder competition spurred by the accelerated diffusion of technology on a global basis. As already noted, national measures to shield domestic industries from global competition will often tend to be counterproductive and aggravate the underlying problems of structural adjustment.

Government-to-government negotiations on specific product issues, particularly those negotiations aimed at official management of trade flows, will be made increasingly irrelevant by the accelerating pace of change. There will instead be a growing need for governments to set aside short-term microeconomic concerns and turn to cooperation aimed at improving the macroeconomic environment for fostering and facilitating change. Thus, governments will need to think about devising international guidelines or consultative arrangements aimed at ensuring mutual compatibility of their respective industrial and economic policies.

Overt explicit economic nationalism will be more difficult for governments to practice. Unilateralist policies on the part of the major economic powers will tend to be rejected by some governments, and the ability of any single nation to control technology transfer will inevitably diminish over time. In essence, a degree of sovereignty and assertion of national power may have to be yielded, even by the United States, in order to obtain greater multilateral cooperation.

This is particularly relevant to the handling of controls on the East–West transfer of technology and on the parallel West–West controls that supplement and support them. Washington has been pushing to widen the scope of export controls to encompass many currently available, commercially developed technologies, and to include many potential technologies that are expected to emerge in the next few years. This drive to expand controls over international technology transfer is increasingly threatening commercial activities of non-U.S. enterprises and is opening new rifts in Western economic relations.

The U.S. effort to widen the control system is based on the rapidly expanding scope of the so-called Militarily Critical Technologies List (MCTL) developed by the U.S. Department of Defense. This list is being broadened to include technologies that might benefit the "defense industrial base," broadly defined, of the Soviet Union and other potentially hostile nations. Thus, it is being expanded to include many of the new materials and new technologies of industrial production that are emerging.

Moreover, the growing importance of computer architecture, new materials, sensors, lasers, advanced energy devices, and other commercially developed technologies in defense planning and procurement inevitably will lead to a growing overlap of defense and nondefense technologies. There is considerable evidence that many new technologies now being sought in the military-security sphere are initially being generated in the commercial sphere. The conceptual framework of the MCTL increasingly reflects this shift in the origins or technologies that have, or could have, defense or security applications.

The concept of "dual use" technologies used by defense experts to justify controls on many specific technologies and products will lose meaning as most technologies becomes dual use. The legitimacy of export controls will thereby be undermined because of a singular failure to take into account the profound effects of the technological thrusts that are now under way. Similar admonitions apply to recent defense department efforts to broaden controls on international technology transfers through parallel systems of government classification of defense-related technology development; of government control over scientific communication and access to information; of government control over foreign investment in, or ownership of, domestic facilities that provide products or services to the Department of Defense and the military services; and unilateral controls over applications of R&D involved in projects like the Strategic Defense Initiative (even when some of that R&D have originated in a commercial context prior to participation in a defense-sponsored project). This rapid extension of defense department concepts and controls into areas of commercial R&D in Europe and Japan will not be sustainable, and Western cooperation will sooner or later fragment under the evolving pressures of global technological change.

The convergence of defense and nondefense technology development also suggests the need for a reexamination of national technology policy. It has long been argued, for example, that defense and space R&D were of limited commercial significance. Thus, although about half of U.S. R&D is funded by the government—and well over half of that government support is for defense R&D—it is often said that there is little benefit to economic competitiveness. Other governments, it is sometimes argued, focus some of their R&D funding on achieving improvements in commercial competitiveness. This line of reasoning has given rise to considerable support in the United States for countermeasures against foreign government targeting policies.

These arguments, however, have decreasing relevance to European and Japanese technology policies, but they could probably be applied in reverse, with increasing relevance, to U.S. technology development. Defense department and NASA R&D programs are increasingly overlapping with major commercial R&D thrusts and are increasingly supportive of those thrusts. This means that there is an urgent need for fundamental reexamination of the dual-purpose consequences of government supported R&D, especially in the areas of defense and space.

CONCLUSION

The sheer force of technological changes now under way will cause fundamental structural adjustments, whatever governments try to do about them. Controlling these forces of change through policies of protection and economic nationalism will tend to be counterproductive.

Unilateralism in technology transfer policies will accelerate the fragmentation of Western cooperation and will intensify the search for technology autonomy in many countries, aggravating the very problems that controls are designed to resolve. A greater degree of international cooperation among governments and of transnational cooperation among private enterprises and research establishments seems to provide the only sensible path.

Government and industry therefore need to rethink the costs and benefits of cross-border cooperation in devising technology policies, assisting basic research, encouraging and exploring emerging technologies, and generating policy responses to the structural adjustments being forced on the world economy.

Vague thinking along such lines was initiated at the 1982 Western Economic Summit, but little came of it. The OECD Committee on Science and Technology is exploring some dimensions of these issues, but with little policy impact on capitals. The EC is moving in its own way, with emphasis on European projects and internal market-opening measures to provide larger-scale market opportunities for European technologies. Japan and the United States spend much time in policy combat and little in the exploration of long-term mutual interests.

Thus, acting together, governments can hope to avoid mutually conflicting policies. But there are two important roles that each of the governments could play independently:

First, governments could try to improve their macroeconomic policies to encourage faster innovation, investment, and growth. They could try to improve the tax treatment and other incentives for innovation, with particular attention to stepping up the speed of innovation and the pace of competitive responses to foreign challenges. Governments could create an environment that favors creation of new businesses and institutional change. But policies that rely on assisting existing large enterprises, and on concentrating new technology development in them, as seems to be the tendency in the EC, will tend to aggravate the difficulties of structural adjustment.

Second, governments could educate their publics, including their business enterprises, about the nature of the forces now at work and the fundamental structural changes that will be necessary to meet them. When political pressures build for intervention in specific sectors, governments should illuminate for the public at large the underlying structural problems and the complexity of adjustment to changing global circumstances. Perhaps, in this connection, the United States and Western Europe could learn a lesson from the Japanese government by generating their own consensus visions of the nature and direction of industrial change.[1]

In educating their citizenry, governments should avoid publicly blaming other governments whenever there is an underlying problem of structural adjustment. The politics of blame may play well in the short term; but in the long run, shifting blame simply diverts public attention from the need for change, while encouraging counterproductive foreign responses.

There is no hope to be found in policies that try to halt or to slow the historic forces now at work throughout the world. The way forward to enhanced economic well-being and quality of life must lie through policies that encourage more rapid structural change in our economies and more rapid adaptation of our education and lifestyles. Technology is opening up revolutionary opportunities for us all, if we go with the flow, rather than fight it.

NOTES

1. In the United States, a substantial effort to develop perspectives on the implications of technological change has already been set in motion by the National Research Council, in conjunction with the National Academy of Sciences and the National Academy of Engineering. See, in particular, National Research Council (1986).

REFERENCES

Clark, J. P., and M. C. Fleming. 1986. "Advanced Materials and the Economy." *Scientific American*, Vol. 255 (Oxtober): 41.

National Research Council, Manufacturing Studies Board. 1986. *Toward a New Era in U.S. Manufacturing: The Need for a National Vision*. Washington, D.C.: National Academy Press.

2 MEETING THE TECHNOLOGY CHALLENGE
Toward a U.S. Agenda

Pat Choate and Juyne Linger

THE TECHNOLOGICAL EDGE

U.S. economic progress has long been grounded in its remarkable capacity to innovate and apply new technologies. In recent years nine of the ten fastest-growing U.S. industries have been in high-technology areas. High-tech industries such as computers, optical and specialty equipment, aircraft, and telecommunications now provide 6.4 percent of all U.S. jobs (Personick 1985: 37), employ 25 percent of scientific workers (International Trade Administration 1983: 25), create more than 13 percent of the value of manufacturing product shipments (International Trade Administration 1983: 4), and constitute 43 percent of the total value of U.S. manufactured exports (International Trade Administration 1985: 14).

Rapid advances in microelectronics, materials, software, fiber optics, biotechnology, and many other technologies promise an irresistible surge of even greater progress. And the application of these new technologies—whether in improvements of existing products, in wholly new goods and services, or in the automation of production processes—is crucial to U.S. competitiveness, boosting productivity as it does through lower costs, greater versatility in processes, and higher-quality goods and services.

THE UBIQUITOUS RESOURCE

Technology has become a ubiquitous global resource: Developed in one firm or nation, a new or improved technology soon appears in many firms and many nations. How technology becomes available—whether through licensing, migration of skilled workers, education exchange programs, publications, simultaneous development, or even theft—has become irrelevant. Holding sole possession of a technology as the Venetian glassmakers did for three centuries is no longer possible. Technology has become so universal that the exceptions, such as the secrecy surrounding the formula for making Coca-Cola, are rare. The spread of technology cannot be stopped, only slowed, and the owner's proprietary rights can be only partially protected. Although theft or expropriation of U.S. technology can be reduced in the short term, the only effective long-term strategy for coping with technological diffusion is for the nation to remain at the cutting edge of innovation and application, thus setting the pace of change.

Increasingly, however, that pace is being set by other nations. U.S. technological superiority, virtually uncontested for decades, is no longer assured. The slowness in introducing new technologies and the growing technological capacities of other nations have combined to diminish the U.S. lead. Indeed, foreign countries now set the pace of technological progress in an increasing number of industries including automobiles, consumer electronics, and advanced machine tools.

The United States' principal technological competitor, Japan, now has a clear lead in a number of technologies that will define global competitiveness in the 1990s. These include large-scale computer processors, magnetic disk storage devices, printers, semiconductor production equipment, biotechnological fermentation processes, and key components of fiber-optic technology such as light sources.

With its ambitious Technopolis plan, Japan intends to expand this lead by creating nineteen high-technology industrial complexes throughout the nation by 1990. In an attempt to replicate the Silicon Valley environment that fostered so much innovation and creative research in the United States, each Technopolis will integrate high-tech industry with a university or research institute and pleasant residential areas designed to attract engineers and researchers.

Each locality is responsible for developing its own Technopolis program, including selection of a site; identification of program goals; the planning, construction, and maintenance of industrial land and water service, housing, and roads; and creation of a legal body to facilitate financing for businesses and other services needed for industrial development. Once government approves a locality's plan, it provides wide-ranging assistance such as favorable tax-depreciation allowances, business financing, and construction of needed infrastructure.

A number of Technopolis programs have already been approved. In the prefecture of Toyama, home of Toyama University and the

Toyama College of Medicine and Pharmacology, the approved plan calls for developing a high-tech complex devoted to robotics, new materials, biotechnology, and information industries. To strengthen the area's research and development capacity, a Center for Research on Life Sciences will be established, along with a Center for the Exchange of Advanced Technology. On the northern island of Hokkaido, the new Technopolis will specialize in marine-related and natural resource–based industries. Businesses locating there will be able to draw on the resources of Hokkaido University as well as an expanded Hakodate Industrial Research Institute and a new Hokkaido Prefectural Center of Industrial Technology. The Technopolis project promises to yield new products, processes, and technologies—and an even more powerfully competitive Japan.

Equally significant, many developing nations, particularly the NICs, are aggressively expanding their technological capacities. Brazil, for example, has become a major contender in the commuter aircraft market. Embraer, Brazil's state-owned aerospace company, obtained technology and manufacturing expertise from Piper Aircraft to build its highly successful Bandeirante, an eighteen-passenger twin-engine turboprop. With low-cost equity capital, subsidized export financing, a protected domestic market, and subsidized consumer financing at below-market interest rates, Embraer was able to capture one-third of the U.S. commuter aircraft market in just four years.

The nations of the Pacific Rim have been even more aggressive in developing technological expertise. Companies in Korea, Singapore, Hong Kong, and Taiwan are rapidly upgrading their technological base through research, licensing, and student exchanges and by disassembling and studying U.S. and Japanese products. Improved technological capacity and dedicated workforces will make these nations formidable economic competitors in the years ahead, much as Japan is today. The Koreans, already successful in steelmaking and shipbuilding, are now entering the motor vehicle and electronics industries. Even the Japanese are concerned about the stiff competition surfacing throughout Southeast Asia.

AUTOMATE OR EVAPORATE

The difficult options confronting the United States have been summarized by James A. Baker, executive vice-president for technical systems at General Electric, who once said, "American firms have three choices: automate, emigrate or evaporate."

The real choice, however, is automate or evaporate. Simply put, if U.S. industry is to retain its competitiveness, it must have the cost savings, flexibility, and qualitative improvements that automation makes possible.

Recognizing the need to strengthen their competitiveness, U.S. firms are indeed automating quickly. Advances in computers and software now make possible the automation of most office work. Microcomputers and commercial software, for instance, can already automate most invoicing, payroll and cost accounting, inventory controls, order processing, personnel records, and financial controls. And improved word processors now being developed will take dictation, automatically prepare text, check spelling and grammar, transmit text via electronic mail, and then file the document.

Morgan Stanley and Company has calculated that new technology investment per service worker more than doubled from $415 in 1975 to more than $1,000 in 1985 ("A Productivity Revolution in the Service Sector" 1983: 106). This trend portends an extraordinary surge in productivity and competitiveness for the expanding U.S. service sector in the years ahead.

Comparable gains do not appear imminent in U.S. manufacturing where automation is proceeding at a much slower pace overall. Because of the significant labor-cost savings inherent in automation, it is coming fastest in unionized industries. Not surprisingly, the auto industry accounts for about 60 percent of the robots in use in the United States (U.S. Department of Commerce 1985 : 21–26). General Motors alone plans to invest $1 billion to install 20,000 robots by 1990 (Fred K. Foulkes and Jeffrey L. Hirsch 1984 : 95). The most highly automated tasks, moreover, tend to be hazardous, strenuous, or repetitive operations such as spray painting, welding, loading and unloading, machining, and some assembly work.

The technologies needed to automate most manufacturing work in the United States exist and are in use but have not been integrated into comprehensive applications in most industries. Computer-aided design and computer-aided manufacturing (CAD/CAM), for example, are now used by most major manufacturing firms. So too are computer-controlled machine tools, robots, inspection and quality control systems, factorywide communication systems, computerized procurement and inventory control systems, production-line balancing techniques, process controls, and automated materials handling and warehousing systems. These automated processes have typically been introduced piecemeal because the software and process engineering needed to link them have not been available.

Indeed, U.S. manufacturers have been markedly slower in introducing automation technologies than have their competitors abroad. In 1980, for example, the United States possessed 15 percent of the world's robots (Gevarter 1982: 81–83). Because of the lagging pace of U.S. automation and accelerating pace of automation abroad, however, the United States will possess less than 10 percent of the world's robots by 1990.

The rapid advances in automation by foreign companies can be traced, in part, to the strong and explicit government support these firms enjoy. West Germany, France, and the United Kingdom have already created national programs of research and development. In addition, these governments are providing training for scientists and engineers, along with technical assistance, capital grants, and loans for firms using automation technologies. Britain, for example, gives a 50 percent grant for all corporate-sponsored robotics feasibility studies and a 33 percent grant for all investment in robotics.

But of all nations, Japan has been most aggressive in fashioning a long-term infrastructure of automation, having more than three times as many robots in operation as does the United States. The Japanese government is financing a $215 million, long-term research effort on automation; it permits a 53 percent first-year tax deduction for robotics investment; it has formed a national leasing company to lease automation equipment to companies, thus reducing initial capital costs; and it offers small and medium-sized firms special low-interest loans for robotization. The government also provides financing for the Japan Industrial Robot Association, which conducts research on robot marketing and application techniques and monitors global technological developments and patents, which are translated into Japanese and distributed.

By contrast, the U.S. government does not monitor the automation efforts of other nations, offers no technical assistance to firms, provides no special incentives for firms to automate, and funds less than $10 million of nonmilitary research on automation.

REAPING THE BENEFITS

U.S. technology has long given U.S. companies a powerful comparative advantage over foreign firms, particularly when it is applied first and best. The competitive edge of U.S. business is shaped not only by the quality of its technology but also by how adroitly and quickly that technology can be applied in the marketplace. Unfortunately, numerous barriers, both domestic and foreign, impede its flexible and widespread application.

Domestically, U.S. managers slow the deployment of new technology by delaying its introduction until customers tire of an existing product, until capital investment is fully depreciated and worn out, or until competition emerges. No U.S. company manufactured radial tires until the 1970s, when foreign firms began to build tire factories in the United States. Six years elapsed between the invention and eventual commercialization of the ballpoint pen, thirteen years between the invention and commercialization of xerography, ten years with the turbojet engine, five years with magnetic recording, and fourteen years with the jet engine (Mansfield 1968: 101). As late as 1984, 9 percent of the nation's raw steel was being produced with antiquated nineteenth-century open-hearth furnaces (U.S. Bureau of the Census 1985: 765). The video cassette recorder, invented in the United States in 1956, was never commercialized here; today, Japan's Sony and Matsushita command 90 percent of the U.S. market.

In years past, when the U.S. economy faced little foreign competition and the pace of technological change was much slower, managerial inattention to major technological breakthroughs and deliberate delays in the introduction of improved technology were of much less consequence. Now, however, firms of other nations are extremely aggressive in their technological competitiveness. U.S. companies that fail to take an innovation or product quickly from development to production to market domination and then on to the next generation in the process are sure to suffer in the marketplace.

Domestic laws and administrative practices also diminish the ability of U.S. firms to create and use their own technology. Uncertainty over which technologies they are permitted to export and the slow, confusing, inefficient licensing practices of the government impede U.S. exports of goods and services as well as technology transfers between U.S. companies and their foreign subsidiaries.

The licensing of exports of widely available technology to Eastern European countries takes from four to six months in the United States, four months in West Germany, two months in France and the United Kingdom, and only one month in Japan. Even when such exports are destined for trading partners in the West, licensing takes an average of four weeks in the United States and West Germany. The United Kingdom, France, and Japan, by contrast, do not even require licensing for exports to many free-world countries.

The United States needs efficient export review and licensing processes that can distinguish, quickly and well, the few technologies that are truly critical to national security from those that are widely available from foreign suppliers. Such distinctions are essential if the United States is to avoid further estrangement from its allies and further rejection of its firms by foreign customers who consider U.S. companies unreliable because of government sanctions.

Domestic antitrust policy is another barrier to the deployment of U.S. know-how. By law a firm is considered to have made a *per se* antitrust violation when it enters into a production or marketing strategy with an affiliate in which it does not have effective control, which is generally considered to be majority ownership. Yet many foreign governments force U.S. firms to cede majority ownership of their affiliate to a local partner. In these circumstances, antitrust laws force the U.S. firm to become a minority investor, give up control, and maintain an "arm's-length" relationship with its affiliate. If the U.S. State Department cannot negotiate away those restrictions, the Justice Department should give affected firms an automatic antitrust exemption.

Conflicting and uncertain tax policies also distort the application of U.S. technologies. For example, even as the government gives firms a 25 percent R&D tax credit to stimulate research activities, its policy on allowable R&D tax expenses permits a firm to deduct only part of those investments. The portion of R&D that is deductible is equal to the U.S. share of a company's sales worldwide. Thus, if a company does all of its research in the United States but registers only one-half its sales in the domestic market, it can deduct only half its R&D expenditures. The U.S. Treasury insists that the balance must be deducted from income earned abroad. Foreign governments, however, refuse to recognize these expenditures for their tax purposes unless the firm actually conducts the research within their borders. Therefore, firms must either forgo the U.S. tax deduction or move part of their R&D investments from U.S. universities and company labs to other nations.

The firms most directly affected are the large companies, which finance most of the privately sponsored research. Because these companies already have international operations, it is relatively easy for them to shift research from U.S. to overseas facilities.

The consequences of this policy have repeatedly been brought to the attention of U.S. Treasury officials who respond that they need the tax collections to relieve the deficit. Yet this inflexible short-term myopia will inevitably harm the national interest. It encourages firms to move research operations offshore at the same time the Department of Defense is embargoing foreign sales of technology. It gives other nations access to some of our most advanced technology. It takes funds away from universities that are training the next generation of scientists and engineers. This destructive policy on research and development requires fundamental reform.

Not all of the impediments to the creation and deployment of competitive technologies are self-inflicted, however. Other nations are reducing the technological competitiveness of foreign firms, including U.S. companies, through a variety of measures: import restrictions and controls of foreign investment and production are imposed; access to foreign research is sought, while their own R&D is jealously guarded; and intellectual property rights are flagrantly violated.

These nontariff barriers come in many guises. Brazil requires that a foreign firm locate research, administrative, and production activities in that nation as a precondition of market access. In India, foreign firms must license or share advanced technologies with local companies; Coca-Cola withdrew from India in 1978 because it was unwilling to share its secret formula with an Indian company. And in the dozens of nations that refuse to protect intellectual property rights, locally owned firms can expropriate and use foreign patents, copyrights, and trademarks without paying their owners.

In combination, this foreign protectionism coupled with weak U.S. responses leave U.S. firms no choice but to forgo certain foreign markets or move their facilities overseas and comply with these demands, however outrageous they may be. Unfortunately, compliance has many adverse consequences for the United States: It is costly to companies, it shifts jobs overseas, and it forces firms to share U.S. technology—sometimes even imperiling foreign workers, managers, and partners who are not adequately prepared to deal with a dangerous technology.

As other industrial nations close the technological gap with the United States, access to the basic research that underpins further technological advance becomes increasingly important. Access to Japan's scientific and technical research is particularly important. Japan has the world's third largest research labor force and now ranks third in the world in total R&D spending, behind the United States and the Soviet Union. Japan is also a leading publisher of scientific and technical journals. The Congressional Research Service reports that the Japanese have more than 9,100 journals that focus on science and technology, and their companies now file more patents in the United States than U.S. companies file in Japan (U.S. Congress 1984: 3).

U.S. scholars and companies face numerous barriers when they attempt to secure access to Japanese scientific and technical information. Language is one difficulty, but Japanese copyright laws are an equally formidable obstacle. To secure Japanese reports, even government reports, for use in the United States, Americans must make the painstaking and time-consuming effort to secure a release from each author, sponsoring organization, and issuing organization. Even then, the Japanese prohibit the U.S. government from circulating many reports on science and technology to U.S. industry and other potential private sector users. This is ironic because so much of Japan's industrial progress has been based on its access to foreign technology, science, and technical information: More than 42,000 contracts transferring technology to Japan from abroad were signed between 1951 and 1984 (Kristof 1985: sec. 3, p. 1). The United States has been the primary source of these technology exports.

Foreign governments also limit U.S. access to their basic research efforts. In the United States, most basic research is accomplished in universities; in Japan most is conducted in industrial research consortia. Japan steadfastly refuses to allow U.S. companies to participate in these consortia, limits the sharing of any research, refuses to permit U.S. scientists and engineers to participate in most studies, and restricts the sale or licensing of its advanced commercial technologies.

Japan's universities have also been closed to U.S. scientists. In 1985, only one American was teaching at a Japanese university (Joseph 1985: 142). The appointment of this American, Californian Robert Geller, to a professorship in seismology at Tokyo National University came about only after Japan's Education Ministry exempted universities from a century-old law that prohibits foreigners from teaching in Japanese schools.

In addition, Japan sharply limits the participation of U.S. firms in government-sponsored technical committees that set product standards. Motorola, for example, had to pass Japanese government standards on paging equipment in order to sell the devices in Japan. But the Japanese would not release the product standards until Motorola's Japanese competitors reviewed and helped set these standards. After considerable protest and negotiation, the Japanese finally agreed to place Motorola on its standards committee for paging equipment—but only on the subcommittee that set standards for the chain and clip that attach the pager to the user's belt. Motorola's access to information on electronic standards was severely limited. Similar restrictions are imposed throughout Japan's telecommunications industry.

At the same time, foreign firms have virtually unlimited access to technical information in the United States. Indeed, foreign governments and firms buy 20 to 25 percent of the technical and scientific information disseminated by the National Technical Information Service, a little-known but important branch of the federal government (Caponio 1986). The Japanese government and Japanese firms are among the largest purchasers.

The Japanese have also been quite aggressive in establishing long-term, lucrative alliances with U.S. universities. In fact, most of Japan's major companies are funding research at U.S. universities.

Business Week reports that research funds from Japan have become so important at the Massachusetts Institute of Technology that the university now has an assistant director for Japanese gifts as well as a liaison office in Tokyo ("Japan Is Buying Its Way into U.S. University Labs" 1984). Japanese firms have endowed nine chairs at MIT at $1 million each. Forty-five of the 297 companies participating in MIT's industrial liaison program, through which companies can pay $30,000 a year for primary access to research that is not sponsored by other firms, are Japanese. Thus, for fractions of pennies on the dollar, Japanese firms have access to some of the very best research and most advanced research funded by the U.S. government.

Foreign companies also contribute $500,000 annually to research on advanced communications technology at MIT's media lab. In return, MIT permits these firms to send their own researchers to participate in the studies and gives the firms royalty-free, nonexclusive licenses to any technology that is developed ("Japan Is Buying Its Way into U.S. University Labs" 1984).

A very small minority of universities refuse to accept research funds from foreign companies. Carnegie-Mellon University in Pittsburgh, a leading robotics research center, is one ("Japan Is Buying Its Way into U.S. University Labs 1984). Because many universities are actively pursuing foreign support and sharing their research results, they are placing other nations precisely at the strategic edge of the most advanced U.S. research.

To the extent that other nations can acquire foreign technologies without sharing their own advances, they can seize the technological advantage and do so with minimal R&D investment. In these circumstances, other nations will have the best of our research and exclusive use of their own.

The current lack of technological reciprocity, particularly with Japan, can no longer be permitted. The government must ensure that U.S. scholars, scientists, engineers, and businesses have the same access to the science and technology of other nations as their overseas counterparts have in the United States. Because of Japan's well-known and well-honed ability to delay negotiations, an effective starting point in creating such reciprocity could be to prohibit further Japanese investment in U.S. university research and to limit Japanese scientific exchanges until Japan grants technological reciprocity to U.S. scholars and firms.

The considerable risks associated with research and development can be justified only if firms and individuals have a reasonable chance of recovering their costs and receiving compensation for their efforts. Yet the increasing complexity of technology, the nation's growing involvement in global markets, and the enormous rewards awaiting those able to steal the technology of others have made the protection of intellectual property rights increasingly difficult.

Existing international rules governing protection of patents, trademarks, and copyrights are deficient in many respects. Although copyright laws have been standardized between many nations, protection of patents and trademarks varies widely. For example, some countries prohibit the patenting of medicines and agricultural chemicals. Many governments—Argentina, Mexico, Colombia, India, and Brazil, for example—will cancel a patent if a local company can prove it is in the "national interest" to do so (President's Commission on Industrial Competitiveness 1985: 324-39). U.S. pharmaceutical firms that want to market their products in Canada, the Philippines, Israel, and India are forced to license their technology to local firms. Japan, which lags far behind the United States in computer software, has considered removing software from the protection of its copyright law, thereby enabling the Ministry of International Trade and Industry (MITI) to force foreign companies to license computer software to Japanese firms. Egypt permits a ten-year patent term for pharmaceuticals. India and Yugoslavia afford patent protection for only seven years. The United States, by contrast, provides seventeen years of patent protection.

Although many less developed nations have stiff laws to protect intellectual property rights, most make infringement of these rights almost impossible to prove or impose such trivial penalties that the laws have little deterrent value. The bureaucratic obstacles to registering patents and trademarks in many nations are so burdensome, time-consuming, and costly for a foreign firm as to be virtually insurmountable.

Weak international standards are fostering the piracy and counterfeiting of U.S. products throughout the world. The International Trade Commission reports that counterfeit goods are flowing into the United States from forty-three other nations (President's Commission in Industrial Competitiveness 1984: 17-18). The ITC also reports that two-thirds of all counterfeit goods made worldwide are sold in the United States. These sales now cost U.S. business nearly $8 billion and 131,000 jobs annually.

Poor protection of intellectual property rights in Singapore alone costs U.S. companies hundreds of millions of dollars each year (U.S. Trade Representative 1985: 4). In 1984, unauthorized copies of discs and cassettes cost the U.S. recording industry $50 million in Singapore and an additional $170 million in Singapore's export markets;

illegal copying cost the U.S. publishing industry $7 million in Singapore and $100 million in the export markets; and software copyright violations in Singapore's domestic market cost U.S. firms $20 million. Counterfeit apparel costs the Calvin Klein Company as much as $20 million a year in sales. And the number of counterfeit Swatch watches imported into the United States each day—an estimated 10,000—nearly equals Swatch Watch USA's daily sales of legitimate timepieces—about 11,000. U.S. publishers exported $5 million to $8 million of books and journals to Korea in 1984; at the same time, however, sales of unauthorized copies in that nation totaled $70 million.

Indeed, most U.S. companies are affected. Phony Apple computers are sold throughout the Far East. Counterfeit parts have been found in heart pumps, the Boeing 737, the F-4 fighter plane, in the Chapparall and Lance missiles, and Sikorsky and Bell helicopters. The products of virtually every pharmaceutical firm are counterfeited. Unlicensed copies of Stanley hand tools are made in Taiwan and sold in the United States. A growing number of nations, particularly in the Third World, expropriate U.S. technology, go into competition with U.S. firms, and even export the products to the United States.

The primary weakness in the international system of patents, copyrights, and trademarks is the absence of international standards. Most developing nations are not signatories to existing treaties. Furthermore, present arrangements require only that nations provide foreign firms the same protection afforded local firms. Because most developing nations provide virtually no patent protection, it is perfectly legal for local firms to take U.S. technology and produce goods to be sold in global markets. Moreover, as existing treaties have no enforcement mechanisms or penalties, they represent little more than gentlemen's agreements.

The United States is woefully unprepared to protect the intellectual property rights of its citizens and firms in the global marketplace. There is no overall policy on scientific and technological exchange with other nations and little protection for U.S. inventors and firms against the sale or use in the United States of foreign goods made with expropriated technology. Most distressing, foreign competitors, governments, and their agents can use the U.S. Freedom of Information Act (FOIA) to obtain access to proprietary and confidential information of inventors and firms. In 1982, for example, the U.S. Food and Drug Administration received more than 34,000 FOIA requests, many of them from foreign governments, foreign firms, and their U.S. agents (President's Commission on Industrial Competitiveness 1985 : 323).

Foreign nations, particularly less developed countries whose firms are counterfeiting and stealing U.S. technology and whose governments are expropriating much of what remains, are sure to oppose U.S. efforts to strengthen the international protection of patents, copyrights, and trademarks. Nevertheless, access to the U.S. market is a powerful negotiating tool.

The first and most critical step in what is sure to be a long process is for the United States to develop a negotiating position and strategy as well as the will power to take unilateral actions against those who believe they can keep their unfair advantages by refusing to negotiate. In 1985, the President's Commission on Industrial Competitiveness identified many of the steps needed in such an effort (President's Commission on Industrial Competitiveness 1985: 340–48). They include the use of existing economic incentives such as foreign aid to encourage other nations to create and enforce intellectual property rights standards; creation of legislation that will permit the federal government to take selected forms of economic retaliation against nations and firms that steal U.S. patents, trademarks, and copyrights and then use them to go into business against their rightful owners; assignment to the Department of Commerce of responsibility for establishing an information system to monitor and evaluate the protection provided by other nations; initiation of bilateral, plurilateral, and multilateral negotiations on intellectual property rights with other nations; and appointment of a presidential commission of scholars, business people, foreign policy experts, and government leaders to help the president and Congress create a long-term strategy to safeguard U.S. technology.

These are common-sense recommendations with considerable merit. Whether these or other approaches are used, however, the key point is that U.S. technology is a major national economic asset—but only if it can be adequately protected from theft or expropriation and readily deployed by U.S. firms.

REFERENCES

Caponio, Joseph F. 1986. Presentation at Washington Researchers' Conference, Washington, D.C., March 10.

Foulkes, Fred K. and Jeffrey L. Hirsch. 1984. "People Make Robots Work," *Harvard Business Review*. January-February.

Gevarter, William B. 1982. *An Overview of Artificial Intelligence and Robotics*, Vol. 2. U.S. Department of Commerce.

International Trade Administration. 1983. *U.S. Competitiveness in High-Technology Industries.* U.S. Department of Commerce.

_____. 1985. *United States Trade Performance in 1984 and Outlook.* U.S. Department of Commerce.

"Japan Is Buying Its Way into U.S. University Labs." 1984. *Business Week.* September 24, pp. 72–77.

Joseph, Jonathan. 1985. "The First American College Professor in Japan." *Business Week.* May 27.

Kristof, Nicholas D. 1985. "Americans Picking Japanese Brains." *New York Times.* September 8.

Mansfield, Edwin. *The Economics of Technological Change.* 1968. New York: W.W. Norton.

Personick, Valerie A. 1985. "A Second Look at Industry Output and Employment Trends Through 1995." *Monthly Labor Review* (November).

President's Commission on Industrial Competitiveness. 1984. *Preserving America's Industrial Competitiveness: A Special Report on the Protection of Intellectual Property Rights.* October 1984.

_____. 1985. *Global Competition: The New Reality*, vol. 2.

"A Productivity Revolution in the Service Sector." 1983. *Business Week.* September 5.

U.S. Bureau of the Census. 1985. *Statistical Abstract of the United States: 1986.* 106th ed.

U.S. Congress. House of Representatives. Committee on Science and Technology. 1984. *The Availability of Japanese Scientific and Technical Information in the United States.* November.

U.S. Department of Commerce. 1985. *1985 U.S. Industrial Outlook.* January.

U.S. Trade Representative. 1985. *Annual Report on National Trade Estimates, 1985.*

3 THE INTERNATIONALIZATION OF TECHNOLOGY
Balancing U.S. Interests

Stephen A. Merrill

ACTION AND REACTION

Through foreign policy and economic cycles, the premise that Soviet acquisitions of leading Western commercial technologies with military applications represent a security threat has not been seriously challenged either in the United States or in the Western alliance. Although there have been lapses in attention and frequent disputes over the scope and means of controlling technology flows to the East, there has not been a major domestic or international quarrel over principle. This consensus underlies the success of defense policymakers of the Reagan administration in advancing an agenda of strict export controls in spite of the fact that their initiatives provoked bitter turf battles and coincided with a deep global recession, a steadily deteriorating U.S. trade balance, and the uproar in the alliance over the U.S. embargo on supplying equipment for construction of the Siberian gas pipeline.

At home, federal law enforcement agencies launched an unprecedented campaign to detain unauthorized shipments and prosecute diverters. The president extended the Defense Department's export license review authority beyond sales to the Soviet bloc and China to include a significant number of West–West transactions. The Commerce Department imposed new conditions, including requirements for internal corporate and external government audits, on bulk exports to approved customers in Western countries under so-called

Distribution Licenses. And the administration eventually secured a new Export Administration Act (EAA) giving it enhanced enforcement powers. This legislation eased the conditions on lower-level technology trade with the European allies and Japan but otherwise made few concessions to U.S. exporters or to foreign trading interests and political sensitivities.

Abroad, the Reagan administration revived the Coordinating Committee for Multilateral Export Controls (CoCom), the informal organization of NATO members (excluding Iceland) and Japan that maintains a common list of proscribed items and passes on requests to approve some technology sales to the Eastern bloc and China for nonmilitary uses. At U.S. instigation CoCom members held their first ministerial meetings in twenty-five years, tightened some of their licensing and enforcement procedures, admitted Spain to membership, upgraded Paris headquarters operations, and agreed to seek the cooperation of nonmember countries. The allies added to the international control list certain types of machine tools, dry docks, semiconductor manufacturing equipment, robotics, superalloy technology, telecommunications equipment, and software. A ten-year debate over what levels of computer hardware should be kept from the Soviet military was finally resolved by compromise. Outside of CoCom, Sweden, Austria, and Switzerland instituted limited controls on technology trade with the Soviet bloc.

To be sure, the allies were hostile to what many perceived to be a broader administration policy of economic denial, with the exception of grain, the principal U.S. export to the Soviet Union. Nevertheless, the administration used Soviet actions in Afghanistan and Poland to its advantage and even contained the bloodletting over the pipeline embargo. U.S. attempts to inject other than strictly military security considerations into CoCom deliberations met with firm resistance in some instances—refusals to embargo items of oil and gas equipment and large turnkey factories, however benign their output. Yet in other cases the allies agreed to politically motivated changes— a moratorium on all exception requests for exports of controlled items to the Soviet Union and a liberalization of technology trade with the People's Republic of China.

On the whole, however, the Reagan administration took advantage of CoCom's narrow mandate, relative obscurity, and isolation from other multilateral institutions and the domestic politics of member states. Aided by a French intelligence windfall, detailing the breadth and alleged accomplishments of Soviet technology acquisition efforts, U.S. representatives carried the day on most issues in

CoCom by presenting a plausible strategic rationale for taking controls much more seriously than had been the case during detente.[1]

The Gorbachev succession has not changed the Reagan administration's basic calculations and concerns. The Soviet military build-up, espionage activities, and efforts to divert desired goods from legitimate Western trade channels all continue apace, the latter apparently shielded from the fluctuations in Western credits and foreign exchange earnings that have constrained purchases of Western technology for the civilian sector.

The startling revelation that in the early 1980s the Soviets obtained from Japanese and Norwegian firms (Toshiba Machine Company and Kongsberg Vaapenfabrikk) sophisticated milling machines and computer controls capable of producing ultraquiet submarine propellers showed that there continue to be gaps in the CoCom net. Consequently, defense policymakers are proceeding with an unfinished agenda. They are worried about technology leakage from unclassified, military-sponsored applied research and development, intercorporate data transfers, public and private computerized databases, and even U.S. patent filings. They will continue to scrutinize the export licensing process for loopholes and maintain pressure on CoCom partners and third countries to harmonize controls.

Nevertheless, a reaction has been gathering steam. In May 1986, barely ten months after the protracted debate over the EAA extension exhausted itself and its partisans, the U.S. House of Representatives passed sweeping amendments to its national security control provisions. A year later, both the House and Senate endorsed similar changes. These are not failed proposals revived but expressions of bipartisan concern that administration policy overcorrected. One amendment would immediately remove controls on low-level technology to all Western countries. Another provision would eliminate the restrictions on reexporting that accompany U.S. goods to CoCom countries and relax them on parts and components to other Western customers. A third instructs the executive branch to take a meat axe to the United States and, by implication, CoCom lists of controlled commodities and remove up to 40 percent of the products covered. That these provisions are part of trade legislation signifies a change in perspective.[2]

As part of President Reagan's competitiveness initiative, the administration itself has taken steps to relax reexport controls on U.S. parts and components incorporated in foreign-made equipment and to introduce a new form of export authorization, permitting unlimited shipments to CoCom-country end-users whose reliability in pre-

venting diversions can be certified. All of these initiatives are responsive to the complaints of exporters and multinational companies that
the shoe has begun to pinch their ability to compete successfully
against foreign firms subject to fewer or no restrictions.

In Europe, where U.S. export controls have heightened prevalent
feelings of technological and economic insecurity, resentment against
U.S. restrictions on intra-alliance trade and technology transfer has
resurfaced in several quarters. As in the pipeline episode, the objections are mainly to the U.S. assertion of jurisdiction over U.S.-origin
goods and know-how in foreign hands. There is also concern about
discrimination against friendly foreign nationals in access to U.S.
research and suspicion regarding the terms of weapons cooperation
agreements, including those related to the Strategic Defense Initiative
(SDI). As many Europeans see it, they are impeded in gaining access
to the technology that would help Europe become competitive with
the United States and Japan, and they are hampered in the commercial use they can make of it.

In 1985 the North Atlantic Assembly supported the creation of a
new European agency both to promote European technological
independence and to bargain with the United States on technology
transfer issues. And in a lengthy resolution adopted in the spring of
1986, the European Parliament proposed more radical responses to
the "unilateral and especially indiscriminate proliferation" of U.S.
technology controls. The resolution asked the EC Commission to
consider seeking a European Court of Justice ruling on the compatibility of CoCom rules with provisions of the Treaty of Rome and
urged member states to adopt legislation, modeled on the British
Protection of Trading Interests Act, blocking the application of U.S.
extraterritorial restrictions to British firms.

Emanating from the fringes of political power, these statements
nevertheless reflect the mood that a few European governments have
conveyed more discreetly. In the European private sector, executives
of several major multinationals have intimated that the entangle-
ments accompanying the use of U.S. componentry and technology in
commercial products are leading them to reduce their dependence
on U.S. sources of supply (see Dekker 1985; "Reagan Curbs Hit"
1986: 1).

Thus, the domestic and foreign complainants are fueling one another's anxieties. This is unlikely to undermine the basic consensus
on East–West technology transfer but does challenge the newly
crafted policy expression of that consensus sooner than most observers anticipated.

UNDERLYING CROSS-PRESSURES

The current situation has no parallel in previous cycles of tightening and relaxation, which reflected the ebb and flow of East–West conflict. Changes in Soviet behavior have only marginally influenced the continuing pressures for restriction and the emerging pressures for restraint. Both are products of revolutionary technological and economic changes confined almost entirely to the West.

The area of principal concern from either a military or a commercial perspective is the electronics sector—integrated circuits, semiconductor manufacturing equipment, CAD/CAM and robotics, computer systems, communications networks, and software.[3] In many of these technologies, defense R&D funding and purchases contributed to the development of U.S. products and industries that became crucial to both the performance and production of weapons and military command and control, while dominating world markets. By the late 1970s, however, both military roles were greatly reduced. The U.S. Department of Defense has not remained a consistent technology leader either in development or in procurement, with the result that weapon systems use components and production technologies that lag well behind the commercial state of the art.

Simultaneously, U.S. firms began to face serious international competition, forcing shorter commercial product cycles and globalization of development and production as well as marketing. At the high end of the technology spectrum, the Japanese have narrowed or surpassed the U.S. lead in certain types of semiconductors, semiconductor manufacturing equipment and materials, optoelectronics, and robots and factory automation as well as some biotechnology applications and advanced materials.[4] Lower down the scale in such areas as microcomputers and memory chips both countries are ceding markets to producers in Korea, Taiwan, and other newly industrializing countries (NICs) as a result of widespread licensing, joint ventures, second-sourcing, and copying. Diffusion of know-how is now occurring within months rather than years of a new technology's appearance on the commercial market.

These developments have several implications for export control policy. First, widespread availability of technology in the international market increases the risk of and thus concern about technology diversion to the Soviet Union. Leakage increases with the quantity of product available, the number of production sources, and the complexity of supply and distribution channels for secondhand as well as new products. It follows that the control policies of other countries have become critical to the success of efforts to contain the flow. If major CoCom partners have more permissive control regimes than does the United States, transfers will increase as their capabilities and market shares increase. The Toshiba milling machines and Kongsberg numerical control equipment, sold directly to the Soviets in violation of multilateral agreements and national laws, apparently contained not a trace of U.S. componentry or licensed technology. The non-CoCom NICs—uniformly aggressive exporters—pose another challenge, initially as users and reexporters of advanced technology but increasingly also as producers.

Second, the security risk, though inversely related to the technology lead of Western military hardware over that of the Warsaw Pact, is probably directly proportional to the lead of Western commercial products relative to U.S. military applications, because the Soviets, if they were able to acquire and apply militarily advanced commercial technologies, could significantly narrow the qualitative advantage in military weapons enjoyed by the West. In any case, .the gaps between the level of commercial and U.S. military technology and between the latter and Soviet capabilities imply a very extensive commodity control list, encompassing not only advanced technologies but also many items that are obsolescent by commercial standards and perhaps some mass-produced consumer products that incorporate sophisticated components.

Third, controllers are now more concerned about transfers of intangible dual-use technology—design and production know-how—because the intervals between development and commercialization and between commercialization and international diffusion have appreciably shortened.

Fourth, as foreign technological advances surpass the levels of the United States, additional complexities arise. The reliance of the U.S. military as well as computer and peripheral equipment manufacturers on Japanese sources of certain standard components is a matter of growing unease. The Defense Department has secured an agreement to obtain selected Japanese military technologies. U.S. officials will soon be in the unusual position of identifying foreign technologies as candidates for control in advance of their development or acquisition by the United States. Even in the unlikely event that Japanese and U.S. technological levels remain comparable, as the Japanese come to dominate world markets in more and more finished products, the United States will be asking Japan to bear a much greater share of the responsibility and economic burden of controls. The reality is that U.S. political influence will decline along with its technological and market leadership.

Finally, although the magnitude is hard to determine, export controls do some damage to U.S. economic and competitive performance (National Academies of Sciences and Engineering 1987: ch. 5). Some marginal economic losses would occur even without foreign competition, simply as a consequence of proscribing certain markets and thereby limiting economies of scale and reinvestment. Competition is nevertheless increasing virtually across the dual-use technology spectrum from countries that impose less sweeping controls and, in many cases, administer them more efficiently as well as from countries that have no formal controls at all. U.S. producers of medium- and lower-level technology products are most vulnerable because increasing numbers of non-U.S. sources, many of them with cost or other advantages, exist for these items or for their essential components.

The costs of export controls are not strictly commercial; they also have implications for the respective military capabilities of the Western alliance and the Warsaw Pact. Reduced revenue may translate into less investment, a lower growth rate, and reduced innovation, the effects of which could be important to the military as well as the commercial sector. To the extent that U.S. controls encourage the growth or emergence of foreign competitors subject to looser restrictions, they indirectly increase the likelihood of technology diversion to the Soviet bloc.

POLICY ADJUSTMENT AND READJUSTMENT

Policy Dimensions

The new characteristics of Western technology development and competition point to two radical policy conclusions. The pessimistic inference is that as export controls assume greater importance as a means of preserving the qualitative superiority of U.S. military forces, they become more overreaching and thus more ineffective and costly in practice. A more optimistic conclusion is that controls are most effective and least costly when they are uniform among Western producers and consumers of dual-use advanced technologies. The latter interpretation poses a positive objective rather than a hopeless dilemma for U.S. policy—the creation vis-à-vis the East of a common wall of export controls allowing the removal of most national security restrictions on commercial trade and technology exchange within the West.

Notwithstanding the Toshiba–Kongsberg case, and perhaps even aided by it, improvements in CoCom and progress in securing the cooperation of European neutrals have made the concept of a common market in dual-use technology a more realistic objective, provided that the allies create incentives for the participation of key third countries while strengthening controls on exports to countries that do not cooperate. CoCom partners are not in the habit of scrutinizing exports of multilaterally controlled items to third-country destinations that are potential points of diversion to the Soviet bloc, nor have they vigorously supported U.S. efforts to reach control accommodations with leading NICs. Thus, creation of a control-free zone even confined to CoCom depends on major policy adjustments on the part of the European allies and Japan.

The Common Market concept depends, too, on the U.S. restraint in pursuing unilateral policies. Restraint may be dictated by underlying economic trends in any case. Balancing national interests encompasses more dimensions than it did even in the recent past. In addition to East–West and alliance relations, policymakers will be forced to consider aspects of U.S. competitiveness and trade policy as well as problems in weapon development and deployment. Further, whatever balance is struck must be reassessed and readjusted with some frequency, for technological and economic changes show signs of accelerating, not abating.

In reviewing each of these policy dimensions, one can conclude that there is a strong case for revising U.S. policy even in the short term. But does the policy process in place have the capacity to make whatever adjustments and readjustments are necessary over a longer period? There are several unresolved export control policy issues, some of them alluded to previously. In abbreviated terms, these four issues are:

Scope of Coverage of Controls. Much of the debate over export controls pertains to the scope of the control effort—the number and value of dual-use products whose export to all countries except Canada requires prior government approval. Neither figure is known with any degree of certainty, but a conservative estimate is that in 1985 U.S. firms exported more than $60 billion in manufactured goods—almost 40 percent of total U.S. exports of manufactures—under licenses issued for individual and bulk shipments (National Academies of Sciences and Engineering 1987: app. C). Can all of the items subsumed under 239 categories described in 120 pages of regulations resulting in well over 100,000 license applications annually be deemed to be military significant or strategic? Do they, in the aggregate, exceed the effective span of control? Congress and parts of the executive branch continue to struggle, largely ineffectually, to develop criteria and mechanisms to limit controls to critical items and remove those whose military utility is marginal or to which the Soviets have access in spite of CoCom controls.

Controls on Technical Information to the West. Some U.S. officials perceive an anomaly and a significant risk in the government's current policy of scrutinizing transfers of unclassified but militarily sensitive technical data to the East while relying primarily on corporate proprietary controls to prevent diversions of such data from West–West transactions. Among other recent efforts to limit foreign access to public and private technical information,[5] Defense Department officials are in the process of identifying a number of critical dual-use technologies (a subset of the Department of Defense Militarily Critical Technologies List) with an eye to proposing that their transfer be reviewed and licensed to most foreign nationals and destinations (see Weinberger 1986: 21). Nevertheless, the practical difficulties of controlling not only personal communications and publications but also computer-based telecommunications systems are formidable. Will U.S. engineers collaborating electronically with Japanese and Korean colleagues on the design of a product or process or the operation of a manufacturing facility be required to have a license? How will the national origin of the collective effort or particular pieces of it be identified? Cannot the data be instantly transmitted to an offshore haven free of controls (see Malmgren 1984)?

U.S. Reexport Controls. In addition to other precautions to ensure the reliability of customers in Western countries, the United States alone often requires purchasers of controlled products to seek written prior approval to reexport, even if the item is incorporated in a product primarily manufactured abroad. Alerted to this peculiarity of U.S. law by the pipeline sanctions and by new distribution license regulations subjecting foreign distributors and users of U.S. products to audits of their activities, many businesses and foreign governments consider unilateral reexport controls a burden on U.S. and foreign commerce, a violation of international law, and a symbol of U.S. mistrust of its allies. In other quarters, reexport authorization requirements are regarded as an essential protection against diversion, precisely because other countries' control of West–West transactions is comparatively lax.

Associating the NICs with Controls. The United States has undertaken to persuade a number of rapidly developing Asian and Latin American countries to institute CoCom-like controls on exports of indigenous products, reexports of Co-Com origin items, and transshipments of goods regardless of origin. From a control perspective the logic of this course is compelling, but there is disagreement about negotiating strategy (for example, whether to deny or delay transfers of U.S. technology pending an agreement or to hold out the prospect of favored-treatment transfers once an agreement is reached) and about the acceptability of compromise agreements (for example, to control only U.S.-origin, not indigenous, technology). Both strategy and results may affect the competitive position of U.S. firms.

The Soviet Dimension

The prospect of protracted strategic conflict argues for continuity in export control policy. Relaxation of strategic controls in a period of optimism regarding detente can negate the effectiveness of previous control efforts and make the job more difficult and disruptive when tensions resurface. More immediately, changes in Soviet policies under Gorbachev are too uncertain to justify a wholesale retreat from the restrictive policies of the last few years. Soviet military modernization continues with the aid of Western technology. Signs of domestic political liberalization and foreign policy moderation are tentative. And despite Gorbachev's rhetorical emphasis on investment and technological modernization, the market prospects for Western exporters are severely constrained by structural features of the nonmarket economies, inconsistencies in the new Soviet Five-Year Plan, and low world oil prices (Wienert and Slater 1986).

The contrast with China in most respects could not be more striking. Liberalization of technology transfer was one element of a broader reassessment of U.S.–Sino political and economic relations, justified in the first instance by post–Cultural Revolution domestic and foreign policy changes that have so far remained more or less on course. No such transformation is in prospect in the Soviet Union. Consequently, such notions as freeing up roughly half of the items on the CoCom embargo list can be viewed as granting the Soviets a gratuitous windfall that would materially ease the burden of their military modernization efforts.

For the time being, any significant relaxation of technology controls must be justified on grounds other than changes in Soviet behavior and resulting improvements in East–West relations. There are several possibilities. First, decontrol does not represent a windfall or increase security risks where products or data are readily available to the Soviets from uncontrolled sources at prices approximating world market levels. The hypothesis here is that certain mass-produced commodities such as personal computers and semiconductor memory devices are available in such volume and from so many sources that they are uncontrollable in fact. Second, controls may not be necessary if the Soviets have chronic difficulty in making effective use of acquired technology even for military purposes. This may be the case with design and production know-how other than that embodied in CAD/CAM, manufacturing, and testing equipment or accompanied by training and other support services. Third, it may be advisable to relax or forgo unilateral West–West restrictions if, partly as a result, CoCom partners or the NICs can be persuaded to do a tolerable job of preventing diversions to the East. Fourth, controls should be curtailed or abandoned if the damage to Western economic vitality and technological progress exceeds the benefits of denial to the Soviets.

The Alliance Dimension

The recent friction between the United States and its allies does not represent fundamental differences over West–East transfers of strategic technology. That consensus would dissolve only if there were a sharp divergence among Western perceptions of Soviet behavior and the opportunities for accommodation. So far no such divergence has occurred despite differences in attitude regarding the Gorbachev succession and the prospect of an improved climate for East-West trade.

Moreover, the allies proved to be susceptible to U.S. pressure and persuasion on a series of technology transfer issues in the early 1980s, even under the provocation of the pipeline sanctions. Nor have U.S. export controls turned out to be an insuperable obstacle to agreements on SDI collaboration. Even if U.S. reluctance to transfer advanced technology without restrictive conditions acts as a slight incentive to European arms cooperation, defense industry integration, and civilian technology collaboration, that is arguably of benefit to Western defense capabilities.

The test of U.S. technology security policy, however, is not the level of formal international cooperation but the adequacy of the allies' performance at both the governmental and private-sector levels. The risk of an overreaching set of controls is that it will gradually undermine the credibility of the system and thus the degree of compliance with it. Maintaining and extending a web of unilateral West–West restrictions may not only undercut cooperation but also drive the development, application, and marketing of some technology to weaker links in the chain of controls.

The Competitiveness and Trade Policy Dimensions

Consideration of the economic effects of export controls has been severely handicapped by a dearth of reliable information and the lack of any mechanism for its generation. National security export control regulations are exempt from the usual requirements for analysis of the costs and benefits of proposed rules. Affected exporters, although in the best position to know the extent of the administrative burden and lost sales attributable to controls, have great difficulty even estimating these effects.

What can be surmised is, first, that the base of affected trade is so large that even a marginal negative effect can have significant consequences for the high-technology sector of the economy. Second, the burden of controls is spread across a wide range of medium- and lower-level technologies whose contribution to Soviet military capabilities would be less than critical and where U.S. producers have the fewest competitive advantages. Third, the costs of controls to U.S.-headquartered industrial firms are primarily in trade with the West and are a function of differences in national treatment of internationally competitive suppliers of technology.

Vis-à-vis other CoCom country sources, U.S. competitive disadvantages are a function of

The greater efficiency and predictability of other countries' export licensing procedures;

The tendency of the U.S. government to interpret the technical parameters of entries on the international control list more strictly than other CoCom governments;

U.S. unilateral controls, currently on some twenty-seven categories of products, prospectively on a range of technical data;

U.S. extraterritorial controls on reexports of U.S.-origin products and foreign products containing U.S. components or simply manufactured with U.S.-origin technology.

Vis-à-vis non-CoCom country sources of technology, U.S. suppliers are at a disadvantage

Because all but a handful of countries (Switzerland, Sweden, and Austria) maintain no national security export controls;

When the United States government alone uses license denials or delays as leverage to secure agreements to control exports;

Where the United States concludes a bilateral agreement, as with India, that restricts only reexports of U.S.-origin technology.

Another neglected consideration is the clash between export control practices and the traditional market-opening thrust of U.S. trade policy. The inconsistency between asserting extraterritorial jurisdiction in one context and insisting on national treatment in other trade and investment contexts is one paradox, although not a new issue and not one that arises only with respect to export controls. It will be more difficult for the United States to lead the drive for global liberalization of services trade and investment while seeking to expand technical information controls. Especially outside the alliance, where the national security priority is less well appreciated, tighter controls on the flow of technical data are likely to be interpreted as part of a U.S. shift toward economic protectionism.

The Weapon Development/Deployment Dimension

Justice cannot be done in this essay to the complex issues of military procurement except to note that the military product cycle is the single element of the changing technological and economic environment that is directly subject to government control. On the development side of the equation, the Defense Department is investing much more heavily in advanced technology. Its VHSIC, high-speed computer, and SDI programs may break out of the pattern of the military's lagging behind developments in the commercial sector. On the other hand, a great many of the building blocks of strategic defense and NATO's emerging technologies initiative for conventional deterrence—VLSI circuits, advanced software/algorithm technology, artificial intelligence, supercomputers, advanced materials and composites, fiber optics, and high-energy lasers—are technologies that have already emerged and are flourishing or at least beginning to show promise commercially (Heisbourg 1986: 71-111; DeLauer 1986: 40-70). Progress in accelerating the deployment of advanced technology is less encouraging.

Near- and Long-Term Policy Adjustments

Although the rationale for maintaining national security export controls remains compelling, certain adjustments in U.S. policy are warranted because the costs incurred are excessive or controls are ineffective or changes can yield more effective multilateral controls.

Scope of Coverage. The target of decontrolling 40 percent of the items currently subject to licensing appears to be arbitrary and therefore politically infeasible. Some pruning needs to be done, however, if only to remove most unilateral controls and commodities that are so widely available that they are uncontrollable.[6] Narrowing the scope of coverage would increase the efficiency of an overburdened licensing system, focus enforcement on more critical technologies, raise the control regime's credibility with U.S. industry and foreign governments and businesses, and enhance the prospects of agreements with the NICs by eliminating from contention some of their own developing export markets that they are loathe to restrict.

Information Controls. Notwithstanding the logic of limiting the transfer of militarily sensitive technical information in Western channels of communication, it is extremely hard to define and segregate such information and to devise effective means of control, beyond proprietary protections but short of classification, without disrupting vital West–West data flows. On the other side of the equation, a convincing case has yet to be made that the Soviets are skilled in adapting, applying, diffusing, and improving on intangible technology.

Reexport Controls. Unilateral U.S. reexport controls are a growing irritant in allied relations and a disincentive to doing business with U.S. firms when alternative sources of comparable products are available. Formal compliance by foreign-owned firms, especially those based in CoCom countries, appears to be minimal (see National Academies of Sciences and Engineering 1987: 243-46). The prospect of persuading CoCom members to institute similar requirements is negligible. Relaxing reexport controls would remove an impediment to multilateral cooperation and U.S. exports at minimal risk to national security.

NIC Negotiations. Efforts to negotiate a series of bilateral control agreements with the newly industrializing countries could stretch out endlessly and yield results that are disadvantageous to U.S. firms in both the short and long runs. The leverage derived from prevailing foreign preferences for acquiring U.S. technology will diminish over time. Diplomatic efforts should be closely coordinated with the allies. They should rely less on holding U.S. technology hostage to cooperation on export controls and more on the promise of easier access once satisfactory agreements are reached.

The prospects for these or any other near-term policy adjustments depend in part on the strength of their constituencies and in part on the ability of the policy mechanisms in place to clarify uncertainties, resolve differences, and implement consensus. The former is a matter of speculation. The latter depends on a recognition that technological and economic change will force a rebalancing of diverse U.S. stakes—if not now, eventually and probably repeatedly.

Past experience suggests that these longer-term prospects are relatively poor. Shared responsibility among bureaucratic rivals has been a chronic feature of export control policy and administration. The president has intervened only intermittently and then usually to arbitrate controversial licensing cases and contain policy conflicts.

Other than the occasional pressure of CoCom allies, there is no effective mechanism for weeding out from the control list technologies that have ceased to be strategic or that have become widely available. The momentum is to add not to delete, and the Department of Commerce, the principal licensing agency with a stake in keeping its task from becoming unmanageable, has been only marginally effective in slowing it down. Only temporary expedients or cumbersome case-by-case review procedures, not long-term solutions, have been advanced to address this deficiency.

Under the Reagan administration, there has been a marked shift in the bureaucratic balance of power to security, intelligence, and law enforcement agencies and away from those entities responsible for technology development, trade, and international economic relations. In the Defense Department, a new organization, the Defense Technology Security Administration, reporting to the Undersecretary for Policy, has assumed most of the responsibilities that previously resided in the office of research and engineering. In the State Department, security assistance officials have assumed the lead role from the economic affairs bureau. The Commerce Department is under a statutory mandate to remove export administration from the International Trade Administration to stand on its own below the Office of the Secretary.

These changes have contributed to a reinvigorated control system, a credible enforcement capability, better threat assessment, a more effective diplomacy, and even improvements in license processing. They bode less well for a realistic export control policy that imposes the least burden on the nation's competitiveness and innovative capacity.

Solving the export control dilemma without compromising recent improvements in the multilateral system depends on presidential and congressional leadership. The domestic policy adjustments and diplomatic initiatives necessary to advance the goal of a Western common market in dual-use technology merit that level of attention.

NOTES

1. The so-called Farewell Papers are summarized and interpreted by the CIA in Central Intelligence Agency (1985).
2. As of this writing, the House and Senate versions of the omnibus trade legislation, incorporating amendments to the EAA, are in conference committee.
3. In FY 1985 the electronics categories on the control list accounted for well over 70 percent of the value of individual export license applications approved and over 80 percent of the number of applications approved. The following section relies in part on the Ferguson (1985) studies of the electronics sector.
4. See the 1984–86 panel reports of the Japanese Technology Evaluation Program (JTECH), operated by Science Applications International Corporation, La Jolla, California, under contract from the National Science Foundation. These include assessments of the relative U.S. and Japanese positions in computer science, mechatronics, opto- and microelectronics, biotechnology, advanced materials, and telecommunications technology.
5. The unclassified information on which additional restrictions are being placed or considered include technical data developed in military-sponsored research and falling within a category on the Militarily Critical Technologies List (MCTL), data in patent applications relating to inventions with military or space applications, data contained in federal government automated information systems, and data within certain "supercritical" MCTL categories that private parties wish to transfer to Western countries or foreign nationals. See National Academies of Sciences and Engineering (1987: ch. 5) for a description of the restrictions and legal authorities.
6. The Co-Com agreement announced in August 1987, to remove controls from certain personal computers is an encouraging, if modest, development in this regard.

REFERENCES

Central Intelligence Agency. 1985. *Soviet Acquisition of Militarily Significant Western Technology: An Update.* Washington, D.C.: U.S. Government Printing Office.

Dekker, W. 1985. "The Technology Gap: Western Countries Growing Apart?" Paper presented by the president and chairman of N. V. Philips at the Atlantic Institute for International Affairs, Paris, December 5.

DeLauer, Richard D. 1986. "Emerging Technologies and Their Impact on the Conventional Deterrent." In *The Conventional Defense of Europe: New Technologies and New Strategies,* edited by Andrew J. Pierre, pp. 40–70. New York: Council on Foreign Relations.

Ferguson, Charles H. 1985. *American Microelectronics in Decline: Evidence, Analysis, and Alternatives.* Cambridge, Mass.: Massachusetts Institute of Technology, VLSI Memorandum 85-284.

Heisbourg, François L. 1986. "Conventional Defense: Europe's Constraints and Opportunities." In *The Conventional Defense of Europe: New Technologies and New Strategies*, edited by Andrew J. Pierre, pp. 71-111. New York: Council on Foreign Relations.

Malmgren, Harald B. 1984. "Technological Change and Trade Policy." Paper presented to the Stockholm Symposium on Technological Trends and International Trade, Stockholm, June 1984.

National Academies of Sciences and Engineering. 1987. *Balancing the National Interest: U.S. National Security Export Controls and Global Economic Competition.* Report of the Panel on the Impact of National Security Controls on International Technology Transfer. Washington, D.C.: National Academy Press.

"Reagan Curbs Hit U.S. Electronic Sales Overseas." 1986. *Financial Times* (October 16): 1.

Weinberger, U.S. Secretary of Defense Caspar. 1986. *Militarily Critical Technologies Program.* Washington, D.C.: U.S. Government Printing Office, July 17.

Winert, Helgard, and John Slater. 1986. *East-West Technology Transfer: The Trade and Economic Aspects.* Paris: OECD.

4 TELECOMMUNICATIONS
The Need for a Policy Framework

Robert R. Bruce

In the last few years, there have been enormous changes worldwide in the telecommunications sector and in related fields such as data processing, electronic publishing, and electronic transactional services. The development of new services and of new regulatory frameworks is, however, creating an increasingly complex agenda of issues for trade officials.

The task for policymakers is anything but easy. It is likely that both existing as well as evolving arrangements for electronic services will coexist. In developing trade strategies, therefore, policymakers must not only understand how such arrangements are developed and work but also adapt them to the framework for negotiations in the new General Agreement on Tariffs and Trade (GATT) round. An additional complicating factor is that services are being developed to differing extents in countries worldwide; one result is that there are, among the nations, disparate levels of interest in establishing new trading links.

One difficulty in making policy is that the telecommunications and other sectors are distinct—having different industry participants and differing legal and regulatory structures—and yet converging. The new services that are being "traded" internationally are neither well defined nor easily differentiated. Nevertheless, it is critical to separate the spectrum of services if coherent policies and strategies to increase opportunities for international trade are to be devised. One important point is that telecommunications and telecommunications-dependent services are, in fact, not "traded" but are offered internationally over a network that is interconnected worldwide.

Another difficulty in resolving trade issues in telecommunications and related sectors is that industry arrangements are in a process of significant restructuring that is creating substantial opportunities for new entrants. At the same time, such restructuring complicates the establishment of trade relationships because the reorganization of the domestic sector can distract business and governmental leaders from its international implications.

Changes in the telecommunications sectors of several industrialized countries are occurring in tandem with the liberalization of financial markets in some industrialized nations. Global networks are creating international financial markets. New information-processing technologies are changing the structure of the financial industry. Processing capabilities are increasingly challenging the historic roles of brokers and exchanges.

Collectively, these developments are spawning a host of new electronic financial services. In turn, such services are generating substantial demand for telecommunications services. Indeed, whereas international telecommunications services in their early phase were centered around maritime transportation, and subsequently were based on the role of airlines, financial services are now seen as driving the development of the telecommunications infrastructure. This background creates difficulties in structuring new electronic financial services on an international basis.

In its concluding section, this chapter identifies the most significant trade-related problems in structuring arrangements for international telecommunications and information services. It also offers some views on how policymakers, particularly in the United States and elsewhere in the industrialized world, may best position themselves to respond to some of these emerging problems.

FROM TELECOMMUNICATIONS TO ELECTRONIC FINANCIAL SERVICES

The development of a regulatory framework for new telecommunications and other telecommunications-dependent services and a trade regime for international arrangements for such services turn on understanding what services exist or are emerging. Hence, it is necessary to explain some of the differences between telecommunications, information-based and transactional, or other electronic financial services.

At the outset, there is certainly no agreement on the fundamental definition of what constitutes "telecommunications" services and how such services might be differentiated from other services that rely on telecommunications. Telecommunications can be viewed, urge representatives of the newly emerging industry sectors, as involving the basic transport of information by networks of transmission facilities; the distinction being made, then, is between pure transmission services—an "open pipe"—and enhancements or changes in the transmission of information.

In the United States, the Federal Communications Commission (FCC) has been struggling with these definitional issues for well more than a decade. In both its *Computer II* and *Computer III* inquiries,[1] the FCC identified such pure transmission services as "basic" services, contrasting them with what are called in the United States "enhanced" services.

To explain further, enhanced services combine nontransmission services and capabilities with pure transmission services and are, for this reason, sometimes referred to as value-added. Enhanced services may include the capability to change the codes, formats, or protocols of a transmission to permit different types of computers or terminals to communicate with each other; such protocol conversion services do not affect the content of the transmission itself. Other enhanced services may combine transmission with data processing functions to deliver a processed message that is different from the message as it originated; yet other providers of enhanced services actually supply information in response to a customer's request.

The FCC, in its *Computer II* and *III* decisions, did not clarify what other services might be included in the spectrum. Its goal was primarily to limit the regulation of processing services such as protocol conversion and to move away from a simple distinction between, on the one hand, communications and, on the other, data processing—a distinction that the FCC had found to be unworkable.

There remains in the United States some definitional uncertainty as to the precise status of two kinds of services—remote access data processing and database services. A remote access data processing service allows a "remote" user to obtain access to the computer processing capacity of a vendor on a time-shared basis. A database service sells information stored in centralized computers to business and residential users. Both kinds of services are telecommunications-based because they rely on networks of transmission lines leased from carriers and on computer nodes that concentrate transmissions to and from their customers.

Although vendors of these remote-access data processing or information-based services are clearly not offering merely pure telecommunications capability, they are, increasingly, offering services that are closely intertwined with raw transmission services. Using the services, customers can transmit messages that relate to the information that is being conveyed, processed, or supplied; at the same time, the network of leased lines that are used by the vendors to deliver their services can also be used by customers to obtain access to another customer's own databases or computers.

Although these hybrid services are definitely not regulated in the United States, the question may arise in other countries whether the operator of an international leased line network is supplying telecommunications—a message switching service—to others. The question is not merely academic because many telecommunications administrations, heeding certain recommendations of the Consultative Committee on International Telegraph and Telephone (CCITT) of the International Telecommunications Union (ITU), forbid the unauthorized use of international leased lines that would permit such operators to offer telecommunications-like services that would infringe on the prerogatives of national monopolies. Vendors of remote access data processing or database services, in distinguishing their offerings from those supplying only telecommunications services, point out that any communications-related capabilities are, in fact, integral to the processing or information component of the service.

That such services are not merely communications is made clear by the fact that the need for the link would not exist in most cases but for the offering of the information service. Yet another kind of service—a so-called transactional offering—can be used to illustrate this point.

Many information vendors of stock exchange or commodity price quotations, for example, are offering customers the ability to execute transactions based on the underlying information or to place bids. Customers use the same network and processors that transmit the information to carry out an activity that might also be conducted over conventional telephone or telex services. It is clear that the vendor's purpose is not to compete with a telecommunications provider in offering communications services but, rather, is to offer something akin to electronic brokerage.

How a service is defined may well, in short, affect whether a foreign telecommunications administration views the service as infringing on its monopoly. Vendors of new transactional services have been careful to avoid anything that would permit characterization of the communications component of their service as the resale of leased circuits, which would violate the above-mentioned CCITT recommendations.

More broadly, the issue of how to define or delimit telecommunications—as distinct from other services—may have some practical consequences for the vendors of enhanced or value-added services. For example, the CCITT Preparatory Committee of the ITU's 1988 World Administrative Telegraph and Telephone Conference (WATTC-88) has been considering an expansion of the definition in the ITU regulations of telecommunications services to embrace new value-added and information-based services.

The information and financial services sectors are deeply concerned that the proposed change in the definition, which is being urged by many telecommunications authorities around the world, would empower administrations to apply restrictive national regulatory schemes to new business activities. For a host of reasons, the U.S. government has not yet fully decided on a policy that would respond to these various, and inconsistent, national and international pressures.

SOME SPECIAL CHARACTERISTICS ABOUT
TRADE IN TELECOMMUNICATIONS AND
INFORMATION SERVICES

There are four principal reasons why it is difficult for policymakers and others to grapple squarely with the issues raised by international trade in telecommunications and related services—as distinct, for example, from trade in both goods and other types of services (such as banking or insurance). First, the new panoply of telecommunications-based services, unlike trade in goods and many traditional services, is only now emerging; indeed, new services are being created to fill market niches every day. In the United States, new electronic financial services are being developed with some vigor, but the international marketing of many of these services is at an early stage. Elsewhere in the industrialized world—in the United Kingdom, in Japan, and in a handful of other countries—similar services are in the process of developing; such developments are occurring, however, at varying paces that are influenced by unique national industrial and regulatory conditions. Thus, it is not yet certain what issues will, in fact, need to be addressed.

Second, generalizing about the problems of market entry and the international provision of particular services is difficult. Services are being developed in the brokerage, commodities, database, banking, and many other sectors. Yet each specific field of business enterprise and each new electronic activity must, from a regulatory perspective, be analyzed on its own terms. In short, there can be no simple, broad-based response by policymakers to the emergence of these new services.

Third, there is no actual trading—at least in the conventional sense—of telecommunications and information services. Rather, when offered internationally, the services are physically interconnected (by cable or satellite circuits). Thus, even though such services are not traded, the terms and conditions applicable in foreign markets are critically important and must be negotiated. For traditional telecommunications services such negotiations are aimed at concluding an operating agreement with a foreign telecommunications partner or supplier of communications circuits. For the new services, however, vendors may need to obtain approvals to do business or additional clearances from regulators in the nontelecommunications sectors. Many services are sufficiently novel, however, that officials may not be prepared to confront how they ought to be classified and regulated under national law.

Fourth, the physical nexus to a foreign country usually necessary for trade in goods and services may not be as crucial for information-based services. The new telecommunications- and information-based offerings can be marketed in foreign markets with relatively little in the way of physical infrastructure, correspondent relationships, or establishments of business other than the capacity of telecommunications networks and information processing facilities. Vendors can develop the core of a new service in the United States and, using a network of international leased lines, extend the offering abroad relatively easily. The ephemeral quality of these services does raise the important question of what physical infrastructure or presence—whether it be the mere connection of a computer into an international network or the situs of switching nodes—will be viewed as an adequate basis for the exercise of jurisdiction by national regulators.

RECENT INTERNATIONAL DEVELOPMENTS IN THE TELECOMMUNICATIONS SECTOR AFFECTING TRADE IN TELECOMMUNICATIONS AND INFORMATION SERVICES

Telecommunications policy worldwide is undergoing a radical transformation as a result of a complex array of technological and economic pressures. Cumulatively, such changes in policy are fusing what had been essentially the two distinct spheres of telecommunications and trade policies.

To start with the United States, the processes of deregulation by the FCC and the divestiture of AT&T under the auspices of Judge Harold Greene have had important global consequences. In combination, the effect has been to shift the pricing of telecommunications services within the United States toward cost. With the competition provided by new U.S.-based providers of telecommunications services (such as MCI and GTE/Sprint), the pricing of international services also is moving toward costs.

In 1984, both the United Kingdom and Japan enacted comprehensive new telecommunications legislation, with both countries deciding to end the monopoly of their historic telecommunications providers, British Telecommunications (BT) and Nippon Telegraph and Telephone (NTT), respectively. Mercury is the single, statutorily authorized provider of transmission facilities that is now challenging BT; NTT will face at least five entrants providing transmission services. In both countries, moreover, a host of vendors—relying on the network and transmission services provided by BT, Mercury, NTT, and the others—will use computer processing and switching services and leased circuits to weave a myriad of new services; in the United Kingdom these are referred to as value-added services, and in Japan as Type II (as contrasted with Type I transmission services).

In France, the new government has proposed to allow a few providers of value-added network services to compete with the Direction Générale des Télécommunications (DGT), the telecommunications authority. Moreover, a new regulatory body—the Commission Nationale de la Communication et des Libertés—will be empowered to approve new private telecommunications networks and to consult with the DGT on the development of new networks to supply services to third parties. The government has also proposed to enact by the end of 1987 a new law setting the parameters for competition in the telecommunications sector.

In the Federal Republic of Germany, the process of change for the Deutsche Bundespost has been slower. German policymakers have been on the horns of a dilemma. This dilemma results from economic pressures to move prices toward costs in response to similar pricing moves by neighboring European administrations at the same time that political pressures require the maintenance of substantial subsidies for postal services and for other social objectives embedded in the telecommunications pricing structure.

In the Netherlands, the telecommunications administration is being turned into a limited liability corporation. Moreover, the Dutch are essentially opening up competition by providers of value-added services—a process in which Dutch policymakers are closely following the British model.

In Canada, Finland, Spain, and Italy, telecommunications policies are also under review. It is important to note that the process of revisiting telecommunications policies is not restricted to the industrialized countries but is underway as well in such Third World countries as Sri Lanka and Malaysia.

Several factors are both fueling these changes and are a direct response to shifts in policies. Perhaps most significant is that the price of telecommunications services increasingly is being driven toward cost. As the Germans—who are being pressured by liberalization in the United Kingdom, by aggressive pricing policies by the French DGT, and by moves in the Netherlands—are coming to realize, it may no longer be viable for foreign telecommunications administrations to maintain historic subsidies in the pricing structures.

Economic pressures are forcing many telecommunications administrations to rethink old policies and to explore new industry structures that may generate increased utilization of their networks and hence new revenues. Concomitantly, competitive pressures are generating an intense rivalry—particularly in Europe but in Southeast Asia as well—among national telecommunications administrations to become the hub of international telecommunications networks. This rivalry has created significant price competition among the major international communications centers and has encouraged competition in the offering of liberal terms for the use of leased lines by large users of telecommunications.

These changes in national telecommunications policies increasingly have involved trade officials in structuring new relationships between the offerers of telecommunications and information services. In the past, the international telecommunications environment was stable and new service arrangements were worked out on a relatively routine basis by the concerned operational entities.

Today, in those countries where two or more providers of international public switched telephone services have been authorized, the agreements between monopoly service providers on both sides of a circuit must be modified to take account of the existence of multiple suppliers, the need for new traffic routing and interconnection configurations, and the potential for competition among suppliers with respect to the terms and conditions for dividing revenues. Thus, there now must be new arrangements for the new services. In the

United States, these agreements may be concluded with some oversight, if not actual involvement, by telecommunications policymakers and trade officials—the latter seeking to open markets, especially those located in Europe, that traditionally have been closed to outside service providers.

Outside telephone services, the need for discussions that might lead to new international agreements or other understandings is even more urgent and complex. Many countries have decided to authorize providers for value-added services. As made clear by a comparison of the regulatory models adopted by the United States, the United Kingdom, and Japan, however, all of which have authorized virtually unlimited service-based competition, the national definitions and regulatory classifications pertaining to these new providers often do not coincide. Devising interconnection arrangements among the value-added service providers in light of these regulatory inconsistencies or disparities will be an exceptionally important task for telecommunications and trade officials over the next several years.

THE EMERGENCE OF ELECTRONIC FINANCIAL SERVICES: NEW SERVICES AND NEW PROBLEMS

It will be especially difficult to work out interconnection arrangements for the new information and transactional financial services in light of their evolutionary state and inconsistent national regulatory frameworks. Furthermore, regulators often have not grasped the potential of, or are confused by, emerging new services. In short, the capacity of regulators is being outstripped by the swift pace of technological development.

New electronic markets for securities or foreign exchange are, for example, beginning to replace the traditional physical markets for buying and selling. Such markets are based on a web of leased lines linking computer processing centers or the networks of banks or brokers in major financial centers; they depend on the electronic dissemination of pricing information and on affording customers the capability to execute transactions. The new markets use information obtained from the simultaneous querying of buyers and sellers through their own computer processing facilities—and do not necessarily rely on a single, vendor-supplied bulletin board. For example, a NASDAQ exchange for venture capital-oriented enterprises is now being studied by a group of banks and European venture capital companies. The Instanet service in the United States facilitates direct transactions among major brokers and institutional investors.

Furthermore, international circuits allow instantaneous access to the pricing of financial instruments or commodities around the world. They greatly facilitate the participation by foreigners in domestic markets. Thus, it is clear that it will be difficult for regulators to confine new electronic market services within national boundaries. Concurrently, the easy availability of communications and processing capabilities is causing a collapse of the boundaries between historically separate sectors within the financial industry and between national markets.

Moreover, the decision of many industrialized countries to liberalize their finance sectors is creating opportunities for new financial services; a few of the liberalizing trends in the financial area that are relevant to the emergence of new electronic services serve as illustration. The nearly contemporaneous liberalization of the financial and telecommunications sectors has been mutually reinforcing. Liberalization in the telecommunications sector is affording suppliers of new electronic financial services a competitive choice of transmission vehicles. Conversely, the emergence of such financial services, and the demands of users for sophisticated communications capability, is creating demand for the underlying telecommunications services. Thus, liberalization and competition in the telecommunications sector increasingly are seen as a proposition that is both economically and politically viable.

The Big Bang in London of October 1986 ended the distinction between brokers and jobbers or market makers on the London Stock Exchange. This restructuring may well not insulate the Exchange, however, from significant diversion of trading to markets off the exchange floor that are based on electronic links between a network of brokers and dealers. Moreover, growth of the market for Eurobonds, already far exceeding the volume of the London Stock Exchange, is likely to depend increasingly on electronic links to develop underwriting and then secondary markets for commercial paper.

Liberalization of financial markets in London is prodding other countries in Europe to follow suit. Stock exchange officials in Amsterdam and Paris are concerned that the British move will cause trading in Dutch and French securities, respectively, to shift to London unless their own trading practices are liberalized. Historically separate exchanges in the Federal Republic of Germany and in Italy are being connected electronically for the first time.

There is also a major transformation taking place in the financial markets of Japan. These changes are being spurred, of course, by Tokyo's emergence as a preeminent financial center and are also due to the extraordinary amounts of investment capital that are accumulating as a result of the trade surplus with Japan.

The Japanese financial market has been quite rigidly separated into banking and securities sectors. The financial sector is viewed as conservative, with the least innovative and flexible participants setting the pace. Major banks, until recently, have been relatively passive in responding to new technological developments due to the generally deferential approach of Japanese business to regulatory authority.

The internationalization of financial markets is causing these traditional attitudes to change. With their customers having easy, communications-based access to other financial markets, Japanese financial institutions have had to react to international trends. Regulators have had to respond, too. Largely in response to the demands of the banks, which want flexibility to deal with each other and with other dealers in foreign exchange, the Japanese Ministry of Finance, for example, recently approved the introduction of the Reuters dealing service over the objections of Japanese foreign exchange dealers. Soon, Japanese regulators will face the question of whether institutional trading networks such as Instanet will be permitted to operate in Japan.

The liberalization of the financial services sector, which is working symbiotically with shifts in telecommunications policy to foster an environment in which new electronic financial services can flourish, is confronting both business leaders and regulators with difficult issues in determining the future arrangements for information-based services. What, then, are some of the problems in organizing business and trading relationships for such new services?

International entry for new electronic market services involves two sets of regulatory hurdles—in the telecommunications and the financial regulatory arenas. First, on the telecommunications side, one issue is how such a new service should be classified. Is it a value-added service or is it another kind of activity more like remote-access data processing, for example? This question of regulatory classification makes a substantial difference because in many countries data processing services are accorded direct access to foreign markets. There is no attempt to limit entry and flat-rate leased lines are usually made available; similar arrangements are often made for database services.

Focusing on the capability of transactional networks to link buyers and sellers together to engage in message switching, some telecommunications regulators may block or subject to regulatory restrictions applicable to value-added services the entry by such services. Even in the United Kingdom, for example, which has adopted a liberal regime for value-added services, major service providers will need to file tariffs and operate their networks in accordance with technical standards. Neither of these regulatory requirements may be appropriate for a service that essentially is not communications but is a financial services offering.

Second, on the nontelecommunications side, and assuming that the telecommunications issues can be resolved, regulatory issues arising from other industry sectors will also be confronted. The addition of transactional capability to a multicustomer service that delivers stock price quotations may raise questions about what exactly constitutes an exchange or a broker under various national financial regulatory schemes. The answers to these questions are difficult under U.S. law; they are only beginning to be approached by business executives and regulators elsewhere.

Thus, regardless of how a service is characterized for the telecommunications regulators, it is obvious that the approval of banking or securities regulators may determine the feasibility of a new offering. More broadly, regulators' perception of these services will have a highly significant impact on the flexibility to develop, introduce, and market them on both the national and international levels.

STRUCTURING NEW TRADING RELATIONSHIPS FOR TELECOMMUNICATIONS AND INFORMATION SERVICES: PROBLEMS AND PRIORITIES FOR U.S. POLICYMAKERS

Policymakers responsible for developing the regulatory framework for telecommunications and information-based and electronic transactional services—in both the United States and in other industrialized countries—are facing a significant set of challenges. In many nations, regulators and executives are having difficulty enough coping with massive domestic changes in the telecommunications and financial services sectors. The task of weaving together differing national definitions of services and various new industry structures, which is required for the provision of services on an international basis, is, however, more difficult by orders of magnitude and ultimately may prove to be too complex for trade officials.

Augmentation of Government Information-Gathering Capabilities

Perhaps the primary impediment facing policymakers working in the area of trade in telecommunications and related sectors is the difficulty in understanding the exact contours of the issues. Trade officials do not know what services are evolving and, if they did, what general or specific regulatory policies should or would be applicable. This problem would be complicated enough even were it to be confined to services operating only at the national level. Many services are, however, international, thereby necessitating a worldwide convergence of regulatory approaches—even in the face of settled, and often divergent, national policies.

At present, U.S. policymakers, like their counterparts in other nations, gather scant information about regulatory changes in the telecommunications and related sectors beyond its borders. Even less data is collected about the emergence of new services outside the United States or other developments in the private sector. Nevertheless, the industry sectors described in this chapter are of extraordinary importance to the long-term economic development of the United States, its financial well-being, and its political and economic relationships with its principal trading partners. While significant efforts are made to assemble intelligence directly affecting the national security interests of the United States, comparable information-gathering could be directed at protecting our long-range economic security.

Consequently, a first priority of U.S. policy in this area must be to monitor worldwide trends in the development and regulation of telecommunications, information, and financial services. There are three points that must be emphasized here, however. First, policymakers should not merely be content with relying on, or reacting to, information that they receive passively. If policy is to be made intelligently, it will be necessary to be vigorous about ferreting out information.

Second, policymakers must deal with specific trade issues and cases as they arise. The telecommunications-related sectors are, however, developing at a rate that is far outpacing the ability of regulators to respond in timely fashion. If such ad hoc policymaking continues, it may well prove to be a case of too little, too late. Although it will be difficult to establish a longer-range framework, it is a task that must be accomplished if new problems are to be anticipated before they arise.

Third, although it is conceded that many of the services are at an extremely early stage of development, making it difficult to assess their impact, others have developed more quickly and are capable of being subjected to careful analysis. Thus, the newness of the activities should not dissuade policymakers from beginning their process of appraisal or from anticipating, to the extent they are able, how the new services will evolve.

Integrating the Relationships among Trade, Telecommunications, and Financial-Sector Policymakers

Currently, at least in the United States, the expertise for tackling new policy issues is lodged in separate parts of the governmental apparatus. The FCC, the National Telecommunications and Information Administration and the International Trade Administration in the Department of Commerce, the Office of the U.S. Trade Representative (USTR), the Department of the Treasury, and the Department of State share responsibility for different aspects of the emerging issues.

Given that these issues are multidimensional in nature—the new services both straddle and affect several important economic sectors—they must be addressed by different groups of policymakers. It is imperative, therefore, that those working in the areas of telecommunications and trade, and in telecommunications and finance, must come to understand the linkages between their traditional spheres of responsibility.

At present, the approaches of the different components of the government may not merely be uncoordinated; they may actually come close to working at cross-purposes. One example may suffice to illustrate the need for a more coordinated effort. In the preparations for the 1988 World Administrative Telegraph and Telephone Conference (WATTC-88), policies for new value-added services are being developed. The Department of State has primary responsibility for all CCITT activities of the ITU and, therefore, is taking the lead in preparing for this conference. Included in that responsibility is the development and articulation of the U.S. position on the question of a new, rigid definition of telecommunications services, which is being opposed by many U.S. interests offering value-added services.

Concurrently the Department of Commerce and the USTR have been engaged in a vigorous series of bilateral discussions on trade in telecommunications goods and services. These talks are aimed at seeking flexible international arrangements for value-added services with the objective of opening overseas markets to U.S. suppliers of such services.

Many observers believe, however, that the Department of State's position in the preparatory discussions for the WATTC-88 has been insufficiently forceful in questioning the desirability of a broad and universal definition of telecommunications services when such a definition would be at odds with efforts elsewhere in the U.S. government to develop a more flexible regime for providing services internationally. What is most unsettling about this and other similar situations is that some policymakers have not fully assessed how their different areas of responsibility interrelate.

Complicating the policymaking process is the fact that trade and telecommunications policymakers often approach problems with fundamentally different perspectives. Trade officials address specific controversies in an ad hoc manner; they expect quick results. Conversely, telecommunications policymakers have relatively long time horizons; they focus on the complexities of market access and on the difficulties and time needed to change past policies. For a coherent policymaking apparatus to emerge, these differences must be bridged.

Currently, the principal gaps in understanding lie in the relationships between officials involved in dealing with telecommunications and trade issues. In the future, much closer links will need to be established between other groups of officials—for example, between the Department of Commerce, with its responsibility for telecommunications trade, and the Department of the Treasury, which is charged with addressing questions of access to financial markets.

To facilitate the necessary coordination among policymakers and to overcome longstanding bureaucratic rivalries, there must be a mandate to develop a mechanism for forging unified policy. What may be most effective is assembling a team from several agencies to deal with specific emerging issues. This approach would depend on an ad hoc structure that integrated staffs and could, therefore, subject senior officials to direction from others outside their departments, depending on the nature of a particular issue. Although formal coordinating procedures may be a step in the right direction, the ad hoc approach, which relies on more particularized response to a specific set of problems, is likely to be more effective than the consolidation of authority in a single agency.

At the present time, existing coordination mechanisms do not assure sufficient linkage between senior-level policy setters and the middle-level officials who implement policy. The senior-level coordinating group is also seriously isolated from contact—as a group—from advice and guidance from the private sector. Coordinating mechanisms have been used to divide responsibilities among agencies on a geographic basis and have thus served to aggravate—not alleviate—problems of policy coordination.

Restructuring Relationships between Private- and Public-Sector Participants and Strengthening the Government Policymaking Infrastructure

Traditionally, the structure of the international telecommunications environment was formed by monopoly providers on each end of a circuit who negotiated operating agreements for the provision of services. Today, the rapidly changing sectors of telecommunications and telecommunications-based services are populated by a diverse set of players who have not historically been part of that process, yet are growing in number. These entrants want a role in framing the international arena in which they operate. Their presence, however, which is the inevitable and desired product of liberalization world-wide, is straining the ability of policymakers to cope with the increasing complexity of the international environment.

In the American, British, Japanese, and Canadian telecommunications sectors, there is now more than one provider of transmission network facilities. Most countries in Western Europe are likely to authorize the entry of providers of value-added services. And the users of telecommunications services, the large multinational enterprises located around the world, also have a great stake in telecommunications policies, particularly those affecting the availability and pricing structure of leased lines, by which they create global links among their subsidiaries or offices.

Major changes in the structure of the telecommunications and related sectors is making it impossible for a single monopolist enterprise—whether private sector or one that is part of a government communications ministry—adequately to represent internationally the entire spectrum of a nation's interests. In the United States, private-sector representatives have long been entrusted with the primary responsibility for working out relationships for the provision of international services. It is, however, increasingly difficult, even in the United States, for governmental policymakers simply to defer to private-sector expertise.

The shift in responsibility for representing national interests internationally raises several issues. First, such a shift can leave a policy vacuum. In many countries, government has had to take the leading role. In the United Kingdom and Japan, for example, the Department of Trade and Industry and the Ministry of Posts and Telecommunications, respectively, have assumed the representational responsibilities historically undertaken by the providers of international telecommunications services—BT and Kokusai Denshin Denwa (KDD). Nevertheless, government officials may not have the expertise and resources that are available to those operating in either autonomous public corporations or wholly in the private sector.

Second, this shift in representational responsibility requires much greater cooperation within the private sector and between the private and public sectors. Although some major policy issues must be resolved by government officials, many difficult operational and technical issues will necessitate consultation with the private sector. It may be difficult, however, for the disparate segments comprising the private sector to develop a unified position for the government agency charged with representing their interests internationally. Thus, increased involvement—and expertise—by the public sector in refereeing disputes will be needed.

The intensified round of bilateral talks now underway between U.S. and overseas officials is severely straining existing mechanisms for coordination between the public and private sectors. In effect, the entire structure of correspondent relationships—and future patterns for doing business by new service providers offering electronic services—is being addressed in discussions now under way in a variety of forms.

U.S. officials are being required to react to proposals by other countries that will establish the structure of future relations and are making major decisions affecting future patterns of doing business in the telecommunications and information sectors without adequate arrangements for consultation with the private sector. The private sector has often had the opportunity for input prior to bilateral negotiations; however, adequate procedures have not been established to involve private-sector representatives directly in the negotiation process itself.

Third, the burden being shifted to government requires that the public sector vigorously recruit and endeavor to retain an expert cadre of policymakers. Due, in part, to great disparities in compensation, the last few years have seen an enormous brain drain from the public to the private sectors. One result of the reservoir of knowledge and policymaking expertise moving out of government has been increased difficulty in formulating U.S. policy. Another consequence, however, has been the high degree of frustration felt by overseas partners who perceive the U.S. policy apparatus as fragmented and without the depth of expertise necessary to engage in effective international consultations.

An intensive effort must be made in the United States to strengthen the infrastructure of the government units having responsibility for trade in telecommunications and related services. The United States must increase its level of commitment to provide staff and other resources for both international consultation and gathering information—that are commensurate with the economic importance of the sectors and their impact on economic growth.

Enhancing the Ability of Foreign Institutions to Manage Their Telecommunications Sectors

In attempting to open markets abroad, U.S. trade officials should recognize the need for domestic mechanisms that can deal with issues of competition in a national environment. Although advocacy by U.S. policymakers of new regulatory procedures may be difficult ideologically, it should be recognized that regulation may be the necessary predicate for a transition from a closed to a more open environment. Thus, at the same time that U.S. officials articulate the advantages of competition and the increased role of the private sector in providing new telecommunications and information-based services, they should recognize that regulatory procedures may ease the problem of establishing new legal frameworks through trade negotiations.

Many countries are now beginning to explore the opportunities afforded by more open and competitive industry structures. Although they may never fully accept the principle of unlimited competition in the provision of both telecommunications facilities and services, some countries are moving to separate the once-integrated regulatory and operational responsibilities of their telecommunications administrations.

Such a new structure will require the development of a set of rules that will be used to demarcate the relationship between the administration and competitors, users, and equipment suppliers, both domestic and foreign. It is also likely that new procedures for dispute resolution will need to be developed—all of which will be created in unique national legal, political, and cultural settings.

U.S. policymakers, however, often fail adequately to acknowledge the legitimacy of differences in the institutional and economic posture of even our most stalwart international partners. The development of new rules should, nevertheless, be viewed as an opportunity for the United States. While arguing for a more liberalized telecommunications sector, trade officials should also encourage the development of flexible regulatory procedures.

More important, as U.S. trade officials initiate negotiations with foreign partners to establish new arrangements for market access, it must be recognized that the development of new regulatory procedures may facilitate their task. Such negotiations usually are able to focus on only a general set of principles and must, necessarily, leave many details unsettled. A regulatory mechanism would be able to address specific problems as they arise or resolve unfinished details as new entrants try to exploit opportunities presented by market access arrangements.

In explaining to our partners the advantages of new institutions for regulation, trade officials can point to the likely benefits that will accrue to domestic, not just foreign, competitors. The possibility of a liberalized environment will be seen as an opportunity by domestic entrants. Moreover, the transition to such an environment, with all its benefits, will be made substantially easier if domestic entrants are able to rely on effective dispute resolution procedures.

From the perspective of the United States, then, an invigorated and open regulatory process has the significant advantage of emphasizing the common interests of domestic and foreign entrants in open markets. This is an extremely important result. It brings issues of market entry within the scope of national decisionmaking, reducing the extent to which competition is perceived as a trade issue and removing substantial burdens from the shoulders of U.S. trade officials.

In many countries new regulatory agencies in the telecommunications field are emerging. Instead of having FCC officials more directly involved in market access talks, it might be more useful and effective to encourage the FCC to take a leading role in establishing a forum through which regulatory officials from a number of countries could consult and compare notes on their differing approaches to common problems. The FCC might be much more effective in this low-key way than as a "co-equal" of agencies with specific responsibilities in the trade field. Turning the FCC into an agency with a role in putting teeth into U.S. trade policy is likely in fundamental ways to compromise key aspects of U.S. deregulatory initiatives. Instead of modifying U.S. deregulatory policies to permit the FCC to control entry by foreign firms in unregulated markets for enhanced or information services, the FCC should adopt a consistent deregulatory posture—a posture that is consistent ultimately with policies that the United States would like other nations to implement.

Devising the Proper Mix of Bilateral and Multilateral Negotiating Strategies

As the arena for the provision of international telecommunications and information-based services is in a state of tremendous expansion, and, concomitantly, as the trade-related issues become more difficult, U.S. policymakers are confronted with a series of choices about the fora in which trade negotiations should take place. The principal choices available to trade officials are between bilateral or multilateral procedures.

Bilateral discussions are likely to be initiated between countries that have clearly decided to liberalize the provision of telecommunications or value-added services. These consultations have the advantages of proceeding from what may be a certain commonality of purpose. They permit negotiators to obtain relatively quick responses from their counterparts, to establish a framework for direct face-to-face discussions, and to enable negotiators to focus on a particularized set of issues. Such discussions are likely, however, to exclude other administrations that may be in the process of considering whether or how to create flexibility for the provision of value-added services.

Politically, there are problems with a bilateral framework. It may, for example, be difficult to conduct such discussions with the United Kingdom without involving, at least as observers, representatives from the Commission of the European Communities.

The Japanese, perhaps the most important U.S. telecommunications trading partner, may be prepared to talk directly with the United States about future arrangements for the provision of value-added services on an international basis. They are, however, sensitive about the sense of exclusion and reaction of other telecommunications administrations to such talks. Thus, the Japanese are likely to keep other countries fully informed as any bilateral talks proceed. Indeed, potentially adverse reactions by the excluded parties, especially those in the Third World, may preclude any bilateral discussions from reaching a definitive or successful conclusion.

U.S. officials have yet to establish adequate procedures for orchestrating bilateral talks with this country's major trading partners. Relationships with these key partners have been seriously strained by inattention to the need to establish a structured way of informing U.S. partners about issues being addressed in bilateral talks. Just as there is a need to devise mechanisms for consultation between the government and the private sector, as noted above, U.S. policymakers need to articulate a clear policy for consulting with parties not directly involved in bilateral discussions. It is simply not adequate for the United States to continue dealing with the procedural issues raised by bilateral talks on an ad hoc basis.

Furthermore, the traditional multilateral mechanism for addressing telecommunications policy issues is the CCITT, which has had the key role in establishing agreements on technical standards and operational procedures for international services. The recent emergence of new services, technical systems, and approaches to the provision of value-added services has posed a series of problems for the CCITT.

Differences over definitional issues and the proper regulatory framework for the new services are causing strain within the CCITT. In the preparations for the WATTC-88 and the proposal for a new, expansive definition for telecommunications services, some administrations are gravitating to the view that uniformity is both unachievable and undesirable. Others are concerned, however, with the unfairness of what appears to be a regulatory disparity between the treatment of telecommunications administrations and that of the providers of information-based, transactional, or other value-added services, which are essentially free of regulation.

In the face of these differences in perspective among the members of the ITU, some high-level officials at the CCITT increasingly see it as developing a new, more trade-related role. The CCITT might focus less on its role as the body charged with the responsibility for setting international telecommunications policies and more on its availability as a forum for working out service agreements in a multilateral setting.

Balancing between bilateral and multilateral fora is likely to become even more complicated for U.S. officials in the telecommunications field over the coming decade due to the opening of the new round of the GATT and the inclusion of telecommunications and other services in the scope of the talks. The United States pressed hard to include telecommunications and trade in services in the new GATT round. It is not yet clear, however, how trade in telecommunications and related services are to be discussed within the GATT framework; obviously the discussions are meant to be broadly multilateral. As the traditional consensus in the field of international telecommunications continues to erode, it may be ever more difficult to reach a multilateral accord on substantive standards for market access for existing and new service providers.

The opening of the GATT round will create a delicate problem for U.S. policymakers, who will have to decide to what extent bilateral talks can continue separately or must be folded into the broader discussion. Similarly, the launch of the new round with telecommunications trade on the GATT agenda raises questions about how to coordinate the GATT and CCITT mechanisms. If the implementation of value-added services, for example, is to be addressed in GATT, there may be increased pressures on the CCITT to modify or quicken the pace of its own agenda. Consequently, the vigor of policymakers in pursuing telecommunications and other services within GATT may have an as-yet unexamined impact on other specialized fora that traditionally have dealt with trade in services issues. Having pushed hard to include telecommunications and trade in services in the new GATT round, it is now incumbent on U.S. officials to develop a complete strategy for dealing with telecommunications issues in both the GATT and ITU frameworks.

Explaining Issues of Trade in the Telecommunications and Information Sectors to Third World Decisionmakers

The complexity of the issues in the telecommunications and information services area makes it imperative that emerging policies are explained, particularly to administrations in the Third World. Policymakers in the developing world may find it difficult to understand the relevance of debates over value-added services. They have been generally skeptical of either bilateral or multilateral discussions on trade in services, which are seen as only involving structural arrangements among the infrastructure-rich economies.

Nevertheless, it may be productive for the industrialized world— and U.S. officials in particular—to demonstrate the importance of the current policy discussions to the Third World and for the developing countries to apply the lessons of those discussions. Many administrations in the Third World, like many of their counterparts in industrialized countries, believe that it is critical to maintain national sovereignty over the development of the telecommunications infrastructure. Monopoly control over the infrastructure may not, however, be the best way of stimulating risky new value-added services.

Third World administrations might, therefore, explore the feasibility of separating control over the infrastructure from control over the use of that infrastructure. By creating market opportunities for the development of new services, and possibly by entering into partnerships with private-sector investors, an administration can minimize the risk of initiating new services while protecting its control over the basic network.

In addition, negative reactions by Third World administrations to new, more liberalized sectoral structures can be minimized by taking the time and effort to explain forthrightly the changes that are occurring in industrialized nations. One cumulative result of those changes has been a shift in the pricing of international telecommunications services that could cause significantly unfavorable reactions within the developing world. Furthermore, concerns about the new pricing of services resulting from structural changes in the industrialized world can be transformed into an adverse reaction to proposals whether emerging from bilateral or multilateral fora—for different national industry structures within the Third World. An explanation of why and how policies are being developed in the industrialized world, and what are the consequences of adopting, or not adopting, them, is more likely to generate level-headed reactions on the part of Third World decisionmakers.

Without programs for implementing new institutional arrangements in the Third World, efforts to explain new policies may not be effective. The provision of managerial and financial resources and the supply of expertise will be required to make concrete to decisionmakers in the developing world the benefits of introducing information-based or other value-added services.

Policymakers in the United States and the rest of the industrialized world, therefore, will need to package technical and financial assistance for those administrations in the developing world that are prepared to implement innovative structures for new services.

U.S. officials should actively support the activities of the World Bank and other multilateral agencies focusing on issues of industry and organizational structure in developing countries. Such support might well contribute toward bridging the gap between policymakers from the industrialized and developing countries in the GATT and ITU where the future arrangements for the telecommunications and information services industries are now being worked out. Such an initiative by U.S. policymakers might also result in identifying areas where joint ventures or intensified trade in information services between the United States—and other industrialized countries—and developing countries might be stimulated and no longer thwarted by dogged, ideologically oriented resistance.

CONCLUSION

This chapter is only a preliminary attempt to establish a framework for discussion of some of the emerging issues in the telecommunications and related sectors. Further exploration of several problems pinpointed here is, no doubt, warranted. At bottom, however, the chapter is intended to encourage dialogue—to foster discussions among officials in government, between the public and the private sectors, and across national boundaries. The agenda of issues may well be an appropriate starting point for the new international fora that are starting to grapple with the difficult questions of trade in telecommunications and information services.

NOTES

1. See Amendment of Section 64.702 of the Commission's Rules and Regulations, 77 F.C.C.2d 384 (1980), *on reconsideration*, 84 F.C.C.2d 50 (1980), *aff'd sub nom.* Computer and Communications Industries Association v. FCC, 693 F.2d 198 (D.C. Cir. 1982), *cert. denied sub nom.* Louisiana Public Service Commission v. FCC, 461 U.S. 938 (1983) (*Computer II*); Amendment of Section 64.702 of the Commission's Rules and Regulations, 60 Radio Regulation 2d (P&F) 603 (1986) (*Computer III*).

THE ECONOMIC DEVELOPMENT CHALLENGE

5 THE DECLINE OF THE NORTH-SOUTH DICHOTOMY
Policy Implications for a Changing International Economic Order

Ernest H. Preeg

The Conference on International Economic Cooperation (CIEC) in 1975 capped a year's intensive preparatory talks and launched a year and a half of comprehensive North–South negotiations. The final meeting took place in June 1977, but the final act turned out to be devoid of substantive content, and CIEC ended with a round of North–South mutual recrimination. The conference has since faded into history, but it should be remembered, if nothing else, as a turning point in what had been a decade long ascendancy of the political-economic phenomenon referred to as the North–South dichotomy.

Since those meetings, the relevance of policy objectives couched in terms of two distinct groups of countries, industrialized and developing, and international negotiations, based on bloc-to-bloc interaction, have declined markedly. This is not to say that North–South economic problems have diminished. To the contrary, the huge debt overhang facing a number of middle-income developing countries, the special plight of the poorest countries in sub-Saharan Africa and elsewhere, and sharpening disputes in industrial trade add up to a far more conflictual and precarious relationship than existed a decade or two ago. But the conceptual framework of a North–South division for dealing with these issues no longer has much practical application, and in many respects no substitute framework has emerged to replace it.

The decline of the North–South dichotomy reflects a reorientation under way in the political and economic relationship between the

advanced industrialized democracies and the more than 100 countries that constitute the developing country grouping. There are
three principal and relatively clear-cut reasons for the decline of the
dichotomy: a growing diversity in the economic circumstances and
interests among developing countries, intensified direct trade competition between the industrialized and so-called newly industrializing
countries (NICs), and the enhanced practicality of dealing with structural adjustment and policy reform on a country-by-country rather
than multilateral basis. It is less clear, however, where the North–
South relationship is or should be heading over time. Should the
United States be content with an increasingly bilateral or case-by-
case approach to economic problems that has been holding the
international economic structure together through a most troubled
period? Should a new attempt be made to construct an economic
order based largely on the distinction between developed and developing countries? Should emphasis be placed on regional initiatives
such as the Caribbean Basin Initiative (CBI) and a possible Pacific
Basin trading arrangement? Or is there some revised multilateral
order of economic relationships under way that needs to be structured in terms other than a dichotomy between North and South?

Answers to these questions, as well as to specific policy issues subsumed in them, are the substance of much of what follows. Emphasis
is placed on group-to-group interaction and systemic changes in the
North–South relationship, although this cannot be separated from
the substantive political and economic issues at play.

HISTORICAL PERSPECTIVE ON THE
NORTH–SOUTH RELATIONSHIP

Developing Nations Struggle for
Independence

During the immediate postwar period, the developing country grouping constituted a minority within the United Nations and the Bretton
Woods/GATT economic system, truly a "third world" remote from
the first two worlds of East and West. Moreover, some of the Latin
American republics within the initial developing country grouping
were ambivalent about their role in the international economic system, viewing themselves as distant appendages to the West European
grouping or preoccupied with the dominant U.S. relationship. Almost all of Africa and Asia was either still in colonial status or struggling to cope with newly achieved independence, while China was de-

bilitated by civil war. During the ensuing fifteen years, however, a rapid expansion and consolidation of the developing country grouping took place. The Nonaligned Movement, launched at the Bandung conference of 1955, added political momentum to the growing ranks of the Third World; at the same time, the triumph of Fidel Castro in 1959 altered Latin attitudes about dependence on the United States. By 1960, a growing majority in the United Nations and other international organizations was comprised of developing nations.

In parallel with the political identification of a developing country grouping during the 1950s, the formulation of an economic development strategy focused on alleged disadvantages for poorer countries on the periphery of a world economy dominated by industrialized countries. A strategy of reduced economic dependence on the industrialized countries was advocated, based on import substitution, regulation of commodity markets, and limitations on the activities of multinational corporations. Disparities in national income levels justified large flows of economic aid to developing countries on equity grounds.

The Ascendancy of the North–South Bloc Relationship

The emerging developing country grouping took on more concrete institutional form in the early 1960s. In the trade field, the GATT added to its basic agreement a provision for special and differential treatment on trade issues for developing countries. In effect, developing countries were given dispensation from obligations under the GATT when there was self-assessed conflict with national development objectives. In the aid field, the industrialized countries formed the Development Assistance Committee (DAC) within the OECD in 1960 as a U.S. initiative to coordinate higher levels of economic assistance to developing countries. The launching of the Alliance for Progress in 1961 was further evidence of the U.S. priority to assist the less developed.

The crowning achievement in the formation of the North–South economic bloc relationship was the convening of the first United Nations Conference on Trade and Development (UNCTAD) in Geneva in 1964. The first UNCTAD established a broad agenda of economic issues; provided for a large, permanent secretariat supportive of developing country points of view; and achieved credibility through the initial leadership of the distinguished Argentine economist, Raul Prebisch. The institutional workings of UNCTAD embodied the North–South bloc-to-bloc relationship in ultimate form. The developing country grouping convened its caucus meetings well in advance of plenary sessions, and strict procedures for bloc caucuses and spokespersons were adhered to throughout. For both industrialized and developing countries, the bulk of the time at UNCTAD meetings was spent in group caucuses to develop consensus positions. The OECD grouping frequently broke consensus during plenary debate, but rarely did the developing countries.

Following the first UNCTAD, the ascendancy of the North–South bloc relationship produced modest results. Aid levels rose, and a system of generalized tariff preferences for developing countries was adopted. In addition, the UN Center for Multinational Enterprises was established with a principal objective of negotiating a code of conduct favorable to developing country interests.

An even more assertive period of developing country group diplomacy evolved in the early 1970s as the international economy faced troubled times. In 1973 the nonaligned countries issued a Charter of Economic Rights and Duties of States calling for a New International Economic Order (NIEO) that would redress fundamental inequities in the economic system. The first oil crisis of 1973–74 was even more decisive in coalescing a somewhat unholy alliance between the OPEC oil exporters and the large majority of oil-importing developing countries. The OPEC strategy to restrict exports and raise oil prices was interpreted as a dramatic example of commodity exporters sharply improving their terms of trade, while OPEC countries mollified the impact of higher oil prices on other developing countries by increasing their aid programs and facilitating the recycling of petrodollars. The developing country bloc, with prominent OPEC leadership, increased political pressure for action on all fronts of the NIEO while the industrialized grouping remained somewhat divided and on the defensive.

Agreement to move from political recrimination to practical negotiation of specific issues led to the more flexible and limited participation in the CIEC, with representation consisting of eight industrial participants, six OPEC members, and thirteen other developing countries. Although the latter two groupings were initially viewed as somewhat distinct within a three-way negotiation, OPEC and other developing countries quickly unified, with overall leadership of the Southern bloc largely dominated by OPEC members Venezuela, Algeria, and Iran. The CIEC deliberations ran in parallel with a Special Session of the UN General Assembly in September 1975 to deal with North–South economic issues, which led to the UNCTAD ministerial meeting in Nairobi in early 1976.

The Decline of the North–South Dichotomy

Failures of UNCTAD at Nairobi and CIEC at Paris were, in retrospect, a turning point for bloc-to-bloc diplomacy and the beginning of the period of decline in the North–South dichotomy. The rhetorical and institutional dialogue continued, particularly in the so-called global negotiations within the UN framework, but with waning enthusiasm. The second oil crisis of 1979–80, the ensuing debt problems of many developing countries, the global recession of 1981–82, and sharply rising protectionist pressures, particularly in the United States, forced all countries to rethink their economic strategies in light of the harsh realities of the early 1980s.

A central reality of the new situation was the growing diversity of interests among developing countries. The oil exporters sought to maximize declining oil revenues. The Latin American countries with unsustainable debt service burdens needed to restructure their debt while increasing nonoil exports. The East and Southeast Asian NICs were achieving phenomenal, export-oriented growth despite the oil and debt crises, but were threatened by protectionism in industrialized export markets. Many of the poorest countries, particularly in sub-Saharan Africa, were falling further behind with no clearly viable development strategy. And the two giants that comprise almost two-thirds of the developing world—India and China—were able to sustain moderate to healthy growth throughout the turbulent period, largely insulated from the international economy.

Under these circumstances of economic stress and increasingly diverse interests, the longstanding bloc positions of North and South, often representing a least common denominator of agreement within the respective groupings, became less and less relevant. To the extent that institutions continued to function in terms of such bloc relationships, the institutions, too, lost relevance. The result was clouded by continued public support for the objectives of the NIEO by many developing countries even while they pursued more pragmatic policies of self-interest, but the general decline in the North–South distinction was unmistakable. The last major North–South event was the Cancun Summit in 1981, but the agreed follow-through of some form of comprehensive North–South deliberations never took place. Since then, with the notable exception of trade policy discussed below, the North–South dichotomy, in terms of bloc-to-bloc negotiations, has become a spent force.

AID, TRADE, AND INVESTMENT
POLICY ENVIRONMENT

The current situation is one of unclear transition in the underlying basis for economic relations between developed and developing countries even while both groups are forced to confront difficult economic problems of adjustment and structural change. The sharply drawn lines between North and South have weakened or broken down and no new framework has taken their place. To a large extent, there is a dual relationship: a rhetorical impasse along earlier North–South lines at the United Nations and some other public forums juxtaposed with more pragmatic bilateral or case-by-case approaches to specific problems. The pattern is uneven, however, and a fuller understanding of the current situation requires a closer look at particular areas of policy.

Aid Policy

The North–South dichotomy has never been as sharply drawn in the field of aid as in some other policy areas, and there has long been differentiation among developing countries with respect to eligibility for development assistance. There is consensus that the poorest countries should get more aid on more concessional terms. The World Bank and the regional development banks distinguish "soft window" eligibility for the lowest-income countries from general borrowing rights, and some more advanced developing countries are moving from the borrower to nonborrower to lender category within the banks. The United States has "graduated" a number of countries in Asia and Latin America from eligibility for economic assistance. Aid targets as a share of GNP for donors have a long history of debate in international forums, but they have never been accepted as a commitment by most donors, and today serve principally as a measure of comparative burden sharing.

Recent developments have had considerable further impact in diluting a simple North versus South relationship with respect to economic assistance in two principal respects: the declining share of aid in overall financial flows, and the case-by-case approach for dealing with structural adjustment and policy reform.

The declining aid share of financial flows reflects the integration of capital markets, the debt buildup, and an absolute decline in concessional assistance to some of the most advanced developing countries. As a result, the financing of a projected "development gap," except for the poorest countries, can be more dependent on commercial bank lending and rescheduling, trade credit rescheduling, corporate transfers, and speculative capital flows than on aid. Similarly, aid agencies, even under strong World Bank leadership, have to share the development dialogue with the IMF, commercial bank advisory committees, and others who influence the transfer of financial assets.

The case-by-case approach to dealing with structural adjustment and policy reform stems from the need to have an integrated country response to financial problems and needs. The shift in relative emphasis by aid donors from project lending to a greater share of policy-conditioned program support reinforces the individual country need focus rather than the notion of an aggregate targeted flow of aid from North to South, although this tendency varies by donor.

Another significant development in recent years has been the increased concentration of U.S. bilateral assistance in a relatively small number of developing countries of particular political or strategic importance such as Israel, Egypt, Pakistan, the Caribbean Basin, and countries in which the United States has military base rights. This reflects, in part, constraints on resources, but it is also a conscious decision to focus available bilateral aid more heavily on deserving friends and allies. Such selectivity has always been a factor in bilateral assistance programs for most donors, but the much heavier country concentration of the United States, the traditional leader in donor coordination, further detracts from the concept of economic assistance as a form of aggregate transfer from North to South.

Trade Policy

In contrast to aid policy, in which differentiated treatment among developing countries has evolved without undue stress, trade policy remains the most contentious area of the North–South dichotomy, characterized by basic differences of principle and, until recently, a high degree of bloc solidarity among developing countries in multilateral institutions. In part, this is because trade is the only area with an explicit set of multilateral commitments, as contained in the GATT, under which all developing countries receive blanket "special and differential" treatment. Trade policy is also more sensitive politically as it directly affects a wide range of specific interests in all countries. Trade negotiations among the most like-minded allies can be highly charged, even without the underlying political and philosophic differences of the North–South relationship. The economic disturbances since the second oil crisis have further exacerbated trade disputes and political pressures in both the North and South.

One consequence of the entrenched North–South bloc relationship within the GATT has been to greatly weaken the organization's ability to resolve urgent trade problems. As a result, many trade policy issues have been shifted into a bilateral context. The United States has been pressing individual developing countries toward greater conformity with GATT trading rules and related trade practices under the threat of retaliatory action. All industrial countries have a growing list of quotas, voluntary restraint arrangements and other informal restrictions on imports from developing countries. In some instances, bilateral and subregional arrangements can lead to more liberal market access, as in the U.S.-Israeli free trade agreement and the Caribbean Basin Initiative; more frequently, however, they result in increased protection.

The new GATT round of trade negotiations, launched at Punta del Este, Uruguay, in September 1986, is intended to reverse these trends and provide a broader, more effective application of the multilateral norms and obligations contained in the GATT articles. The ministerial resolution adopted at Punta del Este maintains the principle of special and differential treatment for developing countries but also notes that "with the progressive development of their economies and improvement in their trade situation" developing countries would be expected "to participate more fully in the framework of rights and obligations under the General Agreement."

Of greater consequence, the negotiations leading up to and at the GATT ministerial meeting were marked by a break in the developing country solidarity that had prevailed earlier. A group of twelve agricultural exporting nations that cut across North–South lines pressed jointly for greater liberalization of agricultural trade in the new round. On the central issues of debate—services, intellectual property rights, and trade-related investment measures—developing countries split, with most joining the "Group of 48" that included industrialized countries, while the ten so-called hard-liners sought a more restricted, traditional mandate for the new round. The final result, which came close to the initial position of the Group of 48 reflects a growing awareness by many developing countries that trade negotiations are a reciprocal affair that require substantive commitments on all sides.

Another hopeful evolution in the trade field is the increasing emphasis placed on trade policy in structural adjustment and policy reform negotiations between individual developing countries and the World Bank. There is an increasing convergence of views in such negotiations, generally in the direction of more open trading systems and greater conformity with GATT norms. The elusive goal in the trade policy field is to extend the more cooperative approach underway in World Bank discussions so as to restrain bilateral disputes and strengthen the multilateral GATT framework.

International Investment Policy

Investment policy is different from both aid and trade in that it has never had a multilateral institutional base. The investment provisions in the draft International Trade Organization (ITO) of the late 1940s were never adopted by governments. Foreign direct investment has also been the most politicized area of economic relations in that the physical presence of foreign firms impacts most directly on issues of national sovereignty. Indeed, during the 1960s, multinational corporations created great controversy in North–South relations. Expropriation of existing companies, particularly in the agricultural and mining sectors, proceeded in parallel with sharp debate in international forums.

For several reasons, however, attitudes within developing countries have changed greatly in recent years. The mining and agricultural expropriations are well past, and foreign investment in manufacturing and many of the service industries is less sensitive politically. The multinational corporations have also become better corporate citizens and more flexible in terms of taking on local partners. Perhaps most important, the alternatives to foreign direct investment for providing capital and technology have proven unsatisfactory. Borrowing from commercial banks can be a more onerous form of dependency when repayment falls due, and the transfer of technology and marketing skills cannot be accomplished through government decree and international codes.

As a result, the current situation is one of a continuing standoff in policy debate along traditional North–South lines in parallel with a growing receptivity, at times competition, among developing countries to attract foreign direct investment as a source of jobs, technology, and exports. There is still no formal multilateral framework of rules and procedures for international investment, but a step-by-step process working toward such a structure is under way. West European countries and, more recently, the United States have been negotiating bilateral investment treaties and agreements with developing countries, which lay out the ground rules for such issues as national treatment and expropriation. Political and other risk insurance is provided bilaterally, as through the Overseas Private Investment Corporation (OPIC), and is now being launched multilaterally through the Multilateral Investment Guarantee Agency (MIGA). More broadly, there is near consensus that more foreign direct investment is part of the answer to the need for increased capital flow from North to South, and developing countries generally welcome support from the International Finance Corporation and other international mechanisms to accomplish this.

CURRENT FACTORS INFLUENCING
THE NORTH–SOUTH RELATIONSHIP

The picture that emerges from this summary of North–South relations in three areas of economic policy is one of diversity and change, with many crosscurrents between longstanding differences in principle and convergence toward a more reciprocal policy relationship where practical interests dictate. The challenge of economic development and growth looms larger than ever, but for distinct reasons among somewhat overlapping subgroups of developing countries. The export dependency and competitiveness of East Asian and other more industrialized developing countries is creating strong pressures for a more balanced trade relationship in terms of stable market access and mutually agreed trade practices; the heavily indebted middle-income countries, particularly in Latin America, are seeking urgent financial support from all creditors and donors in the context of negotiated structural adjustment and policy reform; and many of the poorest countries are trying to retool their development strategy from scratch, with the help of considerably larger financial assistance and other support from the more advanced countries.

The political relationship between North and South is even more complex and less amenable to generalization. The harsh realities of the 1980s have forced a more pragmatic, less ideological approach for most developing countries, particularly among a younger generation of businesspeople and technocrats who were not part of the debates of the 1950s and 1960s. In any event, the experience with more radical policies in terms of statism, self-sufficiency, and confrontation in international negotiations has been a near total failure, while the radical OPEC countries, which played a central leadership role in the 1970s, are now preoccupied with their own financial problems resulting from reduced oil revenues. But while the political cohesion of the developing country grouping has been weakened and its rhetoric subdued, the frustration level over continuing poverty and the painful austerity associated with financial stabilization programs is generally high. If the frustration has been kept under control, it is more a matter of even less confidence in the alternatives than of strong support for the current course.

This assessment of the current situation may be adequate for establishing policy priorities for immediate issues. But looking ahead, are there some overreaching or integrating forces at play that will give longer-term direction to the evolution of the North–South relationship, and thus the basis for a more comprehensive and consistent policy framework? This is more uncertain ground, but two such broader tendencies are apparent at this point, particularly among the upper- and middle-level developing countries. The first is the impact of the so-called information technology revolution, and the second is broadening support for what can be called market-oriented democracy. The two tendencies, moreover, interact in a number of ways.

The Information Technology Revolution

The impact of the information technology revolution on developing countries has received limited attention. The focus has largely been placed on offshore assembly of semiconductors and consumer electronics, but the potential effect of emerging information technology runs far deeper and broader. The application of data processing and automated equipment throughout industry and services, while just beginning in most developing countries, will spread. The U.S.-Brazilian trade dispute over Brazil's highly protectionist policy for computers and digital equipment, for example, is only one dimension of the issue. Of equal or greater importance is the internal Brazilian debate between national producers of these products and the wide range of industrial users who are forced to buy higher-cost, lower-technology equipment as a result of the protectionist policy.

The spread of telecommunications networks and computerized services, already occurring in the "modern" sectors of almost all developing countries, will draw together traditionally fragmented national economies, with far-reaching consequences. In the external sector, application of information technology can have disruptive as well as trade creating effects. Movement toward computer integrated manufacturing in the industrialized countries, for example, tends to reduce the incentive for offshore procurement, which is already being felt in some of the higher-wage Asian developing countries. In broader terms, international communications networks are integrating financial, goods, and services markets at a pace that governments cannot hope to control without severe detriment to the national economy.

The political consequences of the information technology revolution on developing countries are no less far-reaching. The open and rapid dissemination of information throughout national societies can have dramatic impact on traditionally controlled societies. The spread of the transistor radio to a rural, largely illiterate population in poorer countries is opening the political process to an unprecedented degree. The collapse of the Duvalier regime in Haiti, for example, can be attributed in large part to Catholic and Protestant church radio stations transmitting the course of events in Port-au-Prince and provincial cities to a hitherto closed and compartmentalized society. The expansion under way of satellite television broadcasting, direct dial international telephone service, and computerized printshops, not to mention the growing capacity of personal computers to store and print out information, are all working to open up political systems in ways that cannot be reversed.

There are also educational and cultural dimensions of emerging information technology that have particular relevance for developing countries. Teaching techniques using videocassettes and personal computers, which can easily be dubbed in local languages or dialects, have enormous potential, particularly in countries where the lack of professionally trained teachers is a major bottleneck to education. For higher education, telecommunications offers the prospect of new horizons in international exchanges, including teleconferencing lectures and seminars across continents and instant transmission of classroom written material and library references.

The cultural impact of the information technology revolution, particularly on the business and professional elites, is a growing force for change. People trained in the technical skills related to data processing, and working in an environment permeated by digital equipment, have a distinct mind-set. As students, they emphasize math, science, and information technology–related subjects, even though pursuing courses in business administration, finance, or other fields. The information technology mentality, moreover, communicates readily across borders. It can clash with traditional elites whose education is oriented toward law and nonquantitative social sciences.

The effect of information technology is largely an unchartered and unstudied area. There should be no question, however, that the information technology revolution, over time, will have as far-reaching an impact in the developing world as it already is having in the industrialized society.

The Spread of Market-Oriented Democracy

The pendulum swings in development strategy over the past three decades make any statement about a long-term trend in economic approach suspect. The political seesaw in developing countries between constitutionally elected government and military or other authoritarian regimes seemed, if anything, to favor the latter during the 1960s and 1970s. Nevertheless, since the late 1970s, a strong case can be made that there is a growing tendency, particularly among the more advanced, more industrialized developing countries, toward a more market-oriented economic system and a more democratic, or at least pluralistic, political system.

Circumstances and technicalities provide the economic impulse toward greater market-orientation. One circumstance is that earlier recourse to commercial bank borrowing and large net inflows of official assistance to finance high-cost public-sector programs and highly protected domestic industries is no longer feasible, and in some cases an export surplus is needed to maintain debt payments. A more effective allocation of scarce investment funds is critical, and reliance on market forces within a competitive private sector works best to produce high returns per dollar invested. Another circumstance is the example of East Asian and some other developing countries that have been most successful through the use of market-oriented incentives. The technical impulse is that as national economies become more industrialized and more engaged in international markets, governments become less able to direct the economy through controls, arbitrary concessions, and subsidies. This was the Japanese experience, and it is a factor currently at play in such countries as South Korea, Brazil, and India.

A market-oriented economic system does not necessarily mean a completely free and open private-sector approach. The direction of change, however, is toward privatization of some public-sector entities, reduced subsidies and more competitive pricing for others, trade liberalization, reduction in licensing or other special concessions for the private sector, and market-oriented interest and exchange rates. The bottom line as to whether a given set of market-oriented incentives is sufficient is its effect on the flow of speculative capital. If the incentives are inadequate, financial markets are now so highly integrated that speculative capital outflow can quickly negate government negotiated financial assistance.

The political tendency toward more democratic forms of government is equally striking; from Argentina to Brazil, from the Philippines to South Korea, from Guatemala to Haiti, the democratization process has been gathering momentum. The economic trend toward privatization plays a role in this process in that the power structure becomes more diverse and interests less beholden to arbitrary actions. A fundamental problem in many developing countries is a tradition of government patronage and corruption, a dominant role for the public-sector bureaucracy, and overwhelming resistance to the peaceful transfer of power to opposition groups.

But a modern industrial state simply cannot function on this basis. Outstanding examples of the modernizing process overcoming longstanding authoritarian systems with little resistance have been Spain and Brazil. They are both now essentially modern industrial states and are no longer able to be effectively governed by a military junta or narrowly based power grouping through authoritarian police power. To what extent and at what pace this route will be followed elsewhere in the developing world is uncertain, but widespread, growing support for movement toward more open and democratic political processes is evident, particularly where there is also a commitment to a more open economic system.

It is in this context that the political impact of applied information technology and related modernization in other sectors of the economy is most relevant. The clash of two cultures—one traditional and based on patronage and exploitation of the governed by those in power, the other committed to an underlying notion of progress for all through education and new technology—will likely prove the familiar C.P. Snow two-culture rivalry in the polite corridors of Whitehall and Oxbridge to have been trivial and quaint by comparison.

TOWARD A POLICY FRAMEWORK

A policy framework for responding to these various circumstances in the current North–South relationship will have to concentrate on those issues requiring an immediate response. To the extent possible, however, a longer-term set of objectives should be pursued at the same time.

The assessment here points to a progressive weakening of the distinction between North and South in economic relations as well as the movement of a number of developing countries into the industrialized category. The transition, moreover, is evolving toward a model characterized as more market-oriented and democratic and, therefore, highly compatible with a cooperative relationship with the United States. At the same time, however, the severe strains in the international economy from the financial and structural imbalances that have accumulated since the late 1970s make the immediate outlook contentious and precarious.

The policy response, under these circumstances, needs to be substantial and forceful, both in dealing with immediate challenges and in strengthening the longer-term framework. In terms of immediate challenges, there are three principal issues, two of which require a forthcoming response by the industrialized countries, and the third a firmer recognition on both sides of the changed realities of the 1980s.

Growth Strategy for the Heavily Indebted Middle-Income Countries

Policy conditioned financial support for middle-income indebted countries is the thrust of the Baker Plan made at Seoul in September 1985 and a central focus of current IMF and World Bank programs. Most of the debtor countries involved are politically committed to the kind of structural adjustment being advocated, even though some choose not to enter into formal agreement with the IMF. The specifics of how the Baker proposal will strengthen the process of policy conditionality and provide increased financial resources will necessarily vary depending on individual country situations, as in the arrangement worked out with Mexico in September 1986. One critical objective is to reduce the debt-servicing burden over the medium term, which puts a constraint on new official and commercial borrowing. Within this constraint, however, it should be clear that to the extent a debtor country undertakes policy reforms consistent with a higher rate of growth, the necessary external financing will be available to achieve such growth.

A Viable Development Strategy for the Poorest Countries

Many low-income countries require a fundamental restructuring of their incentive systems much the way the middle-income countries are proceeding—less government control and patronage, more incentives for private enterprise—and there is growing recognition in many of these countries of the need to do so. At the same time, these countries require a longer period of time for the adjustment to take hold, depend more on official, concessional aid to finance the transition, and lack the technical skills to manage it. A generous and coordinated international response is called for countries where the political leadership is prepared to undertake the necessary internal change and, in fact, such a response is under way.

In early 1986, a new Structural Adjustment Facility (SAF) was established within the IMF to provide $3 billion to least developed countries at highly concessional terms, and the industrialized country leaders at the Venice Summit in June 1987 called for an expansion of the SAF beginning in 1988. Increased funding for the International Development Association (IDA), to $12.4 billion over three years, was agreed on in late 1986 and will also be targeted on low-income countries embarked on fundamental policy reform. A few early success stories in this least developed group of countries could dispel the pessimism that now generally prevails and stimulate similar responses elsewhere. Several sub-Saharan African countries and Haiti are promising candidates at this point.

A Trade Policy of Graduation and Market Access

Trade policy is the most threatening aspect of North–South relations. Fundamental differences of approach and political pressures in all countries to protect specific interests could easily lead to sharply higher protection, with major negative consequences for development prospects and on the North–South relationship in broadest terms. The basic ingredients to bridge the existing difficulties within the GATT system are evident: The NICs need to relinquish their blanket dispensation from multilateral trade commitments and move toward full compliance with the GATT obligations, perhaps as Japan did in the 1950s by accepting the commitments, but with a list of exceptions to be progressively phased out; the industrialized countries, in turn, would commit themselves to limit the kinds of quantitative and other restrictions on developing country exports (which in many cases are inconsistent with GATT obligations) that have proliferated in recent years, principally through liberalization or phase-out of the Multifiber Agreement and revised safeguard and dispute settlement procedures within the GATT. Such a deal could be consummated in the new GATT round, although it is still too early to judge whether this will be politically feasible.

Building a longer-term economic framework for North–South relations that takes account of the changing realities of the 1980s is more difficult to elaborate in detail. Obviously, more could be accomplished if the three immediate issues outlined above are dealt with in a forthcoming way and with positive results. It would be in the U.S. interest to support the trend toward market-oriented democracy and to seek to integrate countries clearly embarked on that course more fully into all aspects of international economic consultation and policy coordination.

The most active and innovative context for such progressive integration is the IMF/World Bank deliberations seeking practical ways to deal with structural adjustment and policy reform. These deliberations, however, are linked to and dependent on broader developments in the world economy such as interest rates, exchange rates, and aggregate growth. As the NICs progressively open their economies to trade and investment and thus influence more directly global economic developments, they need to participate more fully. Structural imbalances are already building up between some East Asian NICs and the industrialized grouping that should be addressed sooner rather than later in an appropriate multilateral context.

At this stage, informal groups, including private as well as public-sector representatives, might prove more forward-looking than official bodies in developing and promoting mutual objectives. There is a Trilateral Commission and Quadrangular Forum within the industrialized grouping, but nothing analogous to bring together prominent individuals in key industrialized and newly industrialized nations committed to the concepts of market-oriented growth and more democratic government.

One particular area in which a more active and integrated U.S. policy response could be developed is the information technology sector. This sector epitomizes the genius of the U.S. private sector to develop and apply new technologies to the benefit of all countries. It is also an area in which the objective of a more open and market-oriented society can be pursued in a pragmatic, less politicized context. Yet policy issues affecting this sector are handled in a fragmented manner. There has been no serious attempt to formulate an international strategy for information technology despite the important and interacting commercial, strategic, developmental, and foreign policy issues involved. Representative Dante Fascell (1985), a lonely champion of such an approach, proposed in a speech in late 1985 that a presidential advisory council be established to formulate a strategy for international communication and information policy. Such a strategy would have to be comprehensive and designed to ensure that the United States remains at the forefront of new technology development and is fully competitive internationally. It would also include a cooperative approach to trade, investment, and aid issues of importance to the North–South relationship, not to mention other related fields such as education and media transmission touched on earlier. Representative Fascell's initiative deserves a positive response from the private sector as well as the executive branch.

In conclusion, the international economic order is going through a period of rapid change that can aptly be labeled revolutionary in scope. A recent book on the U.S.-Japanese rivalry in the information technology sector lauded today's "bold, visionary leaders," and concluded: "Their efforts will appear heroic to future generations, but the scale of their activities will be dwarfed by the realities in the sector in years to come" (Davidson 1985: 262). This technology-driven era of change has global implications that are sweeping away any simple distinction between "industrialized" and "less developed" countries. In terms of economic realities and prospects, there are various overlapping groupings of countries with continually shifting interests, all being drawn closer together by trade, investment, and financial linkages.

The quest of building and managing an adequate international policy framework to cope with this increasingly turbulent set of relationships will require from national leaders all of the boldness and vision attributed above to corporate leaders in the information technology sector. A common set of interests needs to be nurtured among democratically oriented, industrialized and industrializing countries, cutting across traditional North–South lines. At a minimum, a better coordinated system of structural adjustment between national economies is needed that will minimize sudden, neighbor-beggaring unilateral actions. Perhaps at some point, the more integrated institutional framework for trade and investment envisaged in the International Trade Organization four decades ago will be revived. Even further boldness and vision will be needed to bring together trade and financial institutions, globally and at the national level; today it is not even feasible for trade and finance ministers of major countries to meet regularly over dinner.

To make any real progress, however, national leaders will have to be looking ahead to the circumstances of the late 1980s and 1990s rather than backward to the period of North–South dichotomy of the 1960s and 1970s. And in this context, for the historically minded, I will conclude by hazarding a prediction about a turning point in international economic relations. As the CIEC of 1975–77 marked the high point of a polarized North–South economic bloc relationship, the GATT ministerial meeting at Punta del Este in September 1986, despite the hard bargaining and polemics that took place, will in retrospect mark the point at which major trading nations at all levels of development began a commitment to build a truly reciprocal, multilateral world trading system and, by extension, international economic order. In part, this reflects the harsh realities of an alternative based on unilateral, mutually disruptive policies. In part, it is a response to the growing force of economic integration that reduces the ability of governments to act independently. It is also a consequence of a global industrialization process that has over-taken, for practical purposes, a dichotomy in the world community between those that are industrialized and those that are not.

REFERENCES

Davidson, William H. 1985. *The Amazing Race: Winning the Technorivalry with Japan.* New York: Wiley.
Fascell, Dante. 1985. "International Communications Policy: Preparing for the Future." Paper presented at the Center for Strategic and International Studies, Washington, D.C., October 5, subsequently published by the Center in its *Significant Issues Series* 8 (November 4, 1986).

6 THE UNITED STATES AND THE DEVELOPING WORLD
Pitfalls, Pratfalls, and Possibilities

Alan J. Stoga

During much of the postwar period, trade, finance, and development were viewed by most as a plus-sum game. All parties benefited, ultimately, through growing world trade and increasing real economic activity. The global economy—bound together by increasingly complicated linkages of trade, investment, technology, and finance—offered enormous opportunities to both industrialized and less developed countries. Even during the 1970s, when some developing countries tried to politicize economic relationships with demands for commodity cartels and large-scale transfers of wealth, all nations and most constituencies within those nations sought more, rather than less, involvement in the world economy.

This may be changing in the 1980s. In the industrialized countries, especially the United States, many traditional advocates of free trade and globalization have discovered the short-run attractions of protectionism and "fair" trade. Many industrial country manufacturing companies, in the United States as well as in Europe, seem to be retreating to their home markets, unable or unwilling to compete in the global marketplace. In the United States commercial banks are heavily criticized or even penalized for past international lending and want to define the future in their domestic markets to the extent possible. Opinion polls regularly record growing support for measures that restrict imports, and the Congress is debating trade legislation that would do more to restrict imports than to expand exports. In the developing world, there seems to be a growing predilection to politicize international financial relations and limited support for the new multilateral trade round without which increased protectionism aimed at LDC exports would have been inevitable. Countries that grew rapidly in the 1970s now see little or no prospect for growth or development, in part because of their accumulated debt burdens, and blame the international system as it now functions for their bleak outlook. Apparently, governments and their constituents increasingly suspect that participation in the global economy has become a negative-sum game.

In part this reflects fundamental changes in the fabric of the world economy (see Drucker 1986: 768–91). First, the United States, which once accounted for almost half of the global gross national product (GNP) and dominated world commerce and finance, has become a debtor nation and is in the midst of a painful adjustment to a lower standard of living. Coincidentally Japan has emerged as the industrial world's most dynamic economy and largest creditor.

Second, demand for commodities has been uncoupled from the demand for manufactured products. Economic growth in the developed world no longer necessarily leads to increased demand for developing-country-produced primary products.

Third, in the industrial process, production has been uncoupled from employment. For example, in the United States in recent years manufacturing output has risen and employment has fallen.

Fourth, capital movements have become separated from underlying movements in goods and services. In a sense, capital flows have become the driving force in the world economy, in that they largely determine exchange rates and interest rates—the relative prices at which economies interact. Even as the United States has become less important in economic terms, the dollar has become a more important international transactions currency.

Fifth, financial, commodity, and goods markets have become more speculative, inherently more volatile, and less predictable. The dollar went higher than expected in 1984, oil prices fell lower than anticipated in 1986, and the stock markets plummeted on Black Monday in 1987.

These changes have profound implications for the developing world. There will be enormous opportunities for countries to accelerate their rates of growth and development, to use industrial country technology and access to industrial country markets to leapfrog the usually slow-paced development process. But there will also be enormous risks of a widening gap between industrial and developing countries, of stagnation and economic decline in the Third World.

Not all countries can be exporters; some must import. Developing-country exporters are increasingly competitive and increasingly aggressive players in the global market. The question is whether, and under what conditions, the debtor countries will be allowed to increase further their exports to creditor countries in general and to the United States, the world's largest and richest market, in particular. Equally important, the creditor countries must agree to reverse the recent flow of financial resources if growth is to be resumed—for several years the net flow has been from debtors to creditors, a phenomenon that defies economic as well as political logic. The creditor countries, led by the United States, must reexamine the relationships among trade, finance, and growth and devise a strategy that optimizes the needs of creditors and debtors, exporters and importers.

But this would require a renewed recognition by the United States that improved conditions in the developing world are in its own immediate interests. It also would require that international economic institutions and arrangements, which were largely constructed in the late 1940s, be updated to reflect present economic and political realities. To the extent that this process spreads the burden of economic adjustment more widely, then it is likely to be more politically sustainable. To the extent, however, that particular countries or groups bear the burden of adjustment disproportionately—or perceive themselves as doing so—then the process will fail.

In short, the solution to the trade and debt problems that plague North–South economic relations today must be as politically sensitive as they are economically sensible. The problems will be addressed at a time when political momentum seems already to be moving away from orthodox solutions. If this momentum is unchecked or if a new orthodoxy cannot be defined that is rooted in a renewed commitment to a global trade and finance system—perhaps even one whose basic building blocks are bilateral rather than multilateral—then those who believe that economic internationalism has become a negative-sum game will be proven right. Almost inevitably this would lead to more economic conflict, which would be costly to the United States as well as to the developing countries.

The United States needs to reassess its interests in the developing world and then define a strategy that is compatible with U.S. political and economic resources as well as with U.S. willingness to absorb the costs of economic leadership. From this perspective, today's trade and debt problems could become opportunities to solidify long-term economic and political relationships between the United States and key developing countries, rather than sources of conflict.

The latter, which unfortunately seems to be the course on which the United States is now headed, is certainly not in the national interest. But it will take careful rethinking to change direction.

THE DEBT CRISIS

A key difference between Latin American and Asian countries is that the former ran larger current account deficits and depended more heavily on foreign borrowing to finance their deficits as well as to supplement domestic savings. The result was the accumulation of large foreign debts, in some cases larger than the country could repay or service.

In East and Southeast Asia only the Philippines, which followed development strategies more similar to the countries of Latin America than of the Far East, has been caught up in the full intensity of the debt crisis of the last several years. Other countries, despite large debts, have been able to maintain their access to international financial markets through the implementation of prudent economic policies and the maintenance of strong export growth. More important, they have continued to grow rapidly. And China and India have made important economic policy changes that have begun to reinvigorate their economies.

The most visible economic effects of the debt crisis, especially in Latin America, have been dramatic improvements in countries' external payments positions and balance sheets and significant deterioration in their economic performance. The reduction in the current account deficit of all developing countries (from $87.3 billion in 1982 to $41 billion in 1987) and particularly of fifteen of the most highly indebted ones (from a deficit of $50.6 billion in 1982 to $14 billion in 1987) has been remarkable.[1] This external adjustment initially reflected a sharp decline in imports, but also a drop in exports. Exports recovered in 1984 but, with slower growth in industrialized countries, lower oil and nonoil commodity prices, and increased protectionism, fell again in 1985 and 1986.

The improvement in the balance of payments have permitted the financial aspects of the debt problem to be addressed and, to a great extent, resolved. Massive amounts of debt were rescheduled; banks were required to increase their capital and allowed to slow their lending, resulting in a considerable improvement in their relative exposure to troubled debtors; interest payments were sustained, financed partly by trade surpluses and partly by some new lending from the banks and the international financial institutions; central bankers clarified, to some extent, the very informal arrangements under which they would cooperate to rescue an endangered bank; and, most important, U.S. regulatory authorities demonstrated they could (and would) rescue a major commercial bank—the Continental Illinois—on the verge of failing.

Although these considerable accomplishments add up to a much stronger international banking structure than existed several years ago, they failed to address the fundamental problem from the debtor countries' perspective: how to reignite economic growth. The accumulation of debt in the 1970s was intended to finance more rapid economic growth than would otherwise have been possible; indeed, despite the disruptions caused by the oil price shocks, developing country growth rates remained relatively high. The debt crisis, however, has put an end to high growth, at least in most of Latin America and large parts of the rest of the developing world.

The loss in economic activity and the acceleration in inflation have been remarkable. For example, real GDP in Latin America increased by less than 6 percent between the end of 1980 and the end of 1986. Excluding Brazil (which grew rapidly in 1985 and 1986, at the cost of sharply rising inflationary pressures and of renewed economic crisis in 1987) the level of economic activity in the rest of Latin America actually declined. During the same years real per capita GDP fell by a cumulative 8 percent, returning to a level only slightly above what had been reached in 1978. In Mexico, Venezuela, and Argentina—as well as most of the smaller countries—the decline was even more pronounced. In 1986 and 1987 there was some rebound in several Latin countries, although, excluding Brazil, overall economic activity in the region has continued to be generally weak and uneven. At the same time, inflation, which averaged under 30 percent on a weighted basis in the ten years through 1977 and just under 60 percent during 1978-82, exploded to above 115 percent in 1986-87.

The drop in economic activity has had profound social consequences, especially in countries that have highly skewed income distributions; as documented by the World Bank and the Inter-American Development Bank (1985), most measures of living standards have dropped sharply since the debt crisis began.

Despite the balance of payments improvements and the consequent slowdown in the growth of debt accumulation, after several years of effort few countries in Latin America claim that their economic strategies have really worked. This is as much the fault of poor execution—economic adjustment programs have been implemented so inconsistently that inflation is generally higher and the outlook for growth generally lower than at the beginning of the debt crisis—

as it is of inadequate financial resources. In 1985 and 1986 commercial bank exposure to developing countries fell, although it rose in 1987. The net flow of financial resources (defined as loans, investments, interest payments, and profit remittances) has been strongly from debtors to creditors: The Economic Commission for Latin America and the Caribbean has estimated that the transfer of financial resources from Latin American countries to their creditors totaled $132 billion from 1982-86. Adding capital flight, which represents movement of Latin American capital to the United States and other safe havens, would dramatically increase the total outflow. Industrial country protectionist actions aimed at LDC exports contributed to the problem and, perhaps more important, to developing country resentment of creditors. In these circumstances governments, especially those that were democratically elected, were increasingly hard pressed to maintain stabilization programs; the IMF, the commercial banks, and "austerity" became convenient targets for opposition political forces. One consequence was the search for unorthodox economic strategies in several of the debtor countries (such as Argentina, Peru, and Brazil), another was to raise concerns among creditor governments and banks that a new strategy was needed to cope with the debt problem.

In this environment U.S. Secretary of the Treasury James Baker unveiled his response to the debt problem in October 1985. The so-called Baker Initiative recognized that continued debt service depends on renewed economic growth, and the plan met, at least partially, the debtor countries' demands for a political response from the United States to their situation. The substance of the Baker Plan, however, was modest: renewed adjustment efforts by the debtors and some new lending by commercial and development banks, although much less than projected debt service payments by the countries.

Although the Baker Initiative was a positive and politically bold platform from which growth-oriented debtor-country economic policies could be encouraged and financed, it has been slow to mature. This is partly because creditors have been reluctant lenders and partly because debtors have been slow to implement economic reforms. Moreover, there is a growing realization that some countries simply have too much debt relative to the size, strength, and potential of their economies.

Part of the reason is that debtor countries are increasingly likely to be buffeted by world economic developments. Economic growth in the industrial countries and the consequent growth in world trade have simply not been adequate to allow most developing countries to grow their way out of the debts they have accumulated. Moreover, those few that have avoided debt services problems (like Korea) have done so by aggressive export drives, which face growing protectionist resentment. Those who have succumbed to debt service problems have generally failed to identify or implement economic strategies that could produce both sustained growth and regular debt service, but are increasingly urged to export their way to renewed economic prosperity. They now face not only weak demand in the industrial countries and growing protectionism, however, but continued demands for net transfers of capital to creditors, making sustained export or investment led recovery almost impossible. And the pronounced weakness of commodity prices—in dollar terms real commodity prices were 17 percent lower in 1986 than in 1985—simply added to the inability of many countries to emerge from the debt overhang in any sustainable way. As a result, an understandable frustration with prevailing debt management practices has emerged in the developing world, to some extent shared by the creditors.

The decisions in mid-1987 of major U.S. banks to increase their reserves against possible losses on their loans to developing countries—roughly the equivalent of recognizing that these loans are presently worth less than their full stated value—is one measure of this frustration. Another is Brazil's temporary suspension of interest payments, which began in April 1987. These actions may herald the beginning of a new phase of the debt crisis. It will be characterized by a new realism, a new willingness to confront and deal with facts and, rather simply, to hope things will get better if the problem is pushed into the future. In the process creditors, debtors, and international financial officials will also eventually have to acknowledge what they have thus far avoided: that countries can be overindebted and that old creditors (that is, the commercial banks) are unlikely to be principal sources of new capital flows.

Recognition of all three realities—that the debt is not worth full value, that some countries need debt relief, and that the banks will not (and probably should not) be the source of new lending—necessarily presents a considerable challenge to the leaders of the United States and other industrial countries. On the one hand, they must preserve the integrity of the international banking system; on the other, restoring realistic growth prospects in the Third World should be both a political and economic priority. These are not incompatible objectives, but they will require more creativity—and, inevitably, more public monies—than U.S. political leaders have yet devoted to this problem.

In any event, many debtors are already becoming frustrated with the existing system and seem more likely to adopt confrontational strategies aimed at creating the conditions for renewed short-term economic growth or at least in satisfying the immediate political demands of their citizens. These include rejection of the IMF as the arbiter of appropriate economic policies, unilateral deferment of "excess" interest charges or the imposition of a payments cap tied to a specified share of export earnings. Any of these, if they became widespread, would have significant impact on the international financial system and, more particularly, on the creditor banks.

Africa's debt problem is qualitatively and quantitatively different from that of Latin America or Asia. While the financial and economic positions of various Latin countries have waxed and waned (in 1986 Mexico was in crisis and Brazil seemed to be prospering; in 1987 the positions were reversed), the economic situation of African countries has continued to deteriorate, to a great extent unnoticed.

Part of the problem is that the African countries simply do not owe enough. The largest debtor is Egypt at $34 billion, and the second largest is Nigeria with some $30 billion. Total African debt by the end of 1987 is projected to be around $220 billion; the debt of sub-Saharan Africa, excluding South Africa, is around $115 billion. Around one-fifth of this is due to commercial banks, which is less than 10 percent of what is owed to the banks by various Latin debtors. Thus, African indebtedness is not large enough to threaten the international financial system or even individual creditors.

Africa's social and economic crisis was partly caused by a hostile international economic environment. But the root causes lie within the African countries themselves: Agriculture has been systematically neglected, and industrial programs—often pursued more for international prestige than economic benefit—have been poorly designed and wasteful. Government subsidies typically have aimed to keep food, housing, and services cheap in the cities, thereby discouraging agricultural production, bloating government budgets, and encouraging excessively rapid urbanization. Corruption has been widespread. Many governments have undertaken grandiose prestige projects that wasted scarce financial and human resources without contributing anything to economic development. At the same time, basic infrastructure has been allowed to deteriorate.

Many creditors recognize the uniqueness—and the desperation—of the African situation. Public creditors have been more forthcoming in Paris Club debt reschedulings, have established special lending facilities, and have considered new forms of debt relief. Some private creditors are looking at innovative rescheduling techniques that involve nonmarket interest rates.

PROTECTIONISM

The debt crisis is obviously one legacy of the poor economic management of the 1970s. In a sense, industrial country protectionism aimed at LDC-produced exports is another. The General Agreement on Tariffs and Trade (GATT) has estimated that 30 to 40 percent of total nonoil developing country exports are under restraints in industrial country markets; almost 40 percent of the exports of the five largest debtors consist of "sensitive" products, which are affected by some kind of restriction in creditor countries. The major trade restrictions faced by developing nations are nontariff barriers. World Bank data indicate that in 1983, 20 percent of the industrial country imports from the developing countries were subject to nontariff barriers including 21.8 percent of LDC imports sold in the EC, 12.9 percent sold in the United States, and 10.5 percent in Japan. Since then many new protectionist measures have been taken, although, at least in the United States, import and import penetration levels have continued to increase. Nevertheless, the potential for future trade restriction measures is great.

At the same time, it is important to recognize that developing country trade policies, perhaps with more justification than in industrial countries, have tended to be highly protectionist. Following the onset of the debt crisis in 1982, many debtor countries adopted policies—including licenses, outright prohibitions, prior approval schemes, and restrictions on the availability of import finance—to reduce their imports. Along with the sharp decline in economic activity and in exchange-rate levels, the result was a dramatic drop in imports: For Latin America as a whole, imports fell $42 billion between 1981 and 1983. Since 1983 imports to the region have remained roughly flat; import levels in most debtor countries remain well below peak levels. Because overall GDP has increased marginally over the same period, there clearly has been some import substitution, although it is not yet apparent whether the changes in import intensity are structured or cyclical.

The debt crisis provided a degree of macroeconomic justification for LDC protectionism: the need to reduce deficits dramatically and quickly encouraged the use of both market and administrative mechanisms. In addition, many developing countries, even the rapidly industrializing ones that are already competitive exporters across a range of increasingly sophisticated products, insist on protecting domestic industries to encourage their development or to protect entrenched business and political interests.

Regardless of its justification, LDC protectionism, combined with aggressive export promotion, forms a kind of modern mercantilism. This increases protectionist inclinations in the United States especially at a time when U.S. exports and export jobs are under enormous pressure.

Countries must export to avoid financial problems and to generate enough revenue to maintain both debt service and bankers' goodwill. Indeed, a caricature of the economic model that has helped Asia largely to avoid the debt crisis forms the basis of the orthodox prescription for financial and economic stabilization in Latin America. The Latin debtors are being advised to reorient economic policy to encourage exports, to dismantle inefficient public sector enterprises, to increase savings, to channel local savings more effectively into productive investments, to discipline fiscal and monetary policies, to relax price and wage restraints, and, in general, to rely on free market mechanisms to allocate resources. In Latin America and elsewhere this often translates into export promotion or even subsidization as well as import substitution because of the lack of available foreign exchange, the short-run political imperative to protect indigenous jobs and business interests, and the effects of rapid exchange rate devaluations on import costs. Nevertheless, the intent has been to increase LDC exports and export market shares.

The theory that Latin America's (or, more generally, the developing world's) future effectively lies in imitation of what might be called the Korean miracle is not unchallenged. Some development economists have begun to point out that the relationship between export growth and overall economic growth may not always be as strong as in the leading Asian economies. And there are—or should be—serious questions about the political and social consequences of switching to Korean-style economics in countries with very different resources, histories, institutions, and structures. For example, shifting to a more export-intensive strategy is likely to reinforce the already skewed distribution of income in a country like Mexico. Nevertheless, the conventional wisdom, strongly supported by the World Bank, the IMF, and almost all creditor and debtor governments, is that the developing world must increasingly become more export oriented.

Of course, there are important differences in the ways in which debtors have been treated. From the beginning of the crisis, it has been clear that the financial and economic health of large debtors

like Argentina, Brazil, and Mexico is far more important to the maintenance of stable international financial conditions than the condition of small debtors. As a result, the former have attracted the
attention of creditor country policymakers and the largest share of
what new financial flows have been available. The consequence for
the small debtors has been even less credit and poorer recovery prospects. In some cases, partly because of their own extreme mismanagement but also because of adverse economic conditions, countries
that previously had some access to the international capital markets
such as Sudan, Bolivia, and Jamaica seem permanently cut off.
These countries appear to be caught in a vicious circle of bad management, weak export demand or low export prices, high interest
rates, payments arrears, inability to borrow from private or public
sources, lack of essential imports, and political instability. The result
is economic decline.

Although this has important consequences for the countries as
well as their creditors and trading partners, it does not seem to have
much impact on the overall financial system. For the system as a
whole—and, perhaps more important, for the policymakers of the
major creditor institutions—it seems to be only the condition of the
largest debtors that matters.

From the onset of the debt crisis in 1982, the strategy promoted
by creditors and more or less accepted by debtors has been flawed
by an apparent contradiction: Unless world trade growth could be
sustained at a very high level (implying historically high rates of
industrial country growth), the more successfully the system coped
with the debt crisis the more intense would become protectionist
pressures in the industrial countries; but as protectionist pressures
grow, the debt strategy becomes more vulnerable. In practice this has
had the result of shifting an important part of the "cost" of managing the debt crisis from creditor to debtor to the industrial country
producers and workers who became the objects of LDC mercantilism.

This problem has been compounded by the macroeconomic realities of the last several years. Strong growth and the appreciating dollar—fueled by an unconventional mix of loose fiscal and tight monetary policies—produced a nearly insatiable demand for imports in the
United States. On a balance of payments basis, U.S. imports rose
from around $250 billion in 1980 to some $370 billion in 1986.
More significant, imports have accounted for a progressively larger
share of the U.S. market, with import penetration rising at an unprecedented rate in recent years. Particularly during the past five
years, a major part of this increase was due to manufactured imports
from developing countries: Almost half of the increase in import

penetration since 1980 has been due to growing purchases from the developing world. Although rising import penetration characterizes most mature industrial economies—Japan is a notable exception in which import penetration in manufactures has remained well under 10 percent for the past decade—the rate of increase in the United States has been unusually rapid.

The dramatic depreciation of the dollar against the Japanese yen, German mark, and other currencies that began in February 1985 has yet to correct the U.S. trade imbalance. Indeed, as always, the initial effects are perverse: Imports become more expensive in dollar terms and exports cheaper, so the deficit widens.

But the normal adjustment lags seem to be exaggerated, perhaps reflecting underlying competitive problems that cannot be solved simply by exchange-rate changes. Moreover, since at least one-third of U.S. trade is with countries whose currencies either are pegged to the dollar or are depreciating against the dollar, the overall decline in the dollar's value has been much less pronounced than suggested by the change in the yen/dollar or mark/dollar rates. One consequence is that while recent exchange rate changes may have hurt Japan's competitive position, at least at the margin, they have benefited many developing countries—especially Korea, Taiwan, and other Asian producers of increasingly sophisticated manufactured goods—both in the United States and in Third World countries. Finally, many industrial country exporters seem extremely reluctant to let their shares of the U.S. market erode. The near-term result has been a much more pronounced decline in profits than sales as exporters to the United States have allowed their profit margins to be squeezed in an effort to minimize volume losses.

Of course, eventually exchange-rate changes will have a significant effect on the trade balance. Recent data and anecdotal evidence suggest that imports are likely to fall more than exports will rise (because of the weakness of traditional U.S. export markets like Latin America; the loss of agricultural export sales reflecting weak international demand; low commodity prices and lingering concerns about U.S. reliability as a supplier; poor U.S. productivity performance; and changes in the structure of U.S. industry during the last several years during which industries or parts of industries relocated offshore, investing heavily in new plant and equipment). Moreover, developing countries are likely to gain market share in the United States, if only because of relative exchange-rate changes, at least compared to industrial-country exporters.

U.S. COMMERCIAL AND FINANCIAL RELATIONSHIPS

For the United States the crisis in the developing world has meant a decline in U.S. exports and a rise in imports from the developing world. The U.S. deficit with developing countries was $22 billion in 1982 and $54 billion in 1986. The swing in U.S. manufacturing trade with developing countries has been dramatic: The balance shifted from a $28 billion U.S. surplus to a $26 billion deficit between 1980 and 1985, a $54 billion change. By 1985 developing countries accounted for one-third of all U.S. imports including one-quarter of all manufactured imports coming into the United States.

Moreover, U.S. markets have been markedly more open to developing countries products than have been European and Japanese markets. While U.S. imports from the developing world were rising, LDC exports to other industrial countries have actually fallen. The United States takes a disproportionate 60 percent of the manufactured exports of developing countries, compared with 20 percent by Europe and less than 10 percent by Japan.

These patterns, which have become progressively more skewed, reflected the relative dynamism of the U.S. economy, more effective European and Japanese protectionism, the improving quality and low cost of LDC manufactured products, and aggressive developing country export efforts. Because so many developing countries with important U.S. trading relationships effectively peg their currencies to the dollar, the strength of the dollar in the early 1980s and the sharp decline after February 1985 probably had limited impact on LDC-developed country trading patterns.

Another result has been for developing countries to capture important segments of the U.S. market. According to the U.S. Commerce Department, in 1985 the major East Asian economies supplied 55 percent of U.S. clothing imports, 23 percent of its electric components and electrical equipment, 23 percent of its office and data processing equipment, and 52 percent of its footwear. The list of individual products in which imports from East Asia have been concentrated include electronic components, televisions, tape recorders, toys, calculators, and computers. Latin American exports of manufactures are more diffuse: The largest concentration in 1985 was in footwear, accounting for 17 percent of U.S. imports.

The economic relationship between North and South and, more particularly, between the United States and the developing world, consists of more than just trade flows. Service transactions, public and private transfers, bank loans, and direct investment are among the principal links that can offset or reinforce the effects of trade imbalances. Because service industries such as banking, insurance, information services, telecommunications, and the law tend to be more sophisticated and more technologically advanced in the industrial countries, efforts to export services to the developing world have intensified in recent years. Because of the political sensitivity of some of these industries, the desire to develop indigenous industries, and the drive to protect existing, often inefficient, but usually highly profitable producers (especially in banking), many developing countries have been reluctant to open their markets to foreign competition. Many developing countries, but particularly India and Brazil, aggressively worked to keep services off the agenda of the multilateral trade round that was successfully launched in Uruguay during 1986.

Part of the difficulty in responding to LDC service protectionism has been the diffuse nature of service industries and, consequently, of the restrictions that are imposed. These can range from outright prohibitions—many countries do not allow foreign banks to establish branch offices—to heavy licensing or disclosure requirements that make business impractical.

Nevertheless, U.S. service earnings from the developing world are increasingly important in the balance of payments. In 1986, such inflows totaled $48 billion, although the net flow was only $9 billion. The largest part of the inflow consisted of interest payments.

The United States has been a major provider of finance to the developing world, especially over the past decade. U.S. direct foreign investment in developing countries was $61 billion in 1986. More than half of that total was concentrated in Latin America, especially in Brazil ($9.1 billion) and Mexico ($4.8 billion).

Unfortunately, U.S. foreign investment positions are dwarfed by the foreign exposure positions of U.S. commercial banks. Too many countries have relied excessively on debt rather than equity to finance their growth and development. In many cases countries apparently relied on large-scale borrowing because it was easier to arrange, did not challenge entrenched local business interests, and could be used by national authorities with great flexibility to cover budget and payments deficits. As a result, however, countries accumulated debt burdens considerably in excess of their capacity to service them, on terms that were (and are) entirely unrealistic, and without enhancing their foreign-exchange earnings capacity. Some countries in effect used their foreign borrowing to finance overvalued exchange rates, unsustainable rates of consumption growth, massive capital flight (particularly in Argentina, Mexico, and Venezuela), and highly inefficient government industries.

At the end of the first quarter of 1987, U.S. bank exposure to the developing world totaled $114.5 billion according to U.S. government data. The largest part of this is concentrated in Latin America ($78.3 billion) including Brazil ($23.6 billion), Mexico ($23.2 billion), and Argentina ($9.2 billion).

U.S. POLICY OPTIONS

The extensive financial and economic interrelationships between the United States and the developing world create a need to develop mutually beneficial ways to manage—or preferably resolve—the problems of inadequate growth in the LDCs, self-reinforcing (and self-defeating) protectionism, and financial instability. The prevailing view in U.S. policy circles reflects a clear preference to reinforce the multilateral system created at Bretton Woods, relying on the IMF, IBRD, and GATT as the basic vehicles for promoting financial discipline, economic development, and open markets. This, of course, is consistent with the dominant economic philosophy of the last forty years that was predicated on an assumption of globally open markets for goods and capital, with the United States as the system's ultimate guarantor (as well as its greatest beneficiary) because of the dominance of the U.S. economy. Moreover, this approach in theory should spread the costs of supporting the system as the relative size of the U.S. economy declines and should avoid the intense political negotiations that would necessarily accompany a shift toward a more bilateral system.

Yet many developing countries seem to prefer more of a bilateral approach to addressing these issues. They are increasingly skeptical of the IMF, find the IBRD to be overly bureaucratic and slow moving, and view the GATT and, more generally, the international trading system as vehicles that favor established, industrial-country producers. Their preference apparently is for intensification of bilateral economic, financial, and commercial relations with the United States, through which the United States could recognize the value of the particular country's supposed "special" relationship. Some of this sentiment was visible in the eagerness with which many countries responded to the possibility that trading relationships similar to the new U.S.-Israel free-trade arrangement, negotiated in 1985, might be available to others.

Of course, more such special relationships exist in diplomatic speeches than could ever realistically exist in practice. And this preference for bilateralism may reflect an effort to avoid or minimize politically difficult economic adjustments, which are essential to being competitive in an open system, or a view that the economic system, as it is now being managed, is increasingly prone to instability.

But it may also reflect the unwillingness of more advanced developing countries in East Asia and Latin America to be differentiated from those that are less developed unless benefits are somehow guaranteed. They are unwilling to play more of a role in helping to define and manage the system—to be "graduated"—because such roles are usually defined only in negative terms. Graduation from access to concessional World Bank lending or from the benefits of special trade preferences are costs without corresponding benefits such as a greater role in shaping international trading rules. Inevitably, such one-sided transactions are resisted by developing countries.

Moreover, it is no longer clear that the United States is willing to sustain the kind of policy commitments implicit in managing a multilateral trade and payments system. In the past this meant, in practice, being the financier and importer of last resort of the world economy. U.S. loans and investments financed new plants, equipment, and infrastructure in both the developed and developing world; U.S. imports encouraged the growth of foreign industries; U.S. leadership shaped and guided the international institutions responsible for managing the system. But in the 1980s the United States has become a large net user of the savings of the rest of the world. Import penetration of the U.S. economy is increasing at an unprecedented pace and to unforeseen levels. Many U.S. companies and even industries have become uncompetitive in world markets. Partly as a result, employment in sectors producing traded goods, both manufacturing and agriculture, has been falling. The almost inevitable consequence is that the United States is increasingly attracted to protectionism.

But the move toward protectionism, which is likely to intensify during the next two years, seems to be part of a broader U.S. disenchantment with international economic leadership. This change is no accident. The luxury of aggressively advocating free trade and functioning as the financier of last resort was easier to sustain when only a small segment of the domestic economy was directly affected by fluctuations in the world market. As more workers and businesses find themselves outcompeted internationally and even domestically, the costs of international leadership became more real and more immediate.

There is a dilemma. First, international trade has become more important to the U.S. economy—U.S. exports and imports together rose from 8.3 percent of GNP in 1950 to 23.2 percent in 1985—even as effective U.S. influence on international commerce has declined. This reflects the emergence of countries as diverse as Japan, Korea, Brazil, and Germany as significant exporters of sophisticated manufactured goods as well as the determination of such countries to pursue essentially mercantilistic trade strategies.

Second, the globalization of capital markets in parallel with this country's dramatically increased appetite for foreign capital has meant that the stability of the U.S. financial markets and, indeed, of the U.S. economy is increasingly dependent on the willingness of foreigners to invest here, even as resentment of these countries increases. Between 1981 and 1984 the net increase in foreign assets in the United States averaged $90 billion. In 1985 it increased to $130 billion, and in 1986 it increased to $213 billion. Yet public opinion polls regularly record growing hostility toward aggressive exporting countries like Japan (which is probably the largest single source of foreign financing of the U.S. deficit), and protectionist fervor is intensifying.

A myth among many developing countries is that their own vulnerabilities (such as debt management strategies that are in effect dependent on sustained export growth) will protect them from increasing U.S. trade restrictions. A more likely outcome is that a significant increase in protectionist actions will inevitably generalize to countries that are running large bilateral trade surpluses with the United States (which includes Taiwan and South Korea) or countries that are capturing important shares of sensitive manufactured goods markets (which includes Brazil, Mexico, and Hong Kong). Of course, such actions could seriously disrupt not only these countries' economic strategies, with subsequent impact on industrial country creditors and investors, but also their political ties to the United States.

A more rational strategy, one more in tune with U.S. national interests, would be for this country to decide what it wants from the developing countries and how much it is prepared to pay. This means balancing the sometimes conflicting economic interests of U.S. consumers, workers, banks, corporations, and farmers with broad national political and economic interests. Unfortunately, it is no longer clear that these diverse objectives are likely to be realized through efforts to maintain a Bretton Woods type of an open trade and payments system, which assumes that the United States will absorb a more than proportionate share of the costs of running the system.

In part this is because the U.S. commitment to such a system is under attack from a variety of domestic constituencies, many of whom were traditional supporters of the Bretton Woods system. Because this attack comes at a time when the developing world is subject to growing economic and political pressures, which seem resolvable only by more, rather than less, economic interaction with the developed world in general and the United States in particular, and because that interaction is unlikely to benefit both parties (developed and developing) equally, the political pressures running against renewed commitment to an effective multilateral system seem likely to grow. This renewed commitment would require the United States and other industrial countries to absorb yet a new round of the costs of system maintenance with largely indirect benefits or, even worse in a domestic political sense, benefits that are measured mostly by the avoidance of costs, such as large commercial bank losses. Not only are current systemic arrangements unsatisfactory to important constituencies in the United States, but they are increasingly resented by many of the developing countries, who perceive themselves denied even the prospect of renewed growth and development.

What are the alternatives to this increasingly uncertain and possibly dangerous status quo? The most desirable would be a dramatic U.S. initiative to reinvigorate the postwar economic system constructed on the principles of the freest possible international flow of goods, capital, labor, information, and technology. This effort would have to be at least comparable to the commitment that underpinned the Marshall Plan, which at the time signaled a decisive U.S. turn toward involvement in and responsibility for the world economy. For many reasons (more political than economic) this seems unlikely.[2]

A perhaps more likely alternative—because it would require less aggressive U.S. leadership—would be to induce Japan and Germany to share the benefits and responsibilities of managing the international system. From a technical perspective, constructing such a multipolar economic system would not be difficult. Neither Japan nor West Germany, however, seems interested in changing economic strategies or in making the political commitments that would be required if they assumed shares of the global leadership role. The lack of any sustained movement, rhetoric aside, toward effective macroeconomic policy coordination among the United States, Germany, and Japan reinforces this perception.

But if the United States, Germany, and Japan are unwilling to commit themselves to resuscitate the postwar economic system, is there an alternative to the status quo of gradual systemic disintegration? One possibility would be to deemphasize our multilateral commitments in favor of intensified bilateral relationships with select countries. Although economists will argue this is a second-best solution, it may be more appropriate to our current economic and political resources and capabilities.

In practical terms this approach would entail defining economic and political selection criteria that emphasize the maximization of mutual advantages, then negotiating a series of bilateral arrangements covering trade, finance investment, aid, and other economic relationships. This would not necessarily result in greater government intervention—preferences already exist for many countries for many issues—but would focus these preferences on fewer countries in return for measurable benefits.

For example, the United States and Mexico have overriding political and economic interests in common: massive U.S. investment and loans to Mexico, sizable two-way trade flows, legal and illegal migration, the conflict in Central America, and the reality of a 1,500-mile border. In many ways no other bilateral relationship is more important to the long-term security of either country. Yet in general, the United States continues to deal with Mexico on most economic issues in a multilateral context—through the IMF, the IBRD, and, most recently, the GATT. This necessarily dilutes the U.S. ability to recognize the paramount importance of the relationship.

Admittedly, some Mexicans may prefer to deal with the United States through multilateral structures in an effort to make the relative bargaining positions less unequal. And managing the kind of intense bilateral relationships that this discussion anticipates would require considerable political sophistication from all participants. But in a world of finite resources, it might allow a better matching of resources to problems and more direct realization of the benefits of international commerce for U.S. companies and citizens.

The benefits of pursuing more intense bilateral relationships—of creating zones of mutual advantage—would have to be weighed against their costs. Three kinds of costs stand out. First, the selection of certain countries for preferential treatment (in return for preferential treatment) implies ignoring or deemphasizing others. This could have dramatic political consequences and would represent a pronounced shift in the foreign policy of the United States. Second, if the United States were to move away from a multilateral framework with regard to the developing world (with its explicit assumption of equal treatment), inevitably other industrial countries would do as well. Of course, to some extent countries like Japan (in

East and Southeast Asia) and France (in Africa) have long emphasized certain bilateral relationships. But for the United States to do
so to any significant degree would seriously undermine existing
multilateral arrangements and point toward a new international economic structure. For example, it would certainly affect the functioning of the IMF and World Bank where the United States has long
advocated nondiscrimination among member countries. Third, there
is a risk that bilateral relationships could take on a degree of per-
manence that might be inappropriate in the kind of volatile world
economy that seems in prospect.

It would probably be wrong to propose bilateralism or multilat-
eralism as discrete alternatives; rather it is a question of emphasis.
For the United States, the balance between the two presents strategic as well as tactical choices. For example, to what extent should
the United States pursue its own Third World commercial agenda in
the country-by-country renegotiation of access to the Generalized
System of Preferences (GSP) or a more general agenda of LDC policy changes (for example, with regard to intellectual property protection or more open investment flows) through the new multilateral
trade round?

The debt issue offers the greatest opportunity to develop the bilateral approach. U.S. exports to Latin American debtors and others
have fallen dramatically; developing country imports are pressuring
U.S. producers; U.S. commercial bank loans have declined in value;
and many U.S. private-sector investments in debtor countries are
under pressure. For their part, the growth and development prospects of most of the debtors are poor, and their political tolerance of
the existing system seems to be rapidly eroding. Perhaps a series of
bilateral arrangements could be negotiated that would exchange
highly concessional loan rescheduling terms for privileged trade and
investment access for U.S. companies. Because on the U.S. side most
of the participants would be private-sector institutions, the role of
the government would be to negotiate the framework and to help
distribute benefits and costs among participants. Although both tasks
would be challenging, requiring a considerable change in conceptual
approach, neither would seem to present insurmountable obstacles.

One objection to such an approach is that it could tend to make
the United States a regional power, assuming a natural concentration of economic interests in Latin America. Of course this is not
necessarily the case. A country like South Korea might be prepared
to enter into a broad-based economic and political relationship with
the United States that would be more beneficial to the United States
than one with, say, Peru or Chile.

This implies something about possible selection criteria. Ideally they would combine strategic, political, and economic variables, with heavy weight given to the last of these. These might include market size, extent of existing relationships, complementarity, potential for future cooperation, as well as the cost of not developing a special relationship (such as default).

THE NEXT STEPS

The underlying point is that the United States should reevaluate its economic interests in the developing world and carefully consider the most effective means of pursuing them. Unfortunately, the United States seems to have lost either habit, assuming that long-standing structures are by definition best, with the result that other countries often benefit at U.S. expense or that new problems are inadequately addressed. At the same time—and for much the same reasons—the United States should undertake a review of the international financial institutions to determine if there are gaps, such as the lack of an advocate for liberalized international investment conditions, or redundancies, such as that between the World Bank and the IMF with respect to economic policy conditionality and related lending programs.

For the United States such a reevaluation would be undertaken against the background of extensive existing economic interrelationships with the developing world and in the hope of seeing them expand. But the new reality that needs to be recognized—as much by officials in Washington as by those in the developing countries—is that this will happen only if it is demonstrably in the U.S. near-term commercial interest. For better or worse, U.S. willingness to sustain an open trade and payments system for often abstract or indirect benefits seems to be eroding.

The bilateral approach suggested above is one possible alternative; there may be others. These need to be contrasted not with the multilateral free trade and payments system crafted forty years ago at Bretton Woods, but with the present reality. That reality is a far from perfect system that increasingly seems to fail to satisfy either developed or developing country requirements and to lack an important political condition—a clear popular acceptance by the United States of its assigned role as manager of the system—that is essential for the system to work.

Under these circumstances alternatives that are second or third best in theoretical terms, but are achievable, may become more attractive. It is in the U.S. national interest and, indeed, global interests that the United States carefully examine these alternatives and then actively pursue its conclusions.

To be ultimately successful, this process will have to integrate the range of trade, finance, and development issues. If nothing else, the debt crisis, with its impact on growth and world trade, should have reinforced the message that they are not separable, although it is still the bureaucratic habit in Washington and elsewhere to treat them independently.

Finally, for the United States the current situation offers enormous opportunities, commercially and politically. A forthcoming, even generous, approach to the problems of the developing world—rooted firmly in carefully defined self-interest—could solidify relationships that might last for years. The opposite is also true: Failure to act now could adversely affect U.S. economic and political interests in the South for decades. The choice should be easy.

NOTES

1. These data and aggregate data on inflation in Latin America that appear below are drawn from International Monetary Fund (1987).
2. These themes are developed in Stoga (1986: 79–97).

REFERENCES

Drucker, Peter. 1986. "The Changed World Economy." *Foreign Affairs* 64 (Spring): 768–91.

Inter-American Development Bank. 1985. *Economic and Social Progress in Latin America. External Debt: Crisis and Adjustment.* Washington, D.C.: IADB.

International Monetary Fund. 1987. *World Economic Outlook.* Washington, D.C.: IMF.

Stoga, Alan J. 1986. "If America Won't Lead." *Foreign Policy* 64 (Fall): 79–97.

7 THE DEVELOPMENT ROLE OF THE IMF AND THE WORLD BANK
The U.S. Stance

Irving S. Friedman

Despite their common origin at Bretton Woods, the complementarity of their international functions, and their many common features and joint activities, the International Monetary Fund (IMF) and the World Bank are very different institutions. From their inception, U.S. policymakers regarded the two as distinct and viewed the U.S. role in them separately. At this time, the U.S. policy stance toward the Fund remains largely a question of the U.S. position on the various policies and practices of the Fund, not a question of basic change in attitudes toward the Fund. In the case of the Bank, the current issues are more profound. The choices that need to be made and implemented could result in major changes in the international role of the Bank and its modes of operation. If made, these changes would probably result in parallel basic changes in the U.S. stance toward the Bank.

Any discussion of the U.S. stance toward either the Fund or the Bank must begin with an understanding of their long-term record. The problems of the world economy are not created by the Fund or Bank, nor are they solved by these institutions. Countries have problems and countries act (or do not act) together to solve these problems. Some countries call for the creation of other international financial institutions because they see no logic to the view that only institutions created in the past can be successful in dealing with current and future problems. The existing international institutions have, however, the benefit of forty years of rich experience. This gives them a head start over other potential contenders for their functions or new related functions.

Their importance and responsibilities are found in the support they have internationally, especially from the United States. Time and time again, U.S. support for these institutions has waned, but like the phases of the moon this support repeatedly waxes. Often, after periods of uncertainty, the United States has supported these institutions when other international institutional arrangements were proposed and deemed feasible.

Changes in policy raise questions of the appropriateness of institutions. Evolutions of the institutions raise questions of their appropriateness for policies. This is happening now.

As long as the U.S. vision is one of world prosperity shared by most, it finds itself a champion of these global financial institutions, however limited by other immediate considerations like fiscal deficits or political disturbances in certain countries. Indeed, it is because the United States has not defined its world vision in terms of U.S. prosperity alone, or even the prosperity of the United States and its friends and allies alone, that it has found itself a bulwark of these institutions.

Successive U.S. administrations have differed widely on various aspects of U.S. foreign economic policy but all have accepted this world view. The rest of the world has been assisted in order that it be prosperous, competitive, sophisticated, and even aggressive in world markets. Countries in the old world were restored; new countries have been encouraged to grow and diversify. Import substitution and export promotion have been advocated to the cost of individual U.S. firms. Bolstered by this national conviction that in a prospering world the U.S. competitive market system will thrive, prosper, and become more efficient, even the severe business recessions of the 1970s and 1980s did not result in repudiation of the "one world" philosophy. Therefore, they did not result in a quest for new international financial institutions. At present, however, a new evaluation is needed. The IMF and the World Bank are proving too weak to restore or to defend world prosperity. They need to be reshaped if they are to serve their aims and function effectively to prevent the replacement of the historic U.S. vision of the world.

THE IMF

A Historical Perspective

The Fund was established to provide the international monetary framework for a system of international trade and payments free from governmental controls and permitting market forces to operate and create an efficient, orderly, expanding world economy responsive to the dynamic forces of changing comparative advantages. Exchange rates would link currencies and markets, and when structural, enduring changes in national economies occurred, consequent changes would take place in exchange rates. Stability in exchange rates was prized. It facilitated the expansion of international trade and productive capital flows. Stability, however, was subordinate to economic realism—be it changes in relative prices, costs, productivity, output, or income. Changes in exchange rates could take place, but only after international scrutiny and concurrence. These guidelines shaped U.S. policy, especially in the U.S. Treasury and the Federal Reserve, from the inception of the IMF. The Fund policies and practices embodied the world view of these powerful, decisionmaking bodies within the U.S. government. The U.S. Treasury, supported by the Fund, sought and found allies abroad. With their help, the IMF evolved into the central manager of the international monetary system.

Thus, the Fund was supported by ministries of finance and central banks, or by policymakers within those agencies who favored a liberal international trade and payments system and conservative fiscal and monetary policy to validate such a system. Canada, Mexico, Belgium, and, somewhat later, Germany were outstanding examples of such supporters in the first decade of the Fund's existence.

The views and actions of these agencies and individuals made it possible for the Fund to transform its formal Articles of Agreement into a living code of international monetary practices. In the process, it earned the reputation of being a vigorous advocate of conservative economic policies including conservative wage policies. After time, with the increase in its authority and influence, it became the policeman of such policies. It became the target for governments and leaders who opposed conservative economic policies. Likewise, it became the favored assessor of country performance for those who favored conservative policies. Fund lending policies capsulated in the word *conditionality* became synonymous with insistence on conservative policies (that is, noninflationary fiscal policies), interest rates not fixed by governments, incentives for savings and productive investments, freedom from restrictions on international payments, and realistic exchange rates and wage rates reflective of output and productivity. It also came to mean opposition to the subsidization of consumption, increased taxation, unproductive public investment, and large government expenditures. Its policies often implied more support for a competitive private sector and less special protection.

Successive U.S. administrations supported the Fund in its advice to countries. The United States expected and received advice on how to remedy its own policies in line with general Fund philosophy. It should be recalled that all U.S. administrations have professed adherence to conservative fiscal and monetary policies even when doing otherwise. Actual deviations were made necessary, it was argued, by insurmountable obstacles, not by principle. There was always the uncomfortable fact that what had to be accepted as virtually inevitable for policies in the United States was regarded as unacceptable in developing countries even when they also argued insurmountable obstacles. The Fund tried to find firm footing for itself by lecturing all members, including the United States, on the need to improve their economic and financial management.

The U.S. desire and ability to follow practices that are acceptable under the Fund Articles of Agreement are important in understanding the role of the United States in the Fund. The Fund Articles say nothing about fiscal deficits or even inflation. The Fund's attitudes on these matters derive from its responsibilities for exchange rates and exchange restrictions. From the Fund's inception in 1946, the United States adhered to the Articles of Agreement without qualification or exception. The U.S. dollar was the only major currency that was convertible when the Fund began operations. The U.S. par value was stable and unitary. The U.S. practiced no currency discrimination. The Fund's ideal system was the U.S. system in practice. It is no wonder that the United States was continuously in the lead position of supporting the Fund as the guardian of this system.

Even when the U.S. administration in 1971 broke the link between the U.S. dollar and gold at a fixed price of $35 per ounce, it was the United States that took the lead in restructuring the system by amending the Fund Articles of Agreement. The rejection of exchange-rate stability was now made compatible with strict adherence to the Fund's Articles of Agreement. This discontinuity in the continuous convergence of U.S. views with Fund policies was short-lived.

The Fund was structured from the beginning in a manner that facilitated the leadership of the United States and, within that leadership, the primary role fell to the U.S. Treasury. The key role was assured by assigning a major role to the Secretary of the Treasury. Each country in the Fund is represented by a governor. The board of governors is the highest body in the Fund. The governor for the United States is the Secretary of the Treasury. Other countries have followed this example and many have appointed their ministers of finance to be their governors. As the governor, the U.S. Secretary of Treasury has the leading U.S. role in the appointment of the Fund's managing director as well as a major role in selection of the World Bank president. The Secretary of the Treasury also has the primary responsibility for dealing with Congress on these institutions and

Congress has always taken very seriously its overseer role. The U.S. executive directors in the Fund and Bank need Senate approval and U.S. Representatives have always been part of the U.S. delegations to the IMF/World Bank annual meetings.

The similarity between the U.S. world outlook and the Fund's fundamental philosophy—and the championship of the U.S. Treasury—account for much of the extraordinary success of the Fund. Nevertheless, they do not explain it by themselves. They represent one side of the coin of the significance of the role of the world's leading economy. The other side of this coin is U.S. acceptance and application of the principle that its leadership must be exercised in ways agreeable to the other member nations of the Fund. The United States has from the beginning supported the Fund as a decisionmaking body, not a forum or conference machinery. From the beginning, these decisions have been made by the collective body of executive directors chosen by members.

When there has been doubt about the U.S. support of the Fund, the Fund wavers, becomes awkward, and is much less effective. This happened during the early 1970s. It seemed on the verge of happening in the early 1980s, until the external debt crises made clear to all that the Fund was the only effective institution for dealing with the international balance of payments repercussions of a global recession. Among the consequences were, as all know, widespread difficulties in servicing external debts and the need to restructure external debts, especially in Latin America. Again, the Fund found itself vigorously supported by the United States because the Fund's practices again met the criteria of the U.S. administration as it repeatedly had done in the past.

IMF endorsements for various forms of external debt relief brought greater responsibilities to the Fund. At the same time, the Fund has been seen more vividly than ever as advocating economic philosophies favored by the developed countries. As had happened repeatedly in the past, U.S. support for an enlarged and more accessible Fund was warmly welcomed by the developing countries, but, at the same time, the economic policies advocated by the Fund were often attacked as not sympathetic or understanding of their needs and conditions. The Fund reached new pinnacles of success and importance, but in so doing, it became the focal point for the tensions between the developed countries and the developing countries. In practice, Fund adjustment programs are the product of discussions with the member countries themselves, but the fact that nearly all international capital flows hinge on a country's agreement with the Fund helps achieve agreements on programs but not the conviction that such agreements represent a true and agreed harmonization of the interests of developed and developing countries.

The United States has taken a leading role among the membership of the Fund in resolving the tensions and conflicts between the developing countries and the developed member countries. The suggested resolutions of conflicts have often originated in the staff, but with keen staff awareness of what the United States was likely to support and, more important, keen awareness that any staff proposal would be carefully scrutinized by the United States and that the adoption of suggested actions by the Board had to achieve U.S. agreement.

This activist role of the United States, and more particularly the U.S. Treasury, has been continuous. Other developed countries like Canada, France, Germany, Great Britain, Italy, and Japan have from time to time also been activists but not as continuously or as vigorously. U.S. leadership in the Fund is not challenged by other industrial countries. Countries have opposed U.S. positions in the Fund on specific matters, but not its leadership role in the Fund.

Thus, in considering the U.S. stance toward the Fund, the question is not whether the United States will regard the Fund as a major instrument in international monetary matters or look to other existing or new institutions. Unless the Fund is drastically restructured, the question will rather be what international monetary policies the United States favors within the Fund. The earliest expressions of such may occur at various international meetings such as summits of the heads of states, or ministers of finance, or governors of central banks at the Bank for International Settlements (BIS), but the mechanism for final, precise agreements and executing or administering agreed policies is likely to be the Fund. Thus, a consideration of the U.S. stance toward the Fund begins with the awareness that there are not two separate entities—the United States and the Fund dealing with each other at arm's length. Instead, the United States is using an international mechanism that is very different from its national institutions, but a mechanism that is an integral part of its decisionmaking process. This relationship is probably unique in that no other major developed country seems equally and continuously supportive of this major role for the Fund. It makes a study of this relationship fascinating for many because it is in the Fund that the United States and the rest of the world practice daily how to reconcile an integrated, interdependent world economy with national sovereignty and the position of the United States in world affairs.

Current Issues Affecting the IMF

The Financial Position of the IMF. The financial position of the IMF rests on the availability of resources to the Fund, usually determined by the size of members' quotas supplemented by borrowings from some governments; Fund policies on access to its resources, especially limits on access by members, and repayments (called repurchases); interest paid by users of IMF resources; borrowing from governments; and repayment of IMF loans.

From past experience, it may be expected that the United States will be cautious and conservative on these issues. The United States favors a strong financial position for the Fund and will probably reflect this attitude both in discussions in the so-called Groups of Five, Seven, and Ten (industrial country groupings) and in the Fund bodies. It is likely to start any negotiations for an increase in Fund quotas in disagreement with suggestions emanating from the Group of Twenty-four, which represents the views of the developing countries. In the end, however, after extensive discussions and negotiations agreement will be reached on quotas somewhere between the original cautious position of the United States and the position of other members, especially the developing countries.

Balance of Payments Assistance. Assistance to members with ordinary balance of payments difficulties is to be distinguished from assistance to countries facing extraordinary situations such as external debt rescheduling. This issue involves not only the question of access limits but also the question of short-term help versus longer-run structural assistance and Bank/Fund collaboration. These matters become particularly important when, as now, the Fund is entering into a period when it is the recipient of net inflows from member countries as they meet their repayment or repurchase obligations. Again, this is not an issue to be merely debated, rather it requires decisions to be made after much deliberation. The United States will likely continue to support the equivalent of policy-based lending, but with emphasis on the Fund helping countries to access additional sources of financing. It will, however, agree that the Fund should continue to be the world's single most important source of balance of payments assistance for its members.

Developing-Country Debt Servicing Problems. The external debt servicing problems of developing-country members raises many sub-issues including the role of the Fund versus the commercial banks, the general terms of Fund conditionality (that is, what it considers necessary in adjustment policies to justify Fund endorsement and assistance), the willingness to commit Fund resources and on what terms in specific cases, relations with lending creditor nations also involved in these negotiations, and reactions in borrowing countries to Fund actions.

The Fund has worldwide recognition and attention for its catalytic role in debt restructuring. In many respects, the role of the Fund in the debt restructuring exercises of the commercial banks is transforming the Fund and its relations with all member countries.

The United States is likely to continue to support the lending role of the Fund in debt restructuring, though conditionality is being modified by its rather recent emphasis on growth in developing countries. This new emphasis is already reflected in the new IMF Structural Adjustment Facility. The United States again faces a much repeated dilemma. On the one hand, it supports a cautiously managed Fund, limited in its financial resources, which counsels countries to follow conservative fiscal, monetary, and exchange-rate policies and which relates the use of Fund resources to a country's economic management, usually conceived in conservative terms. On the other hand, the United States has been sympathetic to the special needs and conditions of the developing-country members. This view has been repeatedly reflected in U.S. support for liberalizing access to Fund resources by agreeing to terms and conditions for financial support much less strict than for developed countries—though more strict than the developing countries might wish—and willingness to support Fund approval for exchange restrictions when used by developing countries. An interesting question is whether the United States will feel the need for the Fund to downplay its role because of developing countries' resentment of the roles performed by the Fund in these difficult years. At the moment, the approach seems to be to urge the World Bank to share this policing role with the Fund, bringing with it its worldwide reputation for concern with development.

Surveillance. One of the IMF's central priorities is to monitor the functioning of the world economy and the performance of specific countries, especially developing countries, and develop policies of how to deal with countries, aside from offering financial assistance, that are in serious and dangerous balance of payments difficulties. The Fund's *World Economic Outlook* and its regular Article IV consultations with all members exemplify these surveillance activities.

Subsumed under the broad issue of surveillance are several issues: exchange rates, especially the U.S. dollar in relation to other major currencies; approaches to the Japanese and German balance of payments surpluses; interest rates; and the U.S. fiscal deficit. In addition, questions exist about dealing with countries that have already had multiyear debt restructuring but are not expected to come to the Fund for financial assistance. These countries are deemed to require much more intensive surveillance than other member countries. Programs responsive to these needs, called enhanced surveillance, are evolving.

Developing countries want more attention given to the practices of the developed countries. Thus, they welcome meetings of the Groups of Five, Seven, or Ten on interest rates or the U.S. dollar exchange rate. A related issue, however, is the involvement of the Fund in decisionmaking processes of countries not requiring Fund assistance. Although the United States generally has supported the surveillance activities of the Fund, they pose a dilemma in that the United States supports an activist Fund, but is cautious in inviting the Fund to become the public assessor and judge of its own economic policies. How far will the United States wish the Fund to go?

The International Exchange Rate System. Reform of the international exchange rate system is a long-standing issue, but it is still of current importance and concern. It is well known that a number of European countries like Germany and France have long questioned the wisdom of the present floating-rate system. The developing countries have joined the critics. The meetings and decisions of the Group of Five at the Plaza Hotel received worldwide attention. More experts in the United States are approaching the subject as open for discussion and policy changes without the emotional outbursts of earlier years.

The use of special drawing rights (SDRs) has remained constrained by the fact that the developed countries have not experienced widespread, serious shortages in international liquidity nor loss of their international creditworthiness in private capital markets. On the other hand, the industrial countries, including the United States, have not agreed with the repeated proposals by developing countries to use SDR creation to meet their obvious liquidity needs. The SDR "link" idea has been around for decades but continues to be resisted. However, in the search for international liquidity for developing countries, the fact that SDRs can be created by the Fund keeps it alive as a major issue. At this time, the United States generally opposes the use of SDRs to meet developing country liquidity needs.

THE WORLD BANK: THE MAIN ISSUES
AND THE U.S. RESPONSE

The World Bank has a new president who has been busy reviewing the main issues in the Bank. He took office at a time of major change in Bank policies and activities. These changes were in large part initiated by the United States. These changes, however, have set in motion forces that are likely to compel the United States to reconsider even more drastically its attitudes toward the World Bank.

The Baker Initiative addressed the most publicized current issue in international finance—the external debt crisis and its implications for the borrowing developing countries. It opened up potentials for the World Bank, which had been handicapped by the conventional wisdom of the 1970s, that had the warm endorsement of the United States. It brought into direct confrontation the reluctance of the United States to expand considerably the World Bank and IDA because of fiscal constraints with the eagerness to have the World Bank play a major role in coping with the current international financial crisis and the needs of other developing countries not part of this crisis. The same issue has come back over the years in many forms and on many occasions.

The issues in the Bank arise at three distinct levels. The first is at the level of the Bank, IDA, and the IFC themselves (summarized above). The second level is that of international development finance. At this level, there are consortia, consultative groups, cofinancing, insurance schemes, relations with international institutions like the Development Assistance Committee of the OECD, the UNDP, FAO, and WHO as well as the World Bank and the regional multilateral development banks. Should any financial institution play a global role in establishing rules and practices for all development finance? At present this function is not centralized, if it exists at all.

The third level of issues relates to all international capital movements to developing countries and the conduct of surplus and deficit countries. It is close to the issue of a need for an international code of conduct on capital movements guiding policies and decisions in capital exporting and capital importing nations. This level of issues is neglected as attention centers mainly on the first level and somewhat on the second level. Yet it is the absence of an agreed, centrally administered international code that handicaps all efforts to create a satisfactory system of international development finance. From Bretton Woods onward, the World Bank has not been given this role. It is in no significant sense a "supranational" institution exercising sovereign powers. It is an international bank capitalized by governments, led by a U.S. president, managed by an international staff devoted to assisting countries with small per capita incomes and inadequate access to the private capital markets of the world. This is a major area of responsibility, but it is not a global manager of an agreed code of behavior in international capital movements or even assistance to developing countries. This gap in international machinery must some day be filled. It is, however, not a current issue for the Bank or for the United States.

Heavily Indebted Middle-Income Countries: Policy-Based Lending

The principal issues surrounding policy-based lending to heavily indebted middle-income countries arise from the new role the Bank is playing. The Bank is preparing itself to give macroeconomic policy advice to borrowing members and to try to integrate its policy advice to member countries with that of the Fund. The Bank began to do this in the 1960s when program lending by USAID and other bilateral aid programs was quite fashionable. This approach was given up in the 1970s and the Bank concentrated on project-lending while the Fund concentrated on macroeconomic policy advice and conditions for lending. The theory was that by following Fund prescriptions countries would establish an enduring basis for satisfactory growth in development. The events of the 1980s shattered this conviction.

Many subissues arise from the Bank's current move to accept international responsibility for the macroeconomic policies and performance of developing countries including criteria of lending, member relations, tests of success, competency of advice, use of staff, as well as relations with the IMF and other institutions that may be involved such as the regional multilateral development banks.

Closely related is the issue of project versus nonproject lending. The Bank is moving from nearly 100 percent project lending to substantial nonproject lending. Macroeconomic policy influence is greatly facilitated by some form of nonproject, "quick-disbursing" lending. World Bank Structural Adjustment loans are a form of nonproject lending designed to help cope with balance of payments difficulties and influence the economic management of countries, but they are not reliably "quick-disbursing." Moreover, project lending remains more important than nonproject lending.

Countries have differed on how fast changes in lending practices in the bank should take place and how far the Bank should go, especially when it is tied closely to microeconomic policy performance and collaboration with the Fund. The United States strongly supported project lending in the 1970s. It cautiously accepted the need for temporary use of policy-based or quick-disbursing loans in the early 1980s. It made the major change of advocating large-scale, non-project lending in the Baker proposal. The international reaction has been mixed, but the U.S. initiative was accepted and is now being implemented. As this happens, the Bank will find itself much more controversial—no longer the friendly partner in development—and subjected to the criticism of interference in the domestic affairs of friendly countries. The United States may well find itself in a position analogous to its position in the Fund: welcomed for its support of increased financial assistance but criticized for being inadequate and for supporting rigorous conditionality. The positive favorable reaction to these initiatives can give way to resentment if inadequate external resources doom the growth efforts to failure. The dilemma is easily seen, but it is difficult to resolve when the U.S. deficits remain large.

Capital Increase and IDA Replenishment

Many want the Bank to expand its lending from its present level of about $15 to $16 billion per year to more than $20 to $21 billion. The United States is likely to be cautious or even opposed to giving support to proposals that will require a large increase in Bank capital, even though it strongly advocates an expanded role for the Bank in international finance. The reasons are budgetary.

The size of a capital increase or IDA replenishment are decisively influenced by the U.S. position. Other countries may be prepared to do relatively more, but at any time, there is no significant substitute for the United States as a donor. Similarly in the World Bank, other countries have increased their shares of capital, and the U.S. share has been reduced but only gradually over many years.

For any particular capital increase exercise, the U.S. position has been of decisive importance. Investors in World Bank bonds, the principal source of funds for World Bank operations, still regard the strong and clear support of the United States as essential for their willingness to invest. Thus, U.S. attitudes on capital increases are closely watched by financial markets. The United States is fundamentally supportive of the Bank and IDA but for decades has not supported them in amounts deemed reasonable by concerned Americans or many other nations.

Bank–Fund Relations

Bank–Fund relations have varied greatly over the years. The two institutions began life as twins at Bretton Woods. By the 1960s, they were barely cousins. Managing directors of the IMF and presidents of the Bank have varied in their attitudes toward each other. For many years the Bank felt secure and comfortable with its much publicized successes: steady expansion of lending and technical assistance, general popularity with borrowers, strong position in financial markets, large increases in Bank capital and IDA contributions, large and respected international staff, and huge profits giving great flexibility and an awesome position for dealing with other institutions and individuals in the development community. For many years the Bank tended to overshadow the Fund in public awareness and general esteem. In the past ten years, however, the Fund became increasingly more visible and successful. In the 1980s the Bank has been overshadowed because it has not played a major role in responding to the recent financial crises.

The Baker proposal, however, potentially elevates the importance of the Bank by giving it a major role in macro policy-based lending. The intention is to complement the Fund by making the performance criteria or conditionality more compatible with the conditions and needs of developing countries.

Policy-based lending is much more complicated and difficult in the Bank than in the Fund. The Bank has no internationally accepted code within which to frame its policy advice. In a sense, it has a mandate to avoid universal approaches and to deal with countries on an ad hoc basis. The Fund has an international code to manage and tries to fit its policy prescriptions into this universal framework.

Harmony in monetary and development policies is hard to achieve, but, as in governments, these differences can be resolved in practice. Both institutions will need to be guided by the principle that their common interest is the country and their mission is to achieve policy recommendations that can be supported by the international community and can be implemented by the country concerned.

As long as the World Bank was essentially project-oriented, Fund–Bank collaboration was on relatively less essential matters—joint meetings of governors, a common library, publication of *Finance and Development*, joint missions or reports on countries—but there were clear, separate fields of responsibility. It has been during periods when the Bank moved toward a broader macroeconomic policy role that the issue of Fund–Bank collaboration became more significant as during the mid-1960s and the present.

It is not a question of meshing two bureaucracies with different professional backgrounds and experience. It is a question of meshing two international financial institutions with common membership but different purposes and different traditions of management style. The Fund emphasizes the decisionmaking role of its executive directors representing member countries, the Bank emphasizes the role of the president and his internationally recruited staff.

8 FOREIGN DIRECT INVESTMENT
A New Climate for Negotiations with the Third World

Cynthia Day Wallace

There is growing emphasis on the part of both private industry and government spokesmen that the rapid integration of financial markets in recent years has resulted in an unprecedented interdependence of trade, investment, and other forms of capital transfer. Trade is increasingly dependent on investment, which is rapidly becoming the dominant factor in the world economy (see Drucker 1987). Trade flows are in fact now exceeded more than tenfold by capital flows, a significant percentage of which are a result of foreign direct investment (FDI).[1] In light of this and the shifting direction in both trade and investment flows, and the well-publicized impact of that shift on the U.S. balance of payments and on the international debt problem, FDI has assumed renewed prominence and demands urgent attention on the U.S. and international trade agendas.

It is therefore a very timely challenge to reassess the impact of FDI on the progressive internationalization of business, the redirection of investment capital to Third World nations, and the implications for U.S. economic policy and international negotiating processes. In September 1986 at the GATT Ministerial meeting in Punta del Este, U.S. Trade Representative Clayton Yeutter secured a clear international commitment to begin negotiations on trade-related investment issues in the new round of multilateral trade negotiations, culminating in an extended series of efforts by international, business, and governmental sources to emphasize the importance of FDI (see the appendix to this chapter). The U.S. effort was spearheaded by the

133

Business Roundtable, which issued a Plan of Action on International Investment as early as April 1983 emphasizing the need to update U.S. government policy on FDI and the need for improved international cooperation in the investment arena.

The sum of these efforts indicates a growing recognition on national and international levels of the role FDI plays in improving the balance of payments, in enhancing the export position of both home and host countries as well as creating jobs in each, and in improving productivity. The increasing importance of FDI developments to the legal and economic policymaking processes and to U.S. governmental and private interests cannot be overstated, as the linkage between economic and political conditions continues to strengthen.

FDI will normally flow to areas of greater dynamic growth potential. This currently is the Third World, but the infrastructure of most LDCs is not geared to accepting foreign capital. To improve the prospects of economic growth, the Third World countries themselves must not only invite foreign investment capital, but they must also promote internal investment, increase productivity potential, encourage domestic savings, reverse capital flight, and achieve a more efficient allocation of available resources. It is clear that this cannot be accomplished apart from corresponding macroeconomic policies; only then can the desired net inflows of foreign capital be absorbed in such a way that a positive and lasting contribution to growth can be realized. Creative foreign direct investment can play a contributory role in this development, with advantage to both investor and host.

THE MACROECONOMIC ENVIRONMENT

While the focus of the present analysis is foreign direct investment in the Third World, an overview of the U.S. direct investment picture furnishes a basis both for developing country strategy considerations and for U.S. policy implications.

U.S. Direct Investment Position

Approximately 80 percent of all foreign direct investment is currently carried on between industrialized nations, with the United States having become the single largest source of FDI in the post–World War II era. The U.S. relative world share of FDI, however, has substantially decreased in the 1980s vis-à-vis that of other major capital-exporting countries, and the target of much of the increased

outward FDI flows from abroad has been the United States. Consequently, the U.S. net position has been shifting.

Already by 1980 the United States had become the single largest
recipient of international direct investment, receiving 15 percent of
total world FDI. At the same time it maintained its long-held position as the greatest single source of direct investment abroad. This
continued strong investment position helped to slow the overall
downward curve of the trade deficit figures as our falling export
trade was dragging the current account into a net debtor position.
Yet even the more robust FDI activity could not counterbalance the
decline in trade, as FDI itself was diminishing, albeit at a slower rate.

Since 1980, the U.S. net FDI position has further deteriorated,
owing to the larger absolute growth of incoming foreign investment
capital primarily from Europe and Japan. This net decline is not as
alarming as it would be given a different starting point. U.S. direct
investment abroad from the 1950s through most of the 1970s was
vastly out of proportion to that of the rest of the world. FDI is now
approaching more of an equilibrium of eastward versus westward
flows of investment capital, and the United States is still well in the
lead. Moreover, it must not be forgotten that foreign investment
capital has contributed to financing the U.S. budget deficit where
domestic savings were inadequate.

It was predicted that outward FDI would take a significant upturn
following a 28 percent drop in 1982-83. To date, however, projec-
tions of a 40 percent increase by 1987 have not fully materialized,
and the U.S. Department of Commerce's Bureau of Economic Analysis has since published a downward revision of its earlier estimates.
While 1983-84 showed a decline in the U.S. net international investment position, 1985 figures showed an overall 9 percent increase in
the U.S. direct investment position abroad.[2] The 1985 increase is
deceptive, however, in that it does not indicate new investment
trends but rather reflects some aberrations such as the dramatic
depreciation of the dollar, which altered the value of affiliates'
dollar-denominated assets, independent of any capital movements.

An increase observable in U.S. investment in the developing countries is also skewed by an abnormality involving certain intercorporate debt outflows. Moreover, FDI in Latin America evidences some
inconsistencies (increasing in some countries, decreasing in others),
while Asian and Pacific regions show an overall decline. FDI trends
should be monitored closely; there is little latitude for allowing a
wait-and-watch approach or a no-action policy until the U.S. net
FDI position approaches the extremes of the U.S. trade imbalance.

Since international direct investment has very substantial effects on the U.S. international trade position, on world financial flows, and on technology transfer, it is critical for the United States—still unquestionably the foremost economic power in the world, with the leadership expectations that presupposes—to formulate and enunciate a coherent and consistent foreign investment policy. This policy should embody and protect the vital interests of the U.S. business community while maximally enhancing Third World export capabilities and foreign capital needs.

Although the United States has something of an internal policy toward FDI as formalized primarily in its tax codes, there is not a regularized program or strategy by the U.S. government to influence international policy for the promotion or protection of such investment. Since multinational affiliates located abroad are governed by host state law and policy in addition to any home state restrictions that regulate their activities, MNEs often find their operations hampered by uncoordinated or unnecessary governmental measures at home and conflicting or retaliatory legislation abroad. Both of these might be largely avoidable given a clearer U.S. government policy or some multilaterally agreed principles to facilitate the harmonization of global investment activities and thereby minimize the difficulties caused by MNEs being regulated severally by an indefinite number of foreign governments, each with different investment laws and administrative policies.

Without functional guidelines or multilateral approaches for avoiding potential negative dynamics, the only remaining option is to intervene at the point at which MNE activities actually lead to legal or political confrontation. Clear-cut U.S. policy guidelines, worked into multilateral codes or agreements, would go some way in obviating the need for home government interference with the free-market process and in minimizing undesirable confrontation with host governments.

Host state conflicts with existing U.S. laws or regulations have most frequently occurred in such areas as antitrust and technology transfer aspects of trading-with-the-enemy legislation, which can lead to conflicts of jurisdiction and controversial exercise of extraterritoriality. While these have not been problematic areas in the Third World context, where conflicts have been more likely to arise over expropriation and compensation issues or over questions of parent-subsidiary liability, the European responses to U.S. FDI-related activities have already served as models for LDCs in such areas as conditional entry negotiations, various performance requirements, and other investment incentives and disincentives. Any lessons learned by the United States from European responses to the extra-territorial reach of U.S. law and policy (often leading to further restrictive legislation) might well be learned before the contemplated stepped-up pace of FDI activity in the Third World gets fully under way.

Proposals have been publicized for a "GATT for investment," but as yet, this idea has not taken hold. FDI issues must still be addressed in other forums such as the OECD and the IMF. The GATT itself provides an appropriate forum for deliberating some multilateral aspects of FDI, due to the increasing linkage of trade and investment and the fact that FDI can have as serious and direct consequences on trade policy decisions as can tariff and nontariff barriers to trade.

There is not universal accord, however, that even trade-related FDI should be treated under the GATT. There were serious differences on this and other issues between factions going into the Uruguay Round of the GATT talks, and there is still a disparity in the response level of those different groups when it comes to follow-up on investment issues. The declaration proposed by the developing countries prior to these talks omitted all reference to trade in services, intellectual property rights, and foreign direct investment. These exclusions were of course unacceptable to the industrialized capital-exporting nations, and the items did ultimately see inclusion on the agenda.

The U.S. Stakes and the Role
of Third World Debt

As the U.S. economy is increasingly linked to the world economy, what happens in the Third World, as well as in Europe and Japan, directly impacts the United States. There is some conjecture that increased investment flows to the Third World could have a positive effect on the LDC debt situation. Notwithstanding the Baker Initiative, and in view of the continued sharp reduction in capital flows to the debt-ridden nations, a long-term bank solution to the debt problem is unrealistic. By 1985, the amount of official and private external finance available to Third World countries had fallen to less than 60 percent of the 1981 level. Moreover, financial capital in the form of bank loans fosters economic dependence and vulnerability to commodity price collapse or domestic mismanagement. FDI avoids some of these risks of compounded financial strains by enhancing the infrastructure on which sound economic growth can begin to be rebuilt, with export potential and promise of ongoing capital returns. It should not be forgotten that at the time the United States itself was an emerging nation, its rapid growth in economic strength and independence was due in no small part to the impetus supplied by substantial foreign capital and investment.

Since the 1970s FDI has been vastly overshadowed by banking capital, and related problems—including capital flight—have reached crisis proportions. While the Baker Initiative loan plans may go some way to alleviating the immediate crisis, they will not and cannot supply the entire or long-term solution. The central thrust of the Baker Initiative is sustained growth through comprehensive macroeconomic and structural policies, supported by international financial institutions and increased private-sector involvement. It promotes, along with other strategies, market-opening measures to encourage FDI as a medium- and longer-term supply-side policy, promising long-term benefits from stronger growth.

The available evidence to date does not support a dramatic positive impact of FDI on debt alleviation. In fact, the most careful analyses indicate that FDI is not even one of the primary determinants to growth. But while other factors may play a more critical role, the evidence does appear to indicate a positive ratio between direct investment density and economic development of the host. The FDI provisions of the Baker Initiative should not be overlooked. FDI may provide only one small part of the remedy; yet if it increases the export capacity of the heavily indebted nations or helps to fire the stalled engines of growth, it should be encouraged. A marginally positive impact is still preferable to the decidedly negative impact of further restrictions on either "North" to "South" FDI flows or "South" to "North" export absorption.

The necessary enhancement of voluntary capital flows to LDCs can indeed be expedited by government initiatives, but such enhancement will have to rely largely on nongovernmental and even nonbank sources. While international institutions such as the World Bank may have to take the initiative in promoting and protecting FDI in the Third World and in assisting developing countries to make the transition to international capital markets, the role of the private sector, facilitated by appropriate government policy, should be to be innovative in taking advantage of the new investment overtures from many of the Third World countries. The growing number of LDCs actively seeking FDI since the exacerbation of the debt situation indicates that FDI is now recognized by the Third World as potentially able to provide at least a modicum of debt relief and a more favorable allocation of resources.

In the ultimate analysis, any measures that contribute to increased macroeconomic restructuring and accelerated growth will inevitably have debt-relieving side effects; it is therefore the growth promotional aspects of FDI, rather than its debt-relieving potential, that must be the point of emphasis. Growth is a long-term objective whose momentum needs to be perpetuated well after the current debt crisis is past.

What, then, are the U.S. stakes in this effort? While the focus on international economic issues from the U.S. point of reference has of late been largely concentrated on the domestic budget deficit, relatively little attention has been given to the part played by foreign investment in contributing to the financing of that deficit and to overall increased production. As enunciated in President Reagan's (1983) policy statement on FDI, "foreign investment flows which respond to private market forces will lead to more efficient international production, and thereby benefit both home and host countries" through resultant heightened efficiency of international production. This premise is based on the view that "a world with strong foreign investment flows is the opposite of a zero-sum game," and that FDI provides a "vital and necessary ingredient in a stable, growing world economy."

It is time that attention be given to the long-term U.S. interests and strategy for FDI and to realistically assessing how the benefits of FDI can be maximized in coordination with an overall trade strategy and a consolidated debt-reduction plan. Despite the obvious interplay of the FDI factor with trade policy options, foreign direct investment is important enough in its own right to warrant separate policy formulations, multilaterally as well as domestically. The view has been expressed unofficially from within the Office of the U.S. Trade Representative that it is important that investment policy "be as well developed as trade policy and as well supported by multilateral agreements," precisely because of the increased intertwining of those two related sets of issues. The premise here is that "many of the most objectionable aspects of government treatment of foreign investment are the resulting distortions and barriers to trade flows," and "the United States will not be able to resolve such trade problems without addressing the underlying investment issues" (Bale and Walters 1986: 1).

Issues for Policy Consideration

Building on the consensus, now universally held, that foreign direct investment stimulates growth and benefits both home and host, primary U.S. policy considerations should be based on the following issues:

How can FDI in Third World nations be promoted and facilitated without engendering market-distortive side effects or increasing governmental intervention in MNE operations?

How can protection best be afforded and maintained for both corporate investor and host government, as well as for the home state, with guarantees that are reliable and adequately enforceable?

How can performance requirements be diminished to minimize distortive effects on international trade flows?

What form should an investment agreement take (code or treaty; multilateral or bilateral), and what items should be contained in the provisions to best embody a regional or global political consensus on increased investment protection and reduced government intervention in FDI flows?

How can the U.S. leadership role be most effectively exercised to orchestrate a coordinated investment policy with our major industrialized trading partners and to induce them to share in the effort to foster sustained economic growth in the developing world?

No one disputes that growth in the Third World needs to be radically reinforced by the industrialized nations. At the same time, however, efforts to improve the overall macroeconomic condition in developing countries must meet with receptivity and cooperation from those nations. A recent survey by the Council of the Americas gave evidence that it is unfavorable macroeconomic conditions above all other considerations that most affect the investment plans of MNEs. The Council's report concluded that economic stagnation is currently of greater concern to business than government rules or policies, or even political risk (Council of the Americas 1984). This gives rise to the observation that public-policy decisions undertaken by the industrialized nations individually and severally will have a profound impact on the ability and extent to which FDI can play a role in helping the developing nations emerge out of the current and subsequent phases of the debt crisis.

The task of the industrialized world is to have corresponding input into public policy deliberations of the developing world that are crucial to those nations' immediate economic future. To be persuasive, policy recommendations must be discernible by the Third World as promoting its own enlightened self-interest.

It is advantageous for all, in this regard, that there be a common voice from the industrialized nations, and it is apt to fall to the

United States, in its leadership capacity, to coordinate and articulate such policy options. The conveyance of a coordinated policy position will have to convince the Third World nations concerned that the promotion of FDI through guarantees of investor protection reciprocated by assurances of host protection, through the lowering of performance requirements, through the extension of national treatment, and through the assurance of appropriate dispute settlement mechanisms, is in their interest directly, not just indirectly through the global good. And the rationale must be suitable to the LDCs' own pressing concerns. This is task number one.

THE REGULATORY ENVIRONMENT

The U.S. position on FDI under the current administration is one of promotion and encouragement of both outward and inward FDI flows. The U.S. investment policy as set forth in the presidential statement of 1983 is to

Foster a domestic economic climate in the United States which is conducive to investment, ensure that foreign investors receive fair and equitable treatment under our statutes and regulations, and maintain only those safeguards on foreign investment that are necessary to protect our security and related interests and that are consistent with our international legal obligations;

Create, through cooperation among developed and developing nations, an international environment in which direct investment can make a greater contribution to the development process.

In the area of international economic relations, the development of policy, to a large extent, coincides with the development of law. Traditionally, U.S. laws have been favorable to FDI, and policy has reflected the legal base by exhibiting a very open investment climate. The 1974 decision to monitor the levels of foreign investment in the United States under the Foreign Investment Study Act and the 1976 International Investment Survey Act, which heightened presidential powers to conduct periodic surveys of foreign investment in the United States, did nothing to violate the anonymity of the foreign investor, nor did they involve registration of any kind.[3] Even the U.S. Domestic and Foreign Disclosure Act of 1977 is aimed at supplying information to investors and not to prospective regulators.[4]

On the other hand, the Bryant Amendment, now part of the omnibus Trade Bill (H.R. 3) currently in conference, would require disclosure of any foreign investments in U.S. businesses and real estate that exceed $10 million or are worth more than 5 percent of a company with assets over $3 million or sales over $10 million. Such a regulation would be unprecedented in U.S. economic history and could only be interpreted by foreign investors abroad as compounding the current protectionist sentiment already manifest in the trade area and extending it to FDI. The Reagan administration is opposed to the provision purely on free-trade, antiregulation, and antiprotectionist grounds. It is anticipated that such a provision would induce foreign retaliation, reduce incoming foreign capital flows, and conflict with some existing bilateral agreements. The mild irony of a U.S. representative's warning of "the potential that decisions with a major effect on our society will be made outside the United States," after years of U.S. protestations against just such rhetoric from the developing nations, is not likely to enhance the U.S. bargaining position vis-a-vis those developing nations now being asked in the new GATT round to make concessions on performance requirements for incoming FDI.

The developing world is itself just coming to recognize—in the manufacturing sector, if not yet in the resource sector—that it can often derive greater benefit from a foreign MNE that consistently provides jobs, industrial development, and export earnings than from unreasonable restraints on FDI. Excessive taxation of MNE profits, insistence on a high percentage of ownership, or outright nationalization of MNE assets are being replaced in many of these countries by new investor-friendly laws, and a number of LDCs have entered into bilateral investment treaties (BITs) with capital-exporting nations to promote FDI in their own countries. It would be more than ironic were the United States to reverse its long-standing open investment policy by introducing investor registration, just at a time when foreign investment is being almost universally courted elsewhere.

Promotion and Protection of FDI

In any FDI promotional strategy whether of host, home, or international origin, a key element is assurance of protection. This combination works both ways: (1) promotion and protection by the industrialized state of its own multinationals; and (2) promotion by the host state of direct investment from abroad, with protection measures to secure its own economic and political interests. In addition, the international community often plays a role, which then may be translated into international codes and guidelines. And lastly the MNE, itself a major player but without the exercisable political will of a sovereign state or the influence of an international organization, has to resort to creating some protective strategies of its own.

Promotion and Protection by the Industrialized Home State. With regard to the industrialized home state, promotion of outward FDI is necessary only as it regards investment in the LDCs; no impetus is necessary for direct investment in the industrialized markets beyond normal market profitability. Promotion of FDI in the Third World is necessary for several very apparent reasons: (1) a legacy of investor-unfriendly attitudes in the LDCs toward incoming investment, particularly from the United States, culminating in the U.N. Charter of Economic Rights and Duties of States; (2) the earlier switch by transnational investors from investment in natural resource extractive industries to investment in industrialized-market-oriented manufactured products, and the accompanying move to those markets that could most readily absorb the end-products; and (3) economic stagnation and unfavorable overall macroeconomic conditions and infrastructure in the LDCs. These three grounds alone provide explanation enough for the fact that approximately four-fifths of all U.S. foreign direct investment is now situated in industrialized countries.

One form of promotion and mutual protection of investment is bilateral arrangements, such as Treaties of Friendship, Commerce, and Navigation (FCN treaties) and bilateral investment treaties (BITs). By these agreements, national treatment is ensured in all but certain specified areas of national security, and most-favored-nation and antidiscrimination clauses accord to the contracting state trading or investment terms no less favorable than those granted by it to any third state dealing in a like commodity.[5] FCN treaties and BITs also typically assure the control and management of enterprises established or acquired in the host territory.

During the Nixon and Carter years, with their essentially neutral stance toward FDI, the Europeans and Japanese were entering into a broad network of BITs, numbering close to 200 agreements. When a BIT program did get underway in the United States, its success was limited and far less well received than in Europe where BITs tend to be more realistic and pragmatic.

The Overseas Private Investment Corporation (OPIC), a U.S. government agency offering political risk insurance and financing for U.S. companies investing in developing countries, represents another form of promotion of private direct investment in LDCs by an industrialized home government on behalf of its own MNEs. A 1974 congressional mandate to terminate OPIC and all political risk insurance was reversed in 1987, at which time OPIC shifted its focus to the poorest LDCs. The agency is required to consider trade-related performance requirements in its insurance decisions, but this does not appear to be having much effect on OPIC decisionmaking.

Promotion and Protection by the Developing Host State. Investment incentives, such as tax advantages or market protection, are used by host states to attract FDI. Both of these incentives tend to be distortive, however. Tax and other inducements to locate in a targeted area that would otherwise be unsuited to the investing industry have distortive effects of their own in terms of labor force relocation, market access, and similar considerations. Guarantees of market protection within delimited boundaries are a highly anticompetitive tactic and likewise distortive in terms of such considerations as labor costs (minimal local labor), consumer prices (passed on higher labor cost), and quality standards (absence of normal competition).[6]

By offering market protection, the host seeks to attract the MNE by guaranteeing protection from competition in a given market sector or geographical area. Such promises of exclusive market access have been found to be the most effective of all inducement techniques proffered by host countries seeking FDI. Clearly a protection that is anticompetitive may well benefit the corporation in terms of profits, but it is distortive to the local, the national, and ultimately the international economy, as well as harmful to the consumer.

Preservation of competition is certainly no less vital in the Third World than it has been historically in the United States as initially codified in the Sherman Act.[7] Similarly abroad, this concern is developed and embodied in the various national and EC competition laws so intrinsic to European policy and practice.[8] It has been difficult, however, for the Third World to conceptualize the real significance of antitrust in terms of its original purpose of protecting the consumer. While Third World nations have had input into the UNCTAD restrictive business practices code, there remain some concepts regarding antitrust that may not yet be fully appreciated by most LDCs.

Market competition may indeed be even more vital in Third World nations than in the industrialized world. It has been found that MNEs are less likely to adapt production techniques to the Third World host environment where competitive pricing is not a factor, resulting in less integration of the firm's operations into the local economy, with inflationary consequences. It is clear that market protection is not to be confused with the type of protection advocated as consonant with promotion strategy.

At the same time, restricting this kind of protection does effectively detract potential MNE investment, transferring more of the capital flow burden onto commercial and World Bank lending and Baker Initiative–style solutions. The result is clearly a negative-sum game.

There are sounder alternatives to attracting FDI, however. It has been shown, for example, that host states that are organized to conduct rapid and ministerially coordinated negotiations, with skilled negotiators who have the authority to conclude an agreement swiftly, have a decided edge over those which engage in lengthy negotiations.

Promotion and Protection by the International Community. Promotion of FDI by home and host state governments is now being supplemented by promotional measures originating at the international level, notably the World Bank, where concrete efforts are in progress to ensure investment protection and enhance host-government credibility through the Multilateral Investment Guarantee Agency (MIGA). The purpose of MIGA is patently promotion and protection of FDI. MIGA is designed to encourage and facilitate private direct investment flows to and among developing countries by issuing guarantees against noncommercial risk and carrying out a wide range of investment-promotion activities. Promotional provisions include the dissemination of information on investment opportunities in developing member countries and the encouragement of amiable settlement of investor–host disputes. MIGA's aim also is to consult with governments to seek changes in investment policies.

The World Bank, which initiated MIGA as an autonomous agency with only an organizational link to the Bank, hopes to have MIGA operational soon after the deadline for initial membership, April 30, 1988. The convention requires a minimum of fifteen developing and five developed countries as charter members, with combined membership shares totaling one-third of the initial capital subscriptions, to provide the minimum capital required to launch the agency. The numerical requirements have been met. The capital requirements are unlikely to be met without U.S. participation, since the U.S. share alone amounts to $44.4 million of the nearly $2 billion in assessed capital subscriptions.

The U.S. Congress, desirous of being among the initial members, approved U.S. membership in MIGA in the Appropriations Bill signed into law in December 1987, though not unconditionally. Some rigorous conditions involving workers' rights, performance requirements, and overproduced goods were tacked on by labor interests. The congressional appropriation will not be transferred to MIGA until the April deadline, by which time U.S. representatives to MIGA will have to have either persuaded MIGA's board to adopt the U.S. stipulations or convinced Congress that they will actively propose the stipulations once the funding is granted.

Given the response to date—seventeen developing and six industrialized countries—it would appear that the developing countries may have more to gain by the investment guarantees than the developed world. At the same time, while the Third World will be the major beneficiary from increased capital flows into its lagging economies, the industrialized countries stand to gain in terms of more adequate investor protection and potentially an international forum for the coordination of national governments' direct investment policies. This noncommercial risk insurance will be offered by the agency on its own or, where "useful and expedient," under joint underwriting or reinsurance arrangements with national insurance schemes such as OPIC.

Another recent World Bank initiative, launched by the Bank's private-enterprise promotion arm, the International Finance Corporation (IFC), is the Guaranteed Recovery of Investment Principle (GRIP), providing total guarantees for equity investments in developing countries.

Other international initiatives for protection of the various players involved in FDI can be found in multilateral and international codes and guidelines for multinational enterprises, notably the OECD Guidelines for Multinational Enterprises; the ICC Guidelines for International Investment; the ILO Tripartite Declaration of Principles Concerning Multinational Enterprises and Social Policy; the UN Code of Conduct Formulations; the UNCTAD Draft International Code of Conduct on the Transfer of Technology; and the UNCTAD Principles and Rules for the Control of Restrictive Business Practices.[9]

The scope of the present analysis does not allow for an elaboration on each of these codes, but a study of their respective provisions and the various addressees of those provisions, collectively covering all parties (home, host, and MNE), is a necessary precursor to the formulation of any new multilateral agreement that may be fostered as a result of the new round of multilateral trade talks.

Promotion and Protection by MNEs. The multinationals, for their part, are not passive players. They are developing and adopting counterstrategies to minimize their vulnerability to economic nationalism in the Third World. These MNE counterstrategies include allying themselves with domestic industries to unite against government interventionist threats to local (domestic or foreign) production; exacerbating local political or administrative policy conflicts to create internal political alliances that will have a favorable impact on their operations; and developing other innovative strategies calculated to counter the rigors of performance requirements and the uncertainties of contract renegotiation prospects.

The inclusion of political risk management has become a key element of corporate strategic planning. Once geared primarily to political risk assessment, which proved highly unreliable, political risk management has come to concentrate less on threats of future internal revolution and more on the current and relatively predictable forces of economic nationalism and the realities of conducting MNE operations in the most effective way possible in the very midst of political risk. Political risk *per se* has virtually ceased to be a deterrent to FDI in the Third World.

Performance Requirements

The fact that performance requirements distort international trade flows, while of great concern to the industrialized world with its mandate to readjust the global macroeconomic environment, is more than likely of little immediate concern to most of the debt-stricken LDCs. The most economically depressed of the developing countries are far more likely to be swayed on this issue by reasoning that bears directly on their immediate crisis than by a globally oriented argument. If the LDCs can for now be persuaded simply that stringent performance requirements are self-defeating to their pressing need of massive capital inflows and direct investments geared to enhance export capacity, they may be better disposed a few years down the road to listen to the arguments against the trade-distortive effects of excessive performance requirements and the related global repercussions. The developing world no longer needs to be convinced that FDI provides a net benefit to their economy, but it needs to know that excessive performance requirements can effectively cut off those benefits before they begin.

Performance requirements are not unique to LDCs. Local content, local labor and management, and minimum export requirements, as well as tax and other incentives to investment, have been a part of industrial nations' MNE negotiations for years. The Third World investment climate, however, is far less attractive than that offered by stable, economically vital industrialized host states. LDCs cannot therefore presume to achieve a parallel balance of interests in an investment agreement, with an equivalent set of performance requirements. Such requirements in an economically depressed environment simply neutralize the host's inducements and incentives to foreign investors. Unless the balance of interests compensates for the financial risk involved, a foreign investor will be unwilling to transfer massive tangible assets to a stagnated economy. Foreign capital is thereby deflected from those very countries most in need of foreign exchange. Third World countries need to recognize that in order to attract foreign capital in quantities sufficient to serve their goals, they will have to reduce their performance requirements to a level capable of overriding an otherwise uninviting investment market.

Investment conditions will of course vary, depending on the relative economic well-being, from region to region, from country to country within a region, and certainly between NICs and LDCs. But all the above factors are a real consideration and the industrialized world is responsible for convincing the Third World of this reality.

A difficulty here may be the long-standing and deep-seated distrust on the part of many Third World nations, based on some unfortunate past experiences, of what they regard as a universally exploitative industrialized world. This very distrust, and the parallel distrust of international law norms as being Eurocentric and contrary to Third World aspirations, is largely the reason the developing nations were so long in understanding and accepting, and ultimately soliciting, the benefits of FDI from the developed world.

The LDCs need also to be reassured that as their economy picks up, the balance of interests can shift, and with it the relative bargaining position that over time may allow for contract renegotiation that will accrue greater benefits to the host economy. This means care must be taken by both investor and host at the time of initial negotiations to stipulate the parameters regarding terms of renegotiation, in order to prevent a possible abuse of the fundamental-change-of-circumstances application leading to excessive leverage on the part of the host. This technique, if misused, can deter other potentially beneficial would-be investors, again choking off the source of new investment capital just at a time when the engines of growth are moving into gear. Performance requirements are one area in which policy harmonization could be advanced by a multilateral code or agreement.

INTERNATIONAL POLICY COORDINATION

Despite the record of organizational attempts to foster and protect FDI as well as to protect the host state from possible MNE abuses, no real consensus has emerged on the international treatment of MNEs as vehicles of FDI. The 1960 Convention establishing the OECD, for example, committed its members to contribute to the economic development of all developing countries "by appropriate means," and particularly by capital flows into those countries, to the end of furnishing technical assistance and expanding export markets. Lack of further specificity or implementation plans or procedures to follow up that commitment has left it much of a dead letter. In fact, a 1986 OECD report revealed that the flow of economic resources into developing countries had declined steadily over the preceding four years, reducing the net resource inflows to $80 billion in 1985, less that 60 percent of the 1981 level.

No new sources of available capital appear to be materializing for the LDCs; yet Japan, for example, using less than three weeks of its current account surplus (double its current development assistance level) could instantly wipe out the African resource deficit. The OECD report revealed that Japan's overseas development assistance remains at about 0.3 percent of GNP, compared with 0.5 percent for Germany and France and over 0.8 percent for Scandinavia and the Netherlands. No quick fix such as the above Japanese scenario will have the long-term effect that direct investment is capable of. But if backed up with direct investment, such immediate measures could go some way to providing a welcome stopgap.

Japan does have a medium-term plan for increasing development assistance, but it is a very unambitious one with no real action program for FDI in Third World nations. At the same time Japan has become by far the leading foreign investor in the United States. The Japanese have, of course, simply selected a host where neither the social unrest of parts of Africa nor the severe debt currently plaguing most of Latin America lends uncertainty to the investment. Europe likewise has a very small percentage of its FDI invested in the Third World.

In addition to the record on outward investment, approximately 68 percent of Third World exports in manufactured goods are currently being absorbed by the United States, 24 percent by Europe, and only 7 percent by Japan. Our major trading partners need to be induced to absorb a greater percentage of Third World exports and to redirect some of their ever increasing FDI flows to the debt-ridden economies that are now actively seeking FDI, particularly as other sources of capital are becoming unavailable.

Many sources of commercial capital to Third World debtor nations are drying up; the problem of Third World insolvency remains. The problem is, moreover, not restricted to those nations directly affected; it is one whose resolution is vital to the health of the entire international economic community.

The United States cannot go on indefinitely taking up the slack. Here is an area where one part of the administration's tripartite trade strategy—closer economic policy meshing with Europe and Japan— might suggest a solution if extended to FDI. It is difficult to be overly optimistic on this point, given past experience with European cooperation and the past record of Japan's performance within the OECD framework.

Before the United States can be expected to coordinate a unified effort representing the interests of its industrialized partners while nurturing those of the developing world, attention needs to be focused specifically on the role of U.S. policy vis-à-vis the other major players. The United States needs a macro agenda and a micro agenda; it needs not only to identify major U.S. policy items and to make some determinations regarding its own role in improving the macroeconomic environment, but also to determine which items require multilateral treatment and which lend themselves better to regional or bilateral solutions. It needs also to draft specific action proposals. This is the responsibility of leadership.

Japanese Finance Minister Miyazawa has recently begun to assume some leadership initiatives on Third World debt issues. The United States' own external debt and other domestic economic difficulties work against its traditional influence and effectiveness in international economic policymaking and opinion-forming on these matters. Nonetheless, Miyazawa has acknowledged that Japan is having great difficulties adapting to the new international leadership demands suddenly placed on it. While Japan therefore begins to feel its way into its new responsibilities, the United States, still the single strongest nation in the world both economically and politically, must not abdicate its own leadership role if any real progress is to be made. The vision and intellectual resources required to exercise continuing leadership, however, include taking care not to short-circuit friendly negotiations with established trading partners on matters of mutual concern.

In exerting leadership, the United States should evaluate the effect of domestic policies in international terms, calling on its inherent characteristics of vitality, ingenuity, entrepreneurial instincts, and market flexibility to develop progressive initiatives rather than reactive defenses and emphasizing the positive aspects of Third World investment. In short, the United States should provide a blueprint that will represent U.S. commercial interests and at the same time contribute to world economic growth. The obvious sometimes bears articulating: In creating an agenda for global negotiations, the United States needs to identify issues that reflect common interests while at the same time safeguarding its own.

Leadership and burden-sharing must be distinguished. Leadership does not mean shouldering the lion's share of the burden of Third World debt and other economic symptoms. Leadership is the capability to influence other nations to assume their share of the burden, to adopt fair trading standards, and to cooperate to the best advantage of all parties.

This is clearly no easy task. The difficulties of assuming leadership on burden-sharing with industrialized trading partners are exacerbated by the realities of Europe's growing unemployment figures, the differential economic growth patterns of Europe and Japan, the difference in their respective attitudes toward FDI, and their less-than-optimal structural adjustments, as well as other disparate and unpredictable elements.

This, along with the United States' unique and sensitive relationship with its Canadian neighbor, has a further impact on the leadership potential of the United States. Canada's recent adoption into the Group of Five (now Group of Seven) and changing trade and investment position vis-à-vis the United States, both through legislation and through policy initiatives, promises to enhance its bilateral and multilateral bargaining position in the international economic arena.

Coping with all these complexities is the task that falls to leadership. The LDCs have never been so ready to listen nor so prepared to enact the necessary structural changes to promote growth nor so predisposed to foreign direct investment. This is the moment when maximum impact can be made. The industrialized nations should not let this unique opportunity slip by nor the United States fail to exercise its leadership in coordinating the effort.

POLICY CONSIDERATIONS AND SUMMARY

Those policy issues and considerations identified at the beginning of this chapter and further elaborated throughout can be summed up as follows:

A united policy should be pursued by the industrialized countries to induce, by suasion as well as by leverage where necessary, the

Third World to take both a short- and a long-term view of FDI benefits. LDCs should be induced to curb their appetites for an inflated degree of immediate direct benefit from FDI through the imposition of excessive performance requirements, in order to attract investors in sufficient quantity to motivate the engines of growth. That is the first priority.

Programs of indefinite massive bank lending should be phased out. Though in the short term, qualified lending may still be necessary for bridging the gap, it is certainly not the long-range or ultimate solution for sustained growth.

In promoting FDI in the Third World, special emphasis should be given to export-oriented investments. Export trade, essential to debt reduction and long-term growth, will not come without healthy economic activity; healthy economic activity will not come without a sizable stimulus from the capital-exporting nations.

Formulators of multilateral and bilateral agreements should take into consideration all previous international efforts to promote and protect both the investor and the sovereign interests of home and host states and should give particular attention to promoting a wider acceptance of, and adherence to, the national treatment principle and other international law standards.

Dispute settlement provisions should be strengthened, either retaining the existing instruments or instituting new mechanisms negotiated in an international or multilateral forum, characterized by enhanced credibility, reliability, and enforceability.

The United States should use its leadership position to play a catalytic role in coordinating efforts toward a concerted international investment policy, in addition to a burden-sharing initiative with regard to the Third World.

APPENDIX

In March 1982 the Committee on International Investment and Multinational Enterprises of the Organization for Economic Cooperation and Development decided to engage in a cooperative work program with the Trade Committee to examine trade related investment measures and their effects on both trade and investment;

In April 1983 the Business Roundtable issued a Plan of Action on International Investment, emphasizing the need to update U.S. government policy on FDI and the need for improved international cooperation in the investment area;

In September 1983 President Reagan released a major policy statement on FDI promoting liberalization of foreign investments as a means to increased efficiency of international production;

In October 1984 the U.S. Congress enacted the International Trade and Investment Act, amending the 1974 Trade Act to encompass investment issues and redefining "international trade" to include foreign direct investment;

Beginning in 1985 the International Finance Corporation of the World Bank stepped up its advisory activities in foreign investment, formalizing these activities in its Foreign Investment Advisory Services;

In the last quarter of 1985 the International Bank for Reconstruction and Development established a Multilateral Investment Guarantee Agency to facilitate the flow of foreign investment to developing countries and to strengthen international cooperation for economic development and foster the contribution of foreign investment to such development;

In October 1985, Treasury Secretary James Baker proposed an initiative envisaging not only new LDC lending by commercial and international institutions, but also promotion of FDI in those countries as an added stimulus to Third World development and sustained economic growth;

At the April 1986 Tokyo Summit the U.S. Trade Representative obtained agreement for inclusion of FDI on the agenda for the upcoming GATT round of multilateral trade negotiations;

In September 1986 at the GATT Ministerial in Punta del Este, a clear international commitment was secured to begin negotiations on trade-related investment issues in the new round of multilateral trade talks.

NOTES

1. Foreign direct investment may be broadly defined as the establishment of, or acquisition of substantial ownership in, a commercial enterprise in a foreign country, or an increase in the amount of an already existing investment abroad to achieve substantial ownership. FDI may be engaged in by individual as well as corporate investors but is generally carried out by multinational enterprises (MNEs), primarily through

   The establishment or expansion of a fully or substantially owned subsidiary;
   A merger, takeover, or other form of acquisition;
   A joint venture or other form of equity participation.

   Not included as FDI are other forms of international investment including portfolio investments, licensing arrangements, international holdings or official government reserves, and commercial bank lending.

2. The "U.S. direct investment position abroad," as used by the U.S. Department of Commerce, is described as "the book value of U.S. direct investors' equity in, and net outstanding loans to, their foreign affiliates"; the "net

international investment position" denotes "the net balance of the U.S. direct investment position abroad minus the foreign direct investment position in the U.S."

3. See Pub. L. No. 93-479, 88 Stat. 1450 (1974), and Pub. L. No. 94-472, 90 Stat. 2059. (1976) (codified at 22 U.S.C. section 3101 (1976)).

4. See Pub. L. No. 95-213, Title I.

5. National treatment, under these treaties, means treatment under the laws, regulations, and administrative practices of the host state "consistent with international law and no less favorable than that accorded in like situations to domestic enterprises."

6. For more on the negative aspects of market exclusivity, see Moran (1985).

7. 15 U.S.C. sections 1 et seq.

8. For EC competition rules, see Treaty of Rome, Articles 85 and 86 (Treaty Establishing the European Economic Community, done at Rome on March 25, 1957), 298 U.N.T.S. 3 (1958).

9. As the result of independent studies, all the international bodies enumerated concluded that, through multilaterally agreed guidelines reducing any residual difficulties or incidents of misconduct (many of which are just as likely to be perpetrated by national as by multinational firms), a substantial net benefit from FDI is to be expected for both home and host. Their commonly stated aim is consequently one of both promotion and protection: to "encourage the positive contribution which multinationals can make to economic and social progress" and to "minimize and resolve difficulties which may arise from their various operations." Even the International Labor Organization (ILO), following a study it conducted on MNE operations, came out in favor of MNE activity (see "Bad Guys Do Good" 1975: 81).

REFERENCES

"Bad Guys Do Good." 1975. *The Economist*, November 22, p. 81.

Bale, Harvey E., Jr., and David A. Walters. 1986. "Investment Policy Aspects of U.S. and Global Trade Interests." *Looking Ahead* 91(1) (January): 1.

Council of the Americas. 1984. *Debt, Economic Crisis and United States Companies in Latin America*. New York: Council of the Americas.

Drucker, Peter. 1987. "From World Trade to World Investment." *Wall Street Journal*, May 26, p. 32.

Moran, Theodore, H. 1985. *Multinational Corporations: The Political Economy of Foreign Direct Investment*. Lexington, Mass.: Heath.

Reagan, President Ronald. 1983. "Statement by the President." Washington, D.C.: Office of the Press Secretary, the White House.

III STRUCTURAL CHALLENGES

9 FOREIGN EXCHANGE RATES
The U.S. Interest

Lawrence Veit

At present, the United States seems torn between roughly equal forces of prosperity and crisis. GNP growth, which has exceeded that of most other industrial countries since 1981, has slowed to a snail's pace. Unemployment remains a serious concern for many citizens even though more than 10 million jobs have been created since 1979. Inflation rates have declined significantly, but concern about a new round of price increases persists, holding real interest rates above normal levels. Personal income and stock markets are breaking all-time highs, but the indebtedness of the government, farmers, and other entities remains a serious concern for the nation. In contrast to the good times enjoyed by most service industries, many traditional manufacturing activities are in deep trouble. Banks, too, are threatened.

Inextricably related to both the problems and the accomplishments of the economy are the dollar and the balance of payments. Since 1981, GNP growth has been slowed by a rising merchandise trade deficit. An overvalued dollar has helped curb inflation and hasten the demise of some parts of the economy that were terminally sick in any case. But overvaluation has also hurt well-managed firms, extinguishing jobs and economic progress and helping to transform the United States into a net international debtor. The rise of the dollar and its subsequent tumble, which began in February 1985, have fueled protectionist sentiments and have posed the danger of an international financial crisis if confidence in the dollar cannot be maintained.

U.S. interest in the dollar is great for two reasons. First, the exchange rate, by establishing the price of U.S. goods relative to the products of other nations, has a pervasive impact on the domestic economy and the autonomy of U.S. policymakers. Second, the dollar is used worldwide as an asset and as a means of payment. Its exchange rate and stability help determine the progress of the world economy and financial markets and, by extension, the national security and a wide range of geopolitical issues.

In light of these important roles, it appears odd that since 1971, U.S. policy with respect to the dollar has been ambiguous and, at times, passive. Large misalignments (both over- and undervaluation) have been the rule rather than the exception, and the dollar has been permitted enormous volatility on a daily basis, as well as from year to year.

The world has changed considerably since the unraveling of the Bretton Woods system in 1971. True, the United States still bears a disproportionately large responsibility for the management of the world economy, and developments in the U.S. economy have far-reaching effects abroad. But U.S. hegemony has diminished in response to the rapid growth of Japan and other countries, as well as the domestic reassessments associated with Vietnam, Watergate, and $200 billion budget deficits. Before 1971, the United States was concerned that its economy and the dollar's exchange rate contribute to the health of political allies. The foreign sector had not yet grown to the point where domestic prosperity relied importantly on the exchange rate. Today, however, the United States has a strong national interest in having exchange rates that mirror basic commercial realities and that maximize the benefits of free market forces in the system. Finally, the world has witnessed an incredible revolution since 1971 affecting communications, technology, and the financial markets. New forces, some of them speculative and destabilizing, have emerged as powerful influences over exchange rates. These require governments to initiate new responses to market instability if financial anarchy is to be avoided.

Because any particular exchange rate benefits some U.S. interests more than others, it is hardly surprising that on some occasions a U.S. consensus about the dollar has been lacking. Adding to the problem have been the intrinsic complexity of exchange-rate relationships, the absence of any agreement as to what causes currency fluctuations, debates as to how currency levels and changes affect economic and political developments, differences among nations as to where their mutual exchange rates should be, and questions about what instruments governments should use to influence currency movements and the effectiveness of alternative tools. These conflicts and uncertainties have often led public officials to prefer passive over active exchange-rate policies.

The United States has gradually become better acquainted with the costs of both over- and undervaluation, as well as the harm from allowing the dollar to be unduly influenced by speculators and monetary authorities abroad, neither of which give high priority to the U.S. national interest. Time has also clarified that the United States needs to shrink its balance-of-payments deficit and that trade and finance are so linked that the entire burden of adjustment cannot rest on the exchange rate.

Options for affecting the dollar's exchange rate range from straightforward, low-cost measures such as direct intervention in the currency markets, to more remote and risky actions such as reducing U.S. military expenditures abroad. Given the kind of representative democracy practiced in the United States, and the pivotal role of the United States in the world, it appears wise to rule out the more exotic and high-handed options. They could be too risky and destabilizing in both the economic and political spheres, and the U.S. government might find itself unable to sustain them under pressure. Returning to the opposite extreme, the futility of currency intervention in the face of underlying commercial realities is well recognized. But experience shows that intervention can play a major role in changing the psychology of a speculative market.

With respect to the exchange rate, the one set of measures that both has clout and passes the test of creating a wholesome environment for the U.S. and foreign economies is macroeconomic policy. A balanced fiscal/monetary policy that provides sustained, low inflation and real growth would help the dollar to become less volatile and tend to prevent it from straying far from its commercial value; to the extent that other major economic powers could also manage their macroeconomies well, concern about exchange rates would diminish even further. Among the diverse areas where governments can act to influence exchange rates are debt management, interest rates, tax structure, trade policy, and even immigration. But because these areas are oriented toward—and affected by—noncurrency considerations, they generally cannot carry much of the burden for influencing the dollar.

Another dimension of foreign exchange policy is systemic. Since 1971, the examination of techniques for managing the exchange-rate system has gained new urgency. In retrospect, maintaining a fixed-rate system in the face of a world disoriented by two oil shocks was not possible. But with the return of more stable conditions, many observers echo a wish to revert as soon as possible to a less volatile system. The European Monetary System (EMS) is an expression of the desire to peg rates among major trading partners, making periodic small alterations in parities to compensate for changes in competitive positions and placing as much weight as possible for adjustment on macroeconomic policy. The EMS, moreover, appears to have reduced volatility not only within Europe but between Europe and the United States. Most advocates of flexible-rate systems still favor allowing supply and demand forces to operate freely, but in acknowledging the market distortions observed since 1971, many are prepared to consider some government role in managing the system. In short, pure fixed-rate and floating-rate systems are not practical. Few governments are willing to allow their currencies total freedom to respond to market forces, and national officials often disagree about where rates ought to be and the means for reaching mutual aims. The U.S. interest lies in developing a malleable exchange rate system that reduces volatility to the extent consistent with underlying economic forces, preventing major rate misalignments.

To date, official discussions about the relative merits of differing target zone or target rate systems appear to have been overshadowed by disagreements about how currency misalignments can be recognized. Thus, the direction charted at the 1986 Tokyo meeting of heads of state—for the Group of Five (G-5) to design, in conjunction with the IMF, a system of enhanced economic surveillance—is potentially important. Elitist though it may sound, however, the G-5 may include too many divergent views to permit agreement. If progress is elusive, the United States should be prepared to use a G-3 (the United States, Japan, and Germany), G-2 (the United States and Japan), or to act alone. Proposals for larger meetings, such as an international monetary conference, should be resisted for the practical reason that no such gathering stands much chance of reaching firm commitments. The United States, however, should take advantage of every opportunity to gain popular support for a new exchange-rate regime. In this context, an international meeting might be used later to reinforce and supplement agreements among the major countries, albeit the role of the IMF in such matters already seems well established.

THE DOLLAR IN RECENT DECADES

The disastrous depression and instability of the 1930s virtually assured the adoption of a fixed exchange-rate system in the post–World War II period. What the Bretton Woods agreements did not fully foresee, however, was the extent that reconstruction of the industrialized countries and development of emerging nations would require U.S. economic leadership, especially the de facto role of the dollar as the world's currency. The U.S. economic and political hegemony implied by this situation has diminished in the past forty years, especially since the breakdown of the Bretton Woods system between 1971-73. Four decades of rapid development in Europe and East Asia have also seen the emergence of new economic institutions and institutional arrangements for managing domestic and international affairs. Nonetheless, it is apparent that the void left by the declining U.S. position has not been completely filled. Questions posed by the current, somewhat out of control, system are whether the United States might reassert leadership, whether Japan, Germany, and other major economic nations might take more responsibility, or whether new international arrangements for collective leadership and control can be negotiated.

The demise of the fixed-rate regime was gradual and due to a number of causes. In particular, the devaluation of sterling in 1967 and persistent concern about foreign accumulation of dollars eroded confidence in the dollar. On August 15, 1971, the United States responded to currency and bullion speculations by ending the convertibility of dollars into gold and acting to shore up its balance of payments. Despite subsequent efforts to restore exchange-rate stability (such as the Smithsonian Agreement of December 18, 1971), the dollar has since been determined in a "dirty" floating-rate system characterized by high volatility of daily rates, "overshoots" that have successively caused both over- and undervaluations, and sporadic efforts to reassert official control.

Exchange-rate movements have deviated so much from the predictions of those who advocated flexibility prior to 1971 that it is worth summarizing the recent history. The data in Table 9-1 docu-

Table 9-1. Average Exchange Rates.

	Japan	Germany	United Kingdom	SDR
	(yen/$)	(DM/$)	(S/£)	($/SDR)
1971 (December)	320	3.27	2.53	1.04
1975 (March)	288	2.32	2.42	1.25
1976 (June)	299	2.58	1.76	1.14
1979 (December)	241[a]	1.73	2.20	1.31
1985 (February)	260	3.29	1.10	.96
1986 (September 5)	155	2.05	1.49	1.21

Source: IMF and Brown Brothers Harriman & Co.
a. The cyclical high for the yen was Y184/$ in October 1978.

ment the extreme volatility of rates. They do not, however, show how overshoots on both the strong and weak sides have created large differences between the underlying commercial value of key currencies and their price in the exchange markets. Nor do they indicate the economic, financial, and political costs of these divergencies and excessive volatility. Regrettably, they have little predictive value.

EXCHANGE RATES AND U.S. INTERESTS

How exchange rates relate to U.S. interests is not easy to explain for many reasons. First, causality runs in both directions. Exchange-rate shifts have both positive and negative implications for a wide range of issues—domestic and international, economic, and social—depending on which interest is considered. Conversely, the pursuit of distinct U.S. political and economic aims may influence the dollar in varying ways. Second, the choice of a dollar policy (including benign neglect) is always difficult because of tradeoffs. For example, a weaker dollar could be used to spur GNP growth, but this benefit would be offset by higher inflation. Third, our analytic tools are primitive. The dollar's international value undeniably affects the U.S. rate of growth, and other key variables. But it is not possible for economists (or anyone else) to be precise about the consequence of a particular exchange rate or to specify when the impact will occur. Even if psychological perceptions affecting rates were easier to discern, it would still be hard to measure their effects. Similarly, one can rarely speak with assurance about how a particular policy will affect the dollar—even if it is intended to have a direct influence.

Nonetheless, it is possible to grope toward a better understanding of how exchange rates relate to U.S. domestic and global interests and to gain a rough sense of relative priorities. The discussion that follows distinguishes economic, financial, and security interests. In fact, these categories are somewhat arbitrary and the linkages among them are pervasive and complex.

Economic Interests

The spectrum of U.S. economic concerns includes the narrow self-interest of companies and individuals, national priorities affecting both the micro- and macro-economies, and global and systemic interests. The common element throughout is that exchange rates are, in effect, the price of money. As such, they define the price of goods and services in each nation relative to prices abroad. These prices, in turn, help determine the flow of trade among countries, the location of jobs and investment, and national standards of living.

If exchange-rate relationships do not reflect underlying commercial realities (misalignment), or if the volatility of rates is excessive, a number of economic costs may follow. Uncertainty can cause higher price margins and encourage production. Large exchange-rate fluctuations may impose adjustment costs as buyers and sellers respond to changing price incentives. Domestic and international investment is likely to be curtailed. The structure of output and production technology may be distorted in favor of decisions that render short-term profits without respect to long-term needs for research and development and costly investment. Monopolies may be abetted insofar as large firms are often better able to cope with volatility. If wages and prices are more flexible upward than downward, currency movements may worsen inflation. In seeking to overcome the costs of over- and undervaluation, protectionism is likely to become more common. Finally, exchange-rate instability is likely to deprive governments of some economic policy autonomy, while also impeding the achievement of full employment, growth, and other goals (see International Monetary Fund 1984).

Classical economists such as David Ricardo were concerned about how market forces would, via the price mechanism, establish the so-called terms of trade—that is, the price of imports relative to the price of exports. They concluded that in the absence of monopolistic or other market distortions each country's endowment of physical and human resources would determine the mix of goods entering into world trade, the price of these goods, and the incomes of participants in the system. Against this framework, the costs of exchange-rate volatility and misalignment appear large. How, for example, could a U.S. company invest in a new domestic plant if dollar overvaluation or potential appreciation could undermine the firm's ability to price its output competitively? More generally, sustained misalignment and volatility are an invitation for asset holders to speculate and hoard at the expense of genuine investment. This outcome may not always be reflected in the political sphere, however, because the cost of such behavior is likely to be borne by the economy as a whole rather than by individual asset holders.

The classical economic model was "efficient" in the sense that a given amount of goods would be produced with a minimum effort. Because exchange rates in recent years have often failed to reflect underlying commercial realities, they have been responsible for a loss of efficiency. For example, dollar overvaluation has caused the failure of not only inefficient and high-cost producers but also a number of otherwise viable U.S. firms. The consequent high level of unemployment and low income tax receipts have exacerbated the U.S. budgetary problem, increased interest rates, and completed a vicious circle by putting unwanted, upward pressure on the dollar's exchange rate vis-à-vis major competitor currencies. Taking this argument one step further, a bad exchange-rate regime has distorted economic relationships, reduced efficiency, and fueled protectionist pressures. A future danger is that U.S. protectionism will encourage reciprocity on the part of others and that protectionist policies will become a permanent part of the economic environment.

The Ricardian model assumed that goods could move in international markets, but factors such as design, management, and finance have become relatively important in defining competitive positions. International direct investment plays a key role in this new global structure, and, as in the case of trade, exchange-rate relationships define the opportunities. Countries with rates that are either over- or undervalued are likely to incur major costs—such as losing jobs and production because of overpricing, or selling resources to foreigners too cheaply.

Policymakers and the media have devoted considerable attention to whether domestic growth and stable prices can be attained without regard to exchange rates. The United States recorded positive GNP growth with disinflation for four consecutive years, from 1982–86, despite a worsening trade balance. The dollar's depreciation since February 1985 should induce an improvement in the trade balance and, consequently, a continuation of the U.S. expansion. The danger that this may not happen is a sign that insufficient attention to the dollar in the first half of the 1980s has made future U.S. development more hostage than need be to changes in the balance of payments. A more stable dollar since 1982 would have provided growth in the United States, a better prospect for sustaining the expansion, and other important benefits. It would not have eroded the low inflation outlook nor undermined the growth prospects of other nations.

Exchange-rate policy has repeatedly been at issue with respect to developing countries. The World Bank and International Monetary Fund have sought to persuade countries to substitute market-oriented exchange rates for existing systems built on tariffs, export incentives, and cumbersome administrative controls. Devaluation, however, has often been viewed as a sign of political weakness, and governments have been reluctant to dilute their bureaucratic powers. If the U.S. involvement in global development is to continue—as seems likely— a strong position in favor of responsive exchange rates and other free-market economic policies seems warranted.

Exchange rates also affect international capital movements. The overvaluation of the dollar from 1983–85, for example, is at least partly responsible for the existence of a large U.S. current account deficit. It is also related to the inflow of external funds needed to balance the current account deficit and the transition of the U.S. international investment position from a net lender of $141 billion in 1981 to a net borrower of close to $200 billion in 1986. This net external debt requires an outward flow of interest and dividend payments that reduce domestic welfare. Moreover, if external indebtedness were allowed to build for a number of years at the 1985 pace, the United States would suffer a noticeable curb on its standard of living.

Financial Concerns

An anomaly in the position of those who argue against the United States having an active exchange-rate policy is that most acknowledge the need for domestic monetary and interest-rate policies. Furthermore, most foreign governments follow active exchange-rate policies. Thus, for the United States to absent itself from acting to affect the dollar—or eschewing any view as to what the exchange rate should be—does not allow market forces to set the exchange rate. Rather, it abandons the dollar to the actions of currency speculators and foreign governments, neither of which give high priority to U.S. interests.

International money is as much in need of management as domestic money. The aims of policy and the tools for achieving goals may be even more obscure than in the domestic realm, but this is no excuse for inaction. Indeed, to the extent that money flows easily across national borders, any view of domestic monetary conditions that omits the international situation is flawed (see McKinnon 1983). In practice, exchange rates are critical to both domestic and international financial systems. They strongly influence portfolio decisions that determine the direction of international capital flows and, in turn, domestic interest rates and credit conditions. Carried one step further, they affect levels of saving, investment, economic activity, and inflation. In addition, exchange rates help determine the creditworthiness of companies and governments (for the less developed countries, in particular), and thereby the health and solvency of national banking systems. Finally, they are critical to the international monetary system, providing the liquidity for world commerce and the monetary reserves that must be held by governments to support international trade. Because national sovereignty is often compromised by commercial relationships, and in the absence of a single world currency, it behooves governments to move aggressively to coordinate their separate monetary policies.

The current situation of the dollar is an example of the centrality of exchange rates to domestic and international welfare. If, following the steep depreciation since February 1985, market sentiment were to turn to an expectation of further dollar weakness, the participation of Japanese portfolio capital in U.S. Treasury and other bond issues could diminish dramatically. Coincidentally, capital flight from the dollar could contribute to sharply higher U.S. interest rates with disastrous consequences for debtors (farmers, companies, banks, and developing countries, among others), and the onset of a recession in the United States and elsewhere. The dollar occupies a unique position as the currency most used to support the functioning of the international trading and financial systems. A loss of confidence in the dollar has potential consequences reminiscent of the 1930s depression and its political aftermath. This relationship appears to have been better understood in the immediate post–World War II period than today. But the loss of U.S. economic hegemony since the 1950s should not imply an absence of accountability in 1987, especially because other major industrial powers have been hesitant to share responsibility for the system.

Security Needs

The fact that exchange-rate relationships influence the cost of U.S. security is clear. Foreign currency must be bought with dollars to pay for importing strategic materials, stationing troops abroad, and gathering intelligence. Security of supply for petroleum and other critically important commodities may require large expenditures, particularly if unstable exchange rates are contributing to unstable global politics. Moreover, defense preparedness depends critically on a country's domestic industrial muscle. In this regard, it is of no small concern that the recent appreciation of the dollar has hastened the shrinkage of the U.S. capacity to produce steel, forgings, electronic components, and other critical goods that might be difficult to obtain in a war situation.

The case for the exchange rate's affecting security threats to the United States is more difficult to make but strong enough to warrant consideration. For example, quite apart from humanitarian interests, a poorly functioning international economy could foster political instability in a number of countries—including countries as geographically close as Mexico—and undermine cautious steps toward democracy.

Exchange rates also play a role in the many frictions separating Western Europe and the United States. Balance-of-payments disequilibrium, partly caused by an overvalued dollar, has resulted in disagreements about how the adjustment process should operate that are clearly a source of tension. Perhaps more critical because of its subconscious impact, the inability to sustain a stable and appropriate exchange rate for the dollar vis-à-vis the European currencies may be a subtle factor undermining mutual confidence. Objective measures for these psychological forces do not exist, but conversations with Europeans and Americans reveal that dollar fluctuations are related to the loss of confidence and sense of common interest on which the NATO and the Western alliance are based. The Soviet Union is not so naive as to ignore this phenomenon and may be able to use it in ways that weaken our security. With respect to Japan, the situation is somewhat different, but a resurgent Japanese nationalism and the possibility for its changing that country's political orientation in a direction less favorable to U.S. interests should not be ruled out.

Determinants of Exchange Rates

Recent years amply demonstrate that exchange-rate relationships do not conform to any simple pattern and, despite the needs of policy-makers, economists do not agree on any single theory to account for exchange-rate movements. In part, the explanation lies in the fact that the world economy and financial system have been going though a period of major institutional and structural change. To admit that we do not have all the answers, however, is not to say that exchange rates behave randomly nor to eschew any understanding of this important subject. To be sure, some shocks cannot be predicted, but others—perhaps those that fall under the headings of institutional change and political evolution—are subject to crude analysis at least, and can be incorporated in an exchange-rate outlook.

The purchasing power parity theory, which maintains that the price of particular goods will tend to be equal in all nations, appears to have little predictive value in the short term, although it is likely to have considerable standing over extended periods of time. Studies based on purchasing parity theory have at least determined that the dollar's current market valuation more fairly reflects basic commercial forces than in early 1985.

Portfolio theory, which maintains that exchange rate is a price reflecting the currency preferences of investors, is not easy to apply because changes in market psychology are difficult to predict. Nonetheless, it underscores the dangerous levels of foreign capital needed to support the U.S. current account deficit. Even a moderate alteration of expectations could interrupt this flow and depress the dollar significantly. Given this delicate environment, it is small wonder that monetary authorities in their public statements appear to be walking with feet of clay.

Clearly, monetary factors affect exchange rates, but serious conflicts between the impacts of current interest-rate differences and market prospects make interpretation very difficult. For example, high interest rates would normally attact capital inflows (currency appreciation). But if asset holders believe that they will suffer capital losses as a result of interest rates going still higher, capital outflows (currency depreciation) may occur. The relationship between the U.S. budget deficit and the dollar is also more complex than generally understood, notwithstanding the clear need to reduce the deficit at an early date.

In contrast, the potential for monetary policy to play a useful role by encouraging real economic growth is limited for several reasons. In the United States, lower interest rates could potentially increase GNP and support the dollar. Institutional change, however, seems to have altered the usual, short-term connection between M-1 growth and the rate of inflation, leaving the Federal Reserve only limited opportunities to nudge down market interest rates. Abroad, the monetary authorities are reluctant to ease interest rates for institutional reasons and due to a perceived inflationary threat. German and Japanese officials argue, moreover, that their rates are already so low that GNP growth would barely be stimulated by further interest-rate reductions.

Government policy can both be shaped by developments in the currency markets and also be directed at changing exchange rates. Conventional wisdoms have limited shelf lives. It is not surprising that in the wake of the Plaza Accord a belief that central bank intervention can influence exchange rates has superseded an earlier, disparaging attitude toward the potency of the monetary authorities. In truth, the ability of governments to affect rates is as limited as the memory of markets is short.

Moreover, the emphasis on official intervention as a means to influence exchange rates may be too narrowly focused. Experience shows that intervention stands a better chance of succeeding to the extent that it is significant in amount, sustained over time, supported by the policy statements of monetary officials, inclusive of all major countries, and coordinated among them. More broadly, however, governments can issue debt abroad, encourage or discourage international flows of private capital, and pursue policies affecting both the level and currency composition of their international monetary reserves. Finally, governments may act alone or in concert to change domestic monetary and fiscal postures in order to achieve international objectives. Such policy changes may have major consequences in the short term and often are a necessary condition for achieving long-run equilibrium.

Governments affect exchange rates by their choice of ideology and the images they project, but only in extreme circumstances are they likely to alter major social or political positions in order to modify exchange rates. Nonetheless, just as past concerns about Eurocommunism and Eurosclerosis have faded, the mythology that has made the United States so attractive to foreign asset owners may also wane. Equating the strength of a nation's currency with its geopolitical standing in the world may be excessively crude, but history shows some positive correlation between the two.

The world economy and financial markets are currently in the midst of such rapid and major institutional changes that these cannot be omitted from a discussion of what moves exchange rates. The communications revolution, innovative new financial instruments available to investors, and liberalization of financial markets are prominent among these forces. Little is known about the exact effect of these forces except that such influences are more likely to be gradual than rapid.

The main conclusion from this brief survey is that policy officials must operate in a highly complex and uncertain world in which economic and political time frames may be at odds. Perfect policy solutions cannot exist in this environment, but active and pragmatic initiatives, based on broad overviews, are more likely to bring about desired objectives than more passive postures.

Prospects for the Dollar and Policy Options

The G-5 meeting at the Plaza Hotel in New York in September 1985 reaffirmed that the exchange rate plays a key role in the adjustment process affecting balance-of-payments surplus and deficit countries. At that time, the G-5 ministers announced a mutual interest in dollar depreciation and a preparedness to bring this about. Subsequent international meetings—including the 1986 Tokyo Economic Summit—have reiterated the importance of exchange rates. In the absence of an agreement on specific target rates or target zones, however, the United States and its allies have entered into an acrimonious phase of seeking to change each other's macroeconomic policies. The resulting friction has drawn attention away from the ongoing effort of the G-5 to develop—in conjunction with the IMF—a system of enhanced, economic surveillance that would provide the basis for mutual actions.

The Plaza Accord represented a welcome watershed in foreign exchange policy and established the basis for a stabilization of the dollar. Not too much should be made of the Plaza Accord, however, for a number of reasons. The dollar's decline began largely as a market phenomenon in February 1985, making it an easy target for the G-5 in September. The accord did not establish major new macroeconomic policies for any country, and the subsequent Baker Initiative for less developed countries has yet to demonstrate real substance. The G-5 countries are far from agreement about the optimum set of exchange rates or fiscal/monetary postures. The record of U.S. official concern for the exchange rate has shifted dramatically on past occasions. It is likely that Secretary Baker will hold to his present course, but there is no assurance that future administrations will do so.

Even in the absence of any conviction that governments will act wisely, however, the possibility for reducing foreign exchange volatility, as well as establishing a set of rates that reflect competitive realities, seems increasingly near. The convergence in the economic policies and experiences of the leading industrial nations, if it continues and spreads to the balance of payments, would make a major contribution. The economic disinflation that has occurred, to the extent that it was a reaction to a preceding disorderly and high inflation era, was a natural and healthy response. It was partly the result of a more purely political disinflation of public expectations about the economy. In particular, it reflected a decline in the sentiment that governments can ensure high levels of welfare by overriding market forces. The present government focus features an effort to allow more scope for domestic and international competition, not just in product markets but among the factors of production, especially labor. It extends from the United States and Britain to France and Australia, India, and even Marxist states such as the Soviet Union and China. In short, and at risk of oversimplifying, coming years may see governments paying more attention to macroeconomic and financial conditions, permitting companies to pay less attention to exchange rates and more attention to the essence of their business.

Will the recollection of the troubled 1970s be enough to keep the new pragmatism in place? Will the major industrial nations recognize that U.S. requests for higher GNP growth rates abroad and a more open world trading system are not special pleading, but rather a genuine effort to enlist the support of others in making the world economy function well? Will the counterpart pain that many countries feel as the U.S. current account deficit shrinks induce a popular backlash, causing governments to substitute profligacy for austerity, as they have done so often in the past? Or is there some realistic set of statesmanlike policy moves that governments can take to advance the process of adjustment that is already somewhat in place?

The reassertion of U.S. leadership since 1985 affords an opportunity for progress. A first priority is macroeconomic policy, including further steps to reduce the budget deficit. U.S. interest rates are undoubtedly among the most critical parameters to watch for signs of success or failure. Not only are they a measure of domestic confidence, but lower U.S. rates are the key ingredient without which the LDC debt problem, dollar instability, the bloated future budget deficit in the United States, and other difficulties are unlikely to be resolved.

International cooperation is a second area in which future prosperity is threatened unless a past tendency toward narrow, national interpretations of self-interest can be broadened. One hesitates to ascribe too much importance to exchange rates, but they are an international barometer, akin to domestic interest rates. Just as non-inflationary real growth in the major nations benefits the world economy, a properly running international system contributes to the achievement of domestic goals. Given this mutuality, it is small wonder that the United States puts such a high premium on the new GATT round, the G-5 dialogue, and other political efforts to treat the world economy as an interdependent system. An unstable dollar would be anathema to both domestic and international progress.

Because the foreign exchange rate of the dollar is a price with pervasive economic and political effects at home and abroad, the dollar needs to be managed so as to support the overall policy aims of the nation (admittedly, priorities cannot be ranked in the abstract, but in practice the relative importance of the dollar is generally not obscure). This suggests the need for a nonpartisan dollar policy, based on allowing market forces of supply and demand for goods and services to play the principal role in determining rates. Indeed, any set of exchange rates that strays far from reflecting international competitive forces is bound to be unstable and, thereby, to engender unnecessary costs. As a corollary, one might define the ideal exchange-rate matrix as one that over time would lead to current account balance for all nations (allowing, of course, for rates to change in response to divergent national economic performance).

It is essential for the United States to embrace an active rather than a neglectful attitude toward the dollar and to be consistent in its policy stance. U.S. officials need to have a general idea of the exchange-rate relationships that serve narrow and broader self-interests and how the spectrum of economic, social, and political policies pursued by government may affect the dollar. As pure fixed-rate and floating-rate systems are not practical, the United States should be flexible in seeking to reach approximate target rates for the dollar vis-à-vis other currencies or to keep the dollar within broad target ranges. In this effort, officials should place emphasis on major currencies such as the German mark and Japanese yen, but they should not ignore the currencies of other important economic nations such as Korea and Mexico. An active exchange-rate policy, guided by competitive realities in international business, would have the effect of curbing year-to-year currency swings as well as damping intraday movements.

How should the United States deal with other governments on exchange-rate issues when the inevitable bilateral or multilateral differences arise? Clearly, to the extent that a mixture of mutual compromise and education can be used to reach consensus, this is the most desirable course. The conditions for convening an international monetary conference along the lines of Bretton Woods, however, do not now exist, and such a meeting could cause more harm than good. In contrast, promoting the use of regional organizations such as the European Monetary System (EMS) may bear fruit, as may greater use of international arrangements such as the Special Drawing Rights (SDR), within the IMF. The United States will face difficult choices when others overlook their obligations and also when U.S. officials are torn between specific domestic responsibilities and more ambiguous needs to persuade others of the linkages between trade and finance. The exchange rate can play an important but not an exclusive role in the international adjustment process. Ultimately, however, one must return to the fact that it will not be possible to obtain a good relationship between the U.S. and world economies unless U.S. fiscal and other domestic policies are responsible. But even after putting its own house in order, the United States may need to act independently of the various groupings (G-10, G-5, G-3) until the others are prepared to share in the costs of managing the system. Antidemocratic and elitist though it may sound, the G-1 may be the prime source of wisdom in pursuing a fair and constructive set of exchange-rate relationships.

REFERENCES

International Monetary Fund. 1984. "Exchange Rate Volatility and World Trade." IMF Occasional Paper No. 28. Washington, D.C.: IMF.

McKinnon, Ronald I. 1983. "Coordinate Currencies." *New York Times*, October 25.

10 CHINA AND THE GATT
Time for Modernization

Penelope Hartland-Thunberg

THE CHALLENGE

In the course of its nearly four decades the General Agreement on Tariffs and Trade (GATT) has coped more or less successfully with many intractable problems. Its techniques for coping have been varied. In those instances where the problems were especially difficult, politically or substantively, but where the trade volumes involved were minor, the means of coping was benign neglect. The problems were swept under the rug and ignored. As long as trade volumes remained minor, this solution was pragmatically, if not aesthetically, satisfactory.

China's mid-1986 application for membership in the GATT carries with it the potential for raising two such sets of problems to the level of major trade disputes involving most GATT members. The policy of benign neglect that has permitted the GATT and its members to ignore the problems of coping both with centrally controlled economies and with successful economic development programs will be severely threatened by China's accession to the GATT. It is time that these unresolved problems be confronted by GATT members and be resolved by amending the GATT or otherwise, as necessary.

Although China's present leadership is apparently committed to an increasingly market-oriented economy—to a large measure of decentralization, price incentives, and a price system reflecting the scarcity values of world markets—its economy is still almost totally centrally controlled, internal opposition to "socialism with a capitalist face"

175

is significant, and the success of its new policy is by no means assured.[1] The world trading system cannot afford the easy assumption that China will soon be an economy more capitalist than centrally controlled. It cannot afford to maintain its policy of benign neglect toward the basic inconsistency between the fundamental institutions on which the GATT is based and those of a centrally controlled economy because China's potential for trade disruption threatens to reduce the GATT to impotence. China is already the second largest source of U.S. textile imports, having risen from fourth to second position in the year ending June 30, 1986 (U.S. Trade Representative 1986); its textile exports already have reached disruptive proportions, and the country has taken only its first small step toward modernization. After one year of eligibility, China became one of the ten largest recipients of special tariff preferences extended by OECD to the less developed countries (LDCs) (OECD 1983: 52). The geopolitical interest of the West lies in encouraging China's new policy, but not at the expense of emasculating the world trading system. That alternative can be avoided by confronting now the intractable question long ignored by the GATT: How do we cope with centrally controlled economies?

Even in the highly unlikely event that China should make the transition to a decentralized, market-oriented economy within a decade or so (and thus enable the GATT to leave under the rug with impunity the problem of how to cope), this very success would accelerate the onslaught of the second set of problems—those concerning the "graduation" of developing countries to the ranks of the developed. China is a very underdeveloped country, but one with enormous potential. A system that unleashes this potential implies the same kinds of problems for the trading world as those posed today by Taiwan or Korea, but multiplied many times over.

China's per capita GNP of $300 (1983) makes it the equivalent in poverty to Ghana, Guinea, or Haiti, but its recent rate of growth has been vastly greater. Moreover, China's imports already exceed those of Taiwan, whose per capita GNP is nearly ten times that of China, while its exports nearly equal those of Switzerland, whose per capita GNP is over fifty times larger than China's. If China's exports continue for the next five years to grow at the same rate as they did in 1984 (roughly 20 percent), they would exceed those of Belgium, the world's tenth largest exporter in 1984. Starting from such a low level, China's potential for economic growth is enormous; its potential will be realized only if it does participate increasingly in world trade, importing more capital goods, and paying for them sooner or later through exports.

This is not the place to argue whether or not China will fulfill its potential. What is important is that its potential is vast and its recently experienced rates of growth of both GNP and exports are well within the range of those sustained for two decades by Taiwan, Korea, and other Asian countries. (Korean exports grew on the average by 36 percent a year during the 1960s and 1970s; Taiwan's exports by 27 percent.) Yet already China's capacity for trade disruption is in selected instances equal to that of those two newly industrializing countries (NICs). If an orderly and open world trading system is to survive the absorption of China into its ranks, it must start immediately to establish rules of proper procedure to guide both China and its market-oriented trading partners through the hazards entailed in the growth of China's world trade. Even if China grows at only a fraction of the rates experienced by the Asian NICs in the 1960s and 1970s, the degree of its disruption of world markets still could be seismic. Exports growing at 15 percent a year, for example, would double in five years. China already accounts for 40 percent of the textile exports of the emerging countries whose group share of world textile trade has been expanding rapidly (U.S. International Trade Commission 1985: 4).

China's application for accession to the GATT raises vital interests for the United States. China is a nonmarket economy and a developing country that has long aspired to be the leader of the Third World. Membership in the GATT could put China in a position to make common cause with the most powerful members of the Third World, the NICs. The more strident of the Third World countries are currently the main challenge to the industrial nations' attempt to extend GATT rules to cover services and are a major source of dissension concerning a new GATT bargaining round. China's strength may buttress this group in the GATT, and the United States must be prepared to manage ever more serious challenges to its leadership in the world economy.

Not coincidentally the USSR has recently applied for observer status in the GATT, raising the question of whether it too will eventually apply for accession. If the GATT does succeed in coping more successfully with nonmarket economy membership, entry for the Soviet Union would be more feasible technically if not politically. The United States must be prepared for such a challenge.

China's application, therefore, raises a host of interrelated commercial, political, strategic, and economic questions for this country. This chapter examines the nature of the problems, thus far ignored by GATT members, that arise in managing trade between market- and centrally controlled economies and in managing the transition of developing countries into the ranks of the developed. The concluding section offers some guidelines for making these and the related problems more tractable.

THE PROBLEM AREAS IN THE GATT: BACKGROUND

The GATT can, for present purposes, be described as resting on a foundation of faith in reciprocity, nondiscrimination, transparency, and safeguards. In each case the GATT mechanism designed to ensure the rule is difficult to adapt to a centrally controlled economy.

Reciprocity

The GATT assumes that trade flows respond to price changes, that trade can therefore be increased by a reduction in tariffs, and that reciprocal tariff concessions can be negotiated in such a way that a balance of mutually advantageous gains can be achieved by both negotiating partners. Despite the importance of the principle of "mutually advantageous" and "substantially equivalent" concessions, no criteria have been developed for measuring reciprocity. The conceptual problems of defining the value of a concession, and the empirical problems of acquiring the requisite data once a definition is settled, all remain formidable. In addition all negotiators prefer to return home with their own calculations to show that the export concessions they obtained were greater than the import liberalization they conceded. A country's private negotiating agenda might aim to maximize domestic employment opportunities through trade negotiations, or to maximize its export proceeds or to minimize the impact of trade negotiations on its balance of payments position—or other specific goals. An undefined concept of reciprocity accommodates a variety of negotiating agendas. It has been politically useful to permit reciprocity to remain ambiguous.

The principle of reciprocity has been successfully challenged by the LDCs. Claiming that they could not afford to pay for the trade concessions made by the rich countries and that they should be treated differently, the LDCs succeeded during the Kennedy Round in adding to the General Agreement a new section (Part IV) stating that the developed countries cannot expect to receive reciprocity from the LDCs. (This is only one of a list of commitments on the part of developed countries toward the LDCs contained in Part IV.)

Despite its ambiguity (and in many ways because of it) the reciprocity principle is perhaps the main reason for the success of the

GATT-based world trading system during the postwar years. The system did reduce world tariff barriers dramatically (from over 40 percent in 1947 to an average of 5 to 10 percent today) through a series of bargaining sessions conducted on the basis of "mutually advantageous" concessions. The reductions were politically saleable because they were perceived to be reciprocal.

Nondiscrimination and Transparency

The GATT from its initiation has insisted that every member give equal treatment to any traded commodity regardless of its source or destination by according most-favored-nation (MFN) status to all products. "Any advantage, favor, privilege or immunity granted by any contracting party to any product originating in or destined for any other country shall be accorded immediately and unconditionally to the like product originating in or destined for the territory of all other contracting parties" is the phrasing of the nondiscrimination MFN clause of Article I. It clearly refers to all duties, fees, rules, and formalities affecting both imports and exports. No trading country can legally discriminate against the product of any GATT member in any regard.

The MFN principle has served both as a mechanism for making multination bargaining sessions operationally manageable (the "principal supplier" basis for negotiations) and as the ethic for endowing the world trading system with moral legitimacy. As Article I of the GATT it commands more reverence than any other GATT principle, yet it too is sinned against. The GATT itself permits as exceptions customs unions and the fact of underdevelopment, both blatant forms of discrimination. In addition the drafters of the GATT recognized that GATT members might be tempted to adopt or maintain discriminatory trade procedures (and also to avoid reciprocity) if they were permitted to conduct their trade in secrecy. The GATT therefore requires transparency of trade matters by requiring that its members make information on trade practices and results available in both written form and through consultations. Despite such far-sighted precautions members have avoided MFN treatment through various extra-GATT techniques primarily involving nontariff barriers to trade. Because Part IV (and other relevant articles) for all practical purposes essentially waive for the LDCs (which represent two-thirds of all members) almost all of the basic obligations of the GATT, the sins against the MFN principle are widespread.

Those who drafted the General Agreement recognized the intertwining of trade and finance and therefore the necessity for ensuring that GATT nondiscrimination and reciprocity goals not be frustrated by inappropriate international financial practices of its members. To this end provisions were made (Article XV) for cooperation between the International Monetary Fund (IMF) and the GATT. Indeed, membership in the Fund became a prerequisite for accession to the GATT or, failing IMF membership, a special agreement with the GATT on the subject of foreign exchange rates and convertibility consistent with the rules of the IMF. The experience of the 1930s had clearly demonstrated that exchange controls were an effective means of discriminating among products and countries as well as among currencies.

The intent of these provisions has been largely ignored. Collaboration between the GATT and the IMF has been minimal, in large part because balance of payments stringencies have resulted in widespread use of exchange controls, inconvertible currencies, and exchange-rate changes. In addition the carte blanche given by the GATT to the LDCs meant that trade flows diverged widely from the Pareto optimum because of trade controls as well as exchange controls. The GATT itself, moreover, has not used its instruments of surveillance and consultation nearly to the extent that it might have.

Safeguards and Targeting

The major derogations from the GATT of the past decade or so have primarily been the consequence of mounting discomfort with the still widespread application of the nondiscrimination principle required by the GATT. The escape clause of the GATT that permits safeguards (protective devices) against injurious imports (Article XIX) has been interpreted to require nondiscriminatory import controls. If a member's automobile industry is being injured by imports, for example, higher import duties must be levied against all automobiles regardless of their source. Moreover, a country that undertakes such import-limiting action must give compensation to its trading partners either in the form of reduced import barriers on other of their export products or by accepting heightened import duties against their own products.

The first major derogation from the GATT safeguard mechanism materialized in regard to textile imports from the LDCs in the markets of the developed countries. In response to acute domestic political pressures the United States and Europe in 1961 under GATT auspices negotiated a Long-Term Cotton Textile Agreement with major LDC suppliers limiting the rate of growth of textile imports. That agreement and its successors, the Multi-Fiber Arrangements (MFA) of 1973, 1977, 1982, and 1986 were negotiated to provide for an "orderly" expansion of the world's textile trade. The MFA, which essentially defines the terms by which importers may restrict textile imports, has been referred to as "GATT Aberration No. 1" (*Journal of Commerce* 1986a).

Surging LDC resentment over the MFAs has effectively eliminated the use of similar sectoral arrangements within the GATT to limit the growth of developed country imports in other sectors of industry. LDC experience with the textile agreements also is the source of their suspicion and doubts concerning any amendments to the Article XIX safeguard mechanism.

In the 1970s Europe and especially the United States were confronted with a new phenomenon, highly targeted export selling based on efficient production and marketing techniques and plentiful long-term finance. Such export targeting practiced primarily by Japan has been perfectly legal under the GATT, but frequently proved highly disruptive in the targeted markets. The success of the Japanese practice, moreover, has captured the attention of the emerging, newly industrializing countries (NICs), which clearly hope to profit by emulating Japan's experience.

European countries especially have complained that the safeguard mechanism is out-of-date. In contrast to dumping or export subsidies that the GATT treats as unfair competition and against which import-limiting tariff increases do not require compensation, disruptive surges in imports resulting from export-targeting are treated as legitimate sales, although they are typically concentrated on one country and one sector. The Europeans argue that in such cases the GATT should permit selective safeguard action; a targeted import country, injured by a sudden inundation of legal imports, should be able to limit imports from the single disruptive source. In addition, they claim that compensation should not be required, that disruptive targeting in other words should be made illegal. The issue was argued in the most recent Tokyo Round but was left unresolved.

The major opponents of change in the GATT escape clause mechanism are the LDCs that fear selective safeguard action would be used against their exports. The United States has supported the LDC position, although it has attempted unsuccessfully to find a compromise. The United States has proposed, for example, "consensual selectivity" (GATT jargon is indomitable) according to which a country could selectively limit imports if the supplying country agreed, if the agreement were subject to GATT scrutiny, and if a time limit were set on the new controls (*Financial Times* 1983). The British also have suggested a compromise that would involve a GATT inspection team (*à la* the IMF) for countries using safeguards, with a three-year grace period before compensation is required and a public hearing to ensure equity and transparency (*Financial Times* 1981). No progress toward a resolution of the dispute has been possible.

If the country injured by targeting were to seek redress through the GATT, it would be compelled to limit imports from all sources of the targeted product. Rather than this course, the United States and Europe have chosen to go outside of the GATT to negotiate voluntary export restraint (VERs) agreements bilaterally with Japan and certain NICs or to wield some other extra-GATT form of nontariff barrier. To be sure, the short-run best interests of the LDCs were served by the United States–Japan VER in automobiles because the automobile exports of Korea, Brazil, and other LDCs remained at least unaffected or more probably increased as a consequence of the bilateral agreement. Every solution to world trade problems, however, that is sought outside of the GATT weakens the authority of the existing system. The NICs and the LDCs would be among the chief losers if the GATT should become totally impotent; their opposition to a revision of GATT safeguard rules is very short-sighted.

THE SPECIAL CASE OF NONMARKET ECONOMIES

Czechoslovakia in 1947 was a founding member of the GATT, before the 1948 coup that reoriented its trade relations from West to East. Since then Poland (1967), Romania (1971), and Hungary (1973) were accepted into the GATT and are today full "contracting parties," albeit operating under special provisions contained in their Protocols of Accession.

From the organization's earliest days, GATT members perceived that special arrangements were necessary to accommodate the extension of their relations to centrally controlled, state trading nonmarket economies. That GATT members were willing to make the effort to accept centrally controlled economies as contracting parties was a consequence of the widely shared U.S. view that preferential arrangements for some East European countries would serve the political interests of the West. Nonetheless the degree of accommodation necessary to reconcile the techniques of a state trading system with those of a market-oriented system was gargantuan. The reconciliation was at best only partially achieved.

Although various provisions in the GATT do attempt to cope with the phenomenon of state enterprises, they clearly relate to the occasional state trading operation that is the exception in a private enterprise economy (Kostecki 1978). A government tobacco monopoly or a wheat trading board are the types of occasional state trading operations addressed by the GATT. Command state-trading based on the product-by-product plan targets of a centrally controlled economy is outside of GATT's scope. Indeed Professor John H. Jackson of the University of Michigan, who is one of the leading legal experts on the GATT in the United States, commented in his 1969 classic *World Trade and the Law of GATT* (after nearly thirty pages of analysis of how the GATT attempts to handle state enterprises), "If the existence of state enterprises in an economy that generally follows a free enterprise system poses to GATT the problems that the preceding sections have discussed, consider the problem posed by an economy that is entirely or largely operated by state enterprises!" (exclamation point in the original) (1969: 361). The ability of the GATT to cope with such problems has not improved since Jackson wrote, despite the addition of two centrally controlled economies to its membership in the early 1970s.

As noted above, the law of the GATT assumes that trade responds to prices and in addition that domestic prices are closely related to world trade prices. Trade can therefore be controlled via prices, direct quantitative controls over trade can be outlawed, and such protection as is necessary can be provided through customs tariffs. These GATT assumptions are inconsistent with most of the facts of centrally controlled economies that rely on a separation between their domestic prices and world trade prices as an instrument of resource allocation and growth direction. With few exceptions domestic prices in these economies do not reflect relative scarcities, as they do in market economies, but rather the requirements of the plan or ideology. Domestic prices are insulated from world prices in order to protect the integrity of the plan targets and to ensure the achievement of the industrial structure these countries want for geopolitical purposes, rather than that reflected by their comparative advantage in the world economy. Insofar as they are used, tariffs are usually only a supplementary instrument of protection in a centrally controlled economy and not necessary to the implementation of the plan.

The fact that targeting rather than prices determines production, consumption, and trade in the centrally controlled economies[2] raises numerous challenges in reconciling GATT principles and practices with these systems. New techniques must be devised to achieve reciprocity in trade negotiations. Discrimination in trade between market and centrally controlled economies is almost inevitable in a plan-based system, especially when accompanied by chronic hard-currency shortages and frequent resort to bilaterally balanced trade. In addition subsidies and dumping, illegal under the GATT, are endemic in a planned economy whose internal price structure bears little or no relation to that of the world market and whose planning process continuously generates excesses and shortages through underfulfillment. Secrecy and nontransparency are handmaidens of these economies, employed in order to deny information about their weaknesses to their own people as well as to foreigners, and also because of poorly developed statistical systems. Official exchange rates in most cases are useless as a device for translating domestic prices and costs into dollars or some other international standard because of different price structures. And these are only the major challenges.

Differences between China and Eastern Europe

These anomalies affect China and the other centrally controlled economies to different degrees. The trade of the European members of the Council for Mutual Economic Assistance (CMEA)—that is, the USSR and Eastern Europe—has always been of minor importance to the West, averaging about 3 or 4 percent of the exports of the industrialized West. The insignificance of this trade is primarily a reflection of constraints from the East. Ideologically the CMEA countries view trade with the West as a necessary evil, entailing dangers of unpredictability and of unwanted influence and dependency, but offering an opportunity for some rapid economic and technological growth. In consequence, these countries have erected an elaborate set of institutions to insulate their domestic economies against external influences and to isolate them from world markets. Ideologically and institutionally the centrally controlled economies of the Communist countries are the most protectionist in the world. The bulk of their trade—more than 50 percent—is done with each other.

From the beginning the rush to enhance national security has made the CMEA countries economies of scarcity in which exports are perceived as a drain of scarce goods necessary to finance required imports. Import surpluses are perceived as less undesirable than a "favorable" trade balance, but imports are limited by foreign-exchange scarcities that derive from an obsolete mix of exports of poor quality. More recently declining growth rates in European CMEA countries (as well as the change of regime in China) have increasingly emphasized the importance of imports of advanced technology as a means of stimulating growth.

In the 1970s the USSR and Eastern Europe abandoned their previous policy of paying for imports with current exports to seek medium- and long-term Western credits to finance higher imports.

For the interval before credits fell due, domestic resource availability was raised above what would have been possible without the credits, thus enabling a larger boost to growth. What was surprising was not their abandoning the pay-as-you-go policy of import financing, but rather that they waited so long to seek Western credits. The delay probably was in part a function of declining apprehensions over Western influence.

The timing was right. The quadrupling of oil prices in 1973-74 brought a wave of recycled petrodollars to the large international banks in Europe and the United States. Flush with liquidity, these commercial banks sought investment opportunities for their new funds all over the world. The credit rating of the USSR was of the highest quality, a result of scrupulous attention for half a century on the part of the Soviet Union to honoring its international commercial commitments. International bankers, moreover, having convinced themselves that the USSR would never permit a member of CMEA to default on a commitment, accorded Eastern Europe nearly equal treatment. In addition, recession in Europe made an expansion of exports to the East especially attractive to West Europeans.

Credits and exports grew apace. Between 1970 and the climax of the Solidarity crisis in Poland in 1981, the indebtedness of the European CMEA countries to the West rose from $5.4 billion to a peak $72 billion, an average annual increase of nearly 27 percent. OECD exports to the East, however, rose only from 3 percent of their total exports in 1970 to 3.2 percent in 1981, the constancy of relative share reflecting the simultaneous inflation-driven expansion in world trade.

The resumption of diplomatic relations between the People's Republic of China (PRC) and all of the West in the 1970s was accompanied by a sharp shift in Chinese economic and trade policies. After a policy of nearly complete local autarky and minimal foreign trade during the cultural revolution, the new regime took control with the announced intention of modernizing the country. *Modernizing* implies specialization, an extensive division of labor and economic interdependence domestically and internationally. For China modernization meant starting nearly from scratch.

Although a decade later the country continues firmly committed to the course of modernizing its economic system, the specifics of how and how fast are clearly still being debated. The effects of internal debate and experimentation have had an exaggerated impact on the PRC's foreign trade, involving the placing and then cancellation or postponement of foreign orders, shifts in the commodity composition of imports and exports and considerable confusion at home and abroad. Nonetheless, China's trade with the West has grown rapidly, if unevenly, from a very low base. From 1977 to 1983 it expanded at an average annual rate of 15 percent; more recently the rate has been 20 percent. Today China's trade with the industrial West accounts for 53 percent of its total trade compared with European CMEA's approximately 25 percent.[3] Imports have been concentrated in capital goods and equipment, part of China's attempt to modernize technologically.

Once China decided on a new course of modernization and expanded economic intercourse with the West, it exhibited no qualms about seeking Western credits. It negotiated lines of credit with North America, Europe, and especially Japan. Overblown optimism about the size of the Chinese market and the benefits of being among the first to trade with China created extensive competition among Western banks and businesses, which rushed to open offices in the PRC.

The course of negotiations was not smooth. In 1980, for example, after having negotiated credit agreements with Japanese banks of a reported $8 billion (Ellis 1986) and a smaller number of purchase contracts, China abruptly and unilaterally cancelled or postponed most multimillion dollar projects while it undertook at home a reevaluation of the pace and direction of its growth plans (*Asian Wall Street Journal* 1981). After several false starts the Chinese let it be known they were really interested in low-interest intergovernmental credits. By mid-1984 China's retrenchment (and possibly borrowing also) had boosted its international reserves to about $10 billion (*World Business Weekly* 1980) and China resumed investment growth cautiously. In these stop-and-go reversals China negotiated more loans and lines of credit than it used. It has been estimated that at the end of 1985 China's foreign debt outstanding (both short and long term) amounted to $20 billion, a surge from $12 billion at the end of 1984, with less than half from governmental sources (*Washington Post* 1984).

China's experimentation with price incentives and the operation of the market mechanism finds its closest counterpart among the other nonmarket economies in Hungary. Among the CMEA members Hungary's internal price system is more closely aligned to world market prices than that of any other country. Nonetheless Hungary's exchange rate is unrealistic and thus requires the use of varying conversion factors to relate external prices to their domestic equivalents, similar to those employed in other CMEA countries. Even in Hungary the range of conversion factors is wide, indicating a very incomplete degree of alignment to world market prices. Centralized control and planning remains in force over most of economic activity outside of agriculture and state trading firms are still responsible for much of Hungary's foreign trade.

In contrast to Eastern Europe and the USSR, China's trade with the other centrally controlled economies is a small proportion (8 percent in 1984 in contrast to about three-fifths for Eastern Europe)[4] of its total trade, and China, of course, is not a member of the CMEA. Little is known about pricing practices in China's trade with CMEA members, but it is safe to assume that hard bargaining and political considerations as well as bilateral balancing also characterize these exchanges and result in widespread price discrimination in China's trade with CMEA's members as well as between CMEA and the West in China's trade. Also, bilaterally balanced trade and countertrade are smaller proportions of China's world exchanges than is true of CMEA members, but still offer significant opportunities for trade discrimination.

Like Hungary, China has loosened considerably centralized control over agriculture and encouraged individual enterprise in very small business. China is experimenting with various forms and degrees of market orientation in the remainder of its economy, but central control remains the rule. In late 1985 after a precipitous drop in foreign-exchange reserves followed a loosening of controls over imports, China reinstated tighter central controls. The course of China's progress toward more market orientation is likely to continue to be a bumpy succession of advances and retreats for some years.

In brief, absorption of China into the GATT will require that problems of reciprocity, discrimination, dumping, and safeguards be reexamined by the West. Temptation to rely on the precedents established by the accession of Poland, Romania, and Hungary will be strong (Ellis 1986). Yielding to such temptation would be a serious error.

Precedents

Reciprocity. Tariffs are of negligible importance compared with targets as a determinant of China's trade, although duties on imports by foreign business can be both unpredictable and exploitative.[5] The achievement of reciprocity in trade negotiations in the GATT will require special arrangements permitting the exchange of tariff concessions for concessions phrased in terms of trade targets, as well as the limination of capricious and apparently discriminatory duties.

The GATT can benefit from its experience with the special reciprocity conditions employed in the cases of Poland, Hungary, and

Romania. (Because Czechoslovakia acceded to the GATT before it adopted a state trading system, no special provisions in its Protocol of Accession were required and no new mechanisms were deployed after its shift to central control.) Poland, in return for tariff concessions from GATT members, agreed to increase the total volume of its imports from them by at least 7 percent a year. Romania, in contrast, argued successfully that as an LDC it could not accept any conditions that would interfere with its development. Romania's Protocol thus provided that in exchange for tariff concessions it "firmly intends" to increase its imports from GATT members as a whole at a rate not smaller than the increase in its total imports as provided in its Five-Year Plan—in other words to maintain East–West trade at a constant share, at least, of its total trade. When Hungary applied for membership it had already undertaken a program of economic reforms aimed at enhancing the role of market forces in its economy. It argued that it was in the course of making tariffs its main protective device, that it had no targets for trade with market economies, and that it should not have to guarantee the value of its total imports from GATT countries. The GATT finally accepted Hungarian tariffs as an effective negotiating instrument, and concessions were exchanged on the basis of the new high level of Hungarian customs duties. (High duties were explained by the necessity for protecting the economy during the shift to a market price system.) In each of these cases skeptical GATT members (notably the Europeans) insisted on maintaining existing quantitative import limitations against products from these countries. Reciprocity was formal, not substantive.

Dissatisfaction of GATT members, especially the developed countries, with the reciprocal concessions negotiated with the centrally controlled economies was muted by two considerations. First, Poland, Romania, and Hungary were accepted into the GATT primarily for political purposes as an attempt to loosen the cohesion of the Warsaw Pact by offering an alternative, albeit limited, to ties with the Soviet Union. Second, trade with these countries in relation to the total trade of the developed West was insignificant and limited by the low quality and availability of their exports. Eastern Europe just was not important enough actually or potentially to warrant the time and energy necessary to achieve meaningful reciprocity.

During the 1970s the Polish commitment to an annual 7 percent growth of imports became meaningless in the face of inflation in the double digits in the West, yet no attempt to revise the Polish reciprocity formula was undertaken. Trade with the West maintained or increased its share of the total trade of each Eastern country during the decade, it is true, but only because of generous export financing provided by Western banks. When the flow of credits abruptly ceased after the Polish Solidarity crisis in the early 1980s, the proportion of intra-CMEA trade once again began to rise (*Wall Street Journal* 1986: 12). The Polish and Romanian economies sagged into near-collapse and Hungarian growth went into reverse as all three struggled to service their hard currency debts, cope with stagnant or declining hard currency receipts (as agricultural and raw material prices plummeted), and export more to the USSR as Soviet oil prices stiffened. Meanwhile the GATT had far more compelling problems to confront than lack of reciprocity from its centrally controlled members.

Discrimination. Concern over discriminatory trade practices on the part of Poland, Romania, and Hungary was similarly muted in the GATT. The GATT did express concern that state trading monopolies would result in trade discrimination, that East European systems for licensing imports in the context of bilateral agreements were a source of discrimination, and that export subsidies as practiced by Eastern Europe were discriminatory by their nature in trade between East and West. All three countries claimed that they did not practice state trading or maintain import monopolies in the sense of the GATT (Articles II and XVII). They claimed that their trade was guided by commercial considerations and that licensing merely represented the fixing of contracts previously decided on commercial grounds. GATT remained suspicious, however, and insisted on frequent consultations to ensure nondiscrimination.

Subsidies and Safeguards. The East European members further insisted that they did not employ export subsidies in the GATT sense but rather that their exchange rates required adjustments in order to eliminate the difference between domestic and foreign prices. Subsidies and dumping were swept under the rug with panache when the GATT in the accession protocols redefined "normal value" (Article VI—equivalent to "fair value" in U.S. law) as the external price of a centrally controlled economy rather than its domestic price, thereby implicitly denying the possibility of an export subsidy or dumping by the centrally controlled countries. In general, although East Europe's arguments were not convincing, the GATT compromised and hoped for general compliance. As long as trade remained minor, the issues could be ignored. In addition the quantitative import restrictions maintained by several West European countries were clearly discriminatory to say nothing of the refusal by the United States to grant unconditional MFN treatment to Eastern Europe. The compromise on nondiscrimination was thus in a sense "reciprocal."

The GATT did protect its members against market disruption arising from imports from Eastern members that might exceed the adjustment capacities of Western domestic producers. The special escape clause in the Polish, Romanian, and Hungarian protocols permitted a selective safeguard action by GATT members against East European imports even when the Eastern country was not the only source of the imports.

This is a major, and indeed the only, exception to the interpretation of the GATT safeguard mechanism as requiring MFN treatment. The suspicions of the contracting parties over the claims of Poland, Romania, and Hungary to have trade mechanisms that work in the same way as those of the West appear to have been concentrated on safeguards and the maintenance of existing quantitative controls as the devices that would protect Western interests. In fact the escape clause has rarely, if ever, been used, but dumping remains an intractable problem.

Two years ago a U.S. Department of Commerce ruling in a dumping case brought against steel imports from Poland and Czechoslovakia carried to the absurd the implicit GATT denial that subsidies can exist in nonmarket economies. The ruling stated explicitly that because Poland and Czechoslovakia are nonmarket economies and since subsidies are actions that distort resource allocation by market forces, countervailing duties could not be applied (Ellis 1986: 9–10). At the same time, the Department did find that Poland was dumping and thus Polish steel imports could be required to pay a dumping margin. This distinction between a countervailing duty and a dumping margin in the context of a nonmarket economy was truly a Solomonic judgment.

The decision pleased no one and occasioned widespread derision, congressional complaints, and further litigation. In June 1985 the U.S. Court of International Trade reversed the ruling, and finally on September 18, 1986, after uncommon delay the appeals court agreed with the department, concluding that economic benefits given by nonmarket economies are subject only to the antidumping law, not the countervailing duty law. The decision was legalistic, ignoring the conceptual identity between a "bounty" and sales at less than "fair value" (*Financial Times* 1984).

In 1983 the U.S. textile industry initiated a case against Chinese-made apparel, charging unfair competition and subsidies. When the Chinese indicated they might retaliate against U.S. farm exports, the case was withdrawn before a final decision. Since the opening of trade relations through September 1986, dumping duties have been assessed by the United States against nine minor Chinese export products,[6] but the basic issue of how to cope with truly disruptive imports from the centrally controlled economies has not been satisfactorily resolved in either the GATT or U.S. law. As the textile case three years ago made clear, coping with China is quite a different problem from coping with Poland or Czechoslovakia. Since then, because China has become much more self-sufficient in food, it is a less important market for U.S. agricultural exports. It has given evidence, nonetheless, that it is willing to play hardball.

Reconciling China and the GATT

GATT experience with the specially devised reciprocity conditions in the cases of Poland, Romania, and Hungary has been far from satisfactory. The precedents established thus offer only a negative guide for the case of China, teaching what should be avoided rather than what should be sought. The same is true in regard to discrimination and subsidies. If the GATT is to cope successfully with the incorporation of China into the system, it must start almost at the beginning; only the special escape clause in the East European Protocols appears to offer a useful precedent.

Without question, China will argue that as a developing country it cannot be expected to compromise its growth experience by assuming any obligations in the GATT. It will argue that the General Agreement excuses it from granting reciprocity, permits it to maintain quantitative controls and subsidies, and encourages developed countries to discriminate in its favor.

If market economies accept this argument, however, they will only succeed in pushing the basic problem of reconciliation into the future and in aggravating unnecessarily the difficulties of incorporating China into the world trading system. Kostecki, in his probing assessment of East–West trade and the GATT, argues that Eastern European decisions to participate in the GATT at minimum cost to themselves in terms of commercial concessions meant that little improvement in access to Western markets was granted to them (1978: 134). It meant in addition that during the years of sizable Western credits that financed a spectacular growth in Eastern Europe's imports during the 1970s they were not able to use such market opening to obtain reciprocal market openings in the West.

The point is important because the perception of reciprocity in trade relations is more significant than the objective reality. If China is freed from GATT obligations as a developing country, the dangers of Chinese market disruption will be greatly enhanced. As a centrally controlled economy, moreover, China is likely to be perceived as the source of dumping, unfair competition, and market disruption whether or not the perception is supportable in fact. In consequence, relations between China and the West will be embittered, demands for protection against China are likely to be irresistible, and China's program of market orientation may well founder.

China's sheer size, its ability to target production for exports, its own lack of experience with Western concepts of price and cost, its ignorance of the depth and breadth (or lack thereof) of Western markets and of Western marketing practices, its tradition of linking trade with political considerations—all have the potential for engendering uncontainable misunderstanding and bitterness on both sides. Charges of unfair competition (dumping, subsidies, patent infringement) are likely to be most troublesome.

China, to say nothing of the West, will have great difficulty in judging its own costs both because of its own ideological history and because of the turmoil likely to accompany a more or less gradual and partial shift to a market-oriented price structure. Changing relative prices play havoc with Western accounting practices even in long-established market economies; a factory that buys its materials at fluctuating prices but sells its product at a fixed price has trouble knowing where it stands. China's simultaneous push for rapid growth and for a shift in basic economic institutions is likely to be stormy.

The West will do itself and China a disservice by freeing China from reasonable GATT obligations that will provide a basis for managing the daunting trade disputes on the horizon. In contrast, if on joining the GATT China assumes the obligations as well as the privileges of GATT membership, the dangers of deteriorating China–West relations will be substantially reduced. If China is perceived to grant meaningful (in relation to its poverty) concessions, it will be better positioned to seek extended concessions as its need for them develops, and the developed world will be better disposed to pay for access to China's expanding market as the expansion occurs.

It is true that Western businessmen rushed to China, in the heady days following its opening to the West, with market expectations that were totally unrealistic. They have since been sobered by China's many extortionist demands and abrupt policy shifts. Only those that have been granted market access on terms deemed to be "businesslike" will press their governments to be lenient in dealing with China.

A reciprocal exchange of meaningful concessions at the time of China's accession to the GATT would be perceived as an earnest of China's good faith and long-term intent to participate in the world trading system and support its rules. It would be an important signal that China is planning for the long haul to work within the system to avoid disruption rather than trying to take advantage of the system for short-term gain.

Whether or not China is admitted to the GATT as an LDC free of obligations, dumping and subsidies are likely to be the source of numerous trade disputes. The GATT subsidies code requires proof of injury before countervailing duties can be applied. Because U.S. countervailing legislation dates back to the nineteenth century, the United States has claimed "grandfather" rights in resisting the injury test and since 1979 has applied it only to those countries signing the Subsidies Code. Thus whether China as a member of the GATT could legally retaliate against a U.S. countervailing duty (assuming the U.S. courts should permit such to be levied against a centrally controlled economy) will depend on whether China signs the GATT subsidies code on its accession. It will also, of course, depend on whether China is willing to trade according to GATT rules. Legalisms aside, the problem of determining whether or when dumping occurs from a nonmarket economy remains.

Various approaches to the problem of subsidies (export prices below domestic prices or cost of production) in centrally controlled economies have been suggested. These range from using the export price or cost of production of a third, market-economy, country as the basis for constructing a fair market value; through the use of the lowest price import from a market economy or a trade weighted average of import prices from such market economies; to ignoring prices altogether and simply ruling on whether imports from centrally controlled economies are causing injury (*Journal of Commerce* 1986b: 13A). Objections have been raised to all such suggestions; a constructed value is a makeshift and thus likely to be the source of inequitable treatment to some interested party.

One potential solution that has not been explored (to my knowledge) lies in an attempt to work with the conversion factors actually employed by centrally controlled economies in conjunction with their official exchange rates to equate their domestic prices with world prices. Such conversion coefficients are available for Poland and Hungary. The transparency requirement of the GATT, in addition, imposes on all members the obligation to make available to the GATT members all information relating to trade laws and regulations

(Article X). A technical working group established within the GATT or OECD to explore the feasibility of judging dumping and subsidies on the basis of these coefficients would appear worth the effort.

THE TRANSITION FROM DEVELOPING TO DEVELOPED

The GATT has never defined the difference between a developed and a less developed country. If China is admitted to the GATT as a developing country free from GATT obligations, it will be doubly important for the GATT member countries to initiate a study of the stages through which a developing country will pass as it approaches the rank of developed. Such a study is long overdue; the emergence into the world trading system of the most populous country in the world pushing for rapid economic development through Westernization makes such a study imperative.

Countries like Taiwan, Korea, or Brazil (the NICs) today are much more akin in many ways to the industrial countries than they are to the other LDCs. The growing diversity of their economic structures, the greater relative importance of manufacturing and services, the enhanced ability of domestic savings to support gross domestic investment, their accumulation of international reserves and foreign assets, as well as the growth of GDP and per capita income—all can be indications of advancing economic development.

Countries, like industries, however, cherish the preferential treatment they are accorded as infants and vigorously resist adulthood, insisting on their weakness and vulnerability whenever the subject is raised. This is to be expected. Taiwan, with the second-largest international reserves in the world at the end of 1986 (at over $40 billion second only to West Germany [*The Economist* 1986: 55]), claims that it would collapse without high and reinforced protectionist barriers, tariff preferences, and the panoply of favors with which as a developing country it is blessed. Brazil finds its mountain of debt a similarly useful defense of its infancy.

The U.S. Congress is becoming increasingly impatient with the intransigence of these emerging countries. Unilateral action against some of the NICs is a growing possibility without some initiative in the international arena to cope with the process of graduation from the rank of developing to that of developed.

Graduation should be a process, a phasing out of benefits and a phasing in of obligations in some orderly pattern. The shock of a sudden cessation of the perquisites of infancy should not be forced abruptly on an emerging country; not only would it disrupt that country's economy, but because of the importance these countries have achieved in world trade, it would be disruptive to the world economy. Without a previously agreed, staged progression toward adulthood, however, such a shock is probable, and the longer it is postponed, the more potentially devastating it is likely to be.

This is so because the NICs have clearly learned from Japan's experience and give evidence of intention to emulate it. The development of Korea's automobile industry is repeating the pattern of Japan: first, production for a protected domestic market while building up experience and efficiency; then testing a small export market before the targeted push into the lucrative U.S. market. Korean plans for semiconductor production and exports are an attempt to move into higher technology (despite, as with automobiles, world overcapacity) following the same pattern. Brazil's total protection of its telecommunications industry is another example of the Japanese pattern, soon to be extended by Brazil to chemicals and pharmaceuticals. Taiwan's targeting has been less centrally directed, but nonetheless encouraged by policies of protection, credit availability, and the fact of a limited domestic market. The tactic of delay, so consistently practiced by Japan, seems to have become standard practice among the NICs[7] and the lesson of the usefulness of an undervalued exchange rate has similarly been absorbed. Many other examples could be cited.

The benefits to the emerging countries' governments from such practices are so immense and their own awareness of the fragility of the system that makes those benefits available is so acute, they are certain to pursue the practices as long as they can. The developed countries already are resorting to VERs or other extra-GATT forms of protection against the exports of the NICs. These can only multiply and further weaken the authority of the GATT unless some basic changes in that law are introduced. The imminence of China's membership adds urgency to all of these problems.

GUIDELINES FOR THE FUTURE:
MAKING THE SYSTEM WORK

The problems of reciprocity, discrimination, subsidies, and safeguards—accentuated by practices of targeting—have plagued the developed countries in their trade with both the centrally controlled economies and the NICs. This package of already enlarged problems is about to be further inflated by the emergence of China. To ensure that China's participation in the world system will not be thwarted by the collapse of that system as a consequence of its joining requires some basic amendments to the GATT.

The issues that are at stake for the United States are momentous. The GATT system is perceived by wide sections of the United States—in the Congress, business, labor, and the electorate—as not working the way it should, with the consequence that the United States gains little or nothing from it. The mushrooming of VERs and other nontariff barriers to regulate trade outside of the GATT is clear evidence that the perception has some basis in fact. Many observers have noted that the world economy today is very different from that of the 1930s and 1940s whose conditions the GATT was fashioned to regulate. The GATT, moreover, was never intended to be an international organization, but rather an introduction to an organization that would have a formal organization, structure, and rules of operation. To this day the GATT "secretariat" is still technically the Interim Commission of the International Trade Organization, the ITO that never came into being. As a consequence there are no defined roles in the GATT, governance is awkward, and action on the basis of consensus has become a tradition, absent any formal rules of governance. It is in fact something of a miracle that the GATT system has worked as well as it has for as long as it has.

The system, however, is eroding. China's application for membership and the challenges it raises offer the opportunity for—indeed demand—repair of the GATT. At the least Section IV should be extended to define what a developing country is and is not and to spell out the process of graduation. The subject of government targeting must be confronted, and a section should be added to address the special problems of the centrally controlled economies.

Even beyond these purely commercial matters, however, China's application, with its potential for politicizing the GATT, raises the broader issue of GATT governance. Despite the many trade disputes existing among the industrialized member countries, these have on the whole (and with notable exceptions) been managed according to GATT rules. The LDCs, exempt from the rules, have rarely been motivated to act as a bloc. Where they have united it has largely been in opposition to suggested changes in rules that would apply to them. The GATT has in consequence been blessedly free from the kind of political maneuvering and bloc formation that has characterized the UN or UNCTAD. Nonetheless, because most countries of the world perceive trade and economic matters to be among their most vital national interests having a high national security content, the potential for political maneuvering within the GATT is always latent.

China's interests in the GATT in many cases will be identical to those of the developing countries. Because of China's size and geopolitical role, however, China's leverage in trade matters will be vastly greater than that of any one or most combinations of LDCs. China's clout will make it a natural leader; the degree to which China exercises this potential for leadership will depend on the issues arising in the GATT and on the mix of motivations leading China to apply for membership. Given Chinese national pride, innate abilities, and determination to assume a position in the world arena commensurate with its self-image, the likelihood is that China will be increasingly influential in GATT affairs.

A working group should be established within the GATT specifically to address the problems of reconciling GATT obligations with the basic institutions of centrally controlled, nonmarket economies. European CMEA members and China should be invited to send technically qualified advisors; if, however, these advisors prove to be obstructionist, their services should be dispensed with. The goal of the working group should be a coherent additional section to the GATT spelling out how nonmarket economies can negotiate mutually advantageous trade expansion with GATT members—perhaps in a phased pattern of acceptance of responsibilities and benefits—drawing on the lessons, positive and negative, of experience with the East European members.

Benefits of GATT membership are probably more important to CMEA members today than ever before; they are therefore likely to be more willing to grant concessions in order to retain those benefits. To ensure a mutually advantageous exchange of benefits, the GATT should put more emphasis on transparency than it has in the past, perhaps seeking observer status in CMEA in order to be in a position to judge whether discrimination is in fact an outcome of the CMEA-based system of trade. Such a GATT initiative would surely test CMEA's willingness to entertain reciprocity.

After China's accession, the frustrations already felt by the developed countries in dealing with the LDCs are likely to be enhanced. This implies that for the GATT to cope with a rapidly growing emerging China, as well as with the present NICs, rules must be established now to guide a developing country's assumption of the obligations and responsibilities that make the system work. The process of graduation must be defined, criteria for eligibility for the perquisites of Part IV must be established, and the process of adjustment by current GATT members to whom the criteria presently only partially apply must be initiated.

As Issaiah Frank noted in his study of the Graduation Issue (1979: 23), the fact that no established procedure exists in the GATT according to which a country in the developing group emerges from that category contrasts with World Bank procedure that has long applied principles of graduation based on per capita income. Frank too observes that the GATT system cannot endure in the condition where its rules apply only to a group of two dozen countries while all others, some seventy countries, remain free of obligations regardless of their stage of development. The GATT, however, practices the rule of unitary voting, established in 1947 when the number of countries in the world was much smaller, in contrast to the World Bank, which is governed by weighted voting (Hudec 1978: 21).

It is in the best interest of those GATT members benefiting from Part IV to participate in the design of a graduation process in order that the staging be equitable and not disruptive. They will probably postpone and delay the inevitable as long as possible. On the other hand, the emergence of competition from China may concentrate their thinking. In any event, foot-dragging should not be countenanced. If a working group with LDC participation cannot be established within the GATT, it should be initiated elsewhere.

In addition to the issue of graduation, the other most controversial issue between the developed and the developing countries is that of government targeting and safeguards. As noted above the United States has supported LDC opposition to selective safeguard action, insisting on the inviolability of the MFN principle. U.S. opposition to selective safeguard action is not in the best interest of either the United States or an orderly world trading system governed by an institution and mechanisms that command respect and adherence. The export targeting that Japan has practiced has clearly been disruptive in the United States as well as Europe. Undoubtedly it would have been less disruptive had the yen been less undervalued. Even with exchange rates in an equilibrium range, however (that is, no sustained changes in international reserves or net foreign assets), export targeting can be disruptive because it can result in an indigestible dose of "too much too soon." When the disruptive imports are clearly from a single source, maintenance of the integrity of the international trading system would be served by permitting selective protection for a limited period of time.

The drafters of the GATT never foresaw the emergence of industrial policies aimed at dramatic and revolutionary shifts in comparative advantage or of targeting as an instrument of such industrial policies. That the U.S. Congress perceives the need for a U.S. response to such foreign industrial policies is evidenced in the reciprocity legislation that has hovered in the Congress for the last three or four years (Gadbow 1982: 691–746). Selective safeguard action, especially if permitted for a limited period without the requirement for compensation (that is, if injurious targeting is made illegal), would impede the use of export targeting by all countries (developed or developing), would lessen the necessity for seeking extra-GATT remedies, and would thus contribute both to the lessening of demands for protection in the developed countries and to the strengthening of the existing world trading order.[8]

China and the LDCs can be expected to object to such changes. The heavily indebted LDCs will argue that their debt burden requires a special exemption to any such new limitations on their exports or rate of growth. Rules for graduation, however, can accommodate the existence of foreign indebtedness. Injury in the developed countries caused by rising fair-valued imports from the LDCs or other developed countries could be eased by a GATT-blessed tiny import levy (of a fraction of 1 percent) on all manufactured imports, the funds to be used for retraining and relocation of affected workers in the developed countries or the NICs.

It is in the best interest of both the United States and the world that the GATT system be made to work. Open markets, reciprocal concessions, and nondiscrimination are still worthy principles, but the rules governing their application require adjustment. A U.S. initiative aimed at making the system work would be likely to find wide support in this country and probably also in Europe and Japan. Such an initiative could be broad enough to encompass the agenda being currently proposed for the GATT by the United States, or it could aim at only the major modernizations suggested above.

Perhaps the most feasible approach to ensuring modernization would be one aimed solely at GATT governance. If the existence of unitary voting in the GATT appears likely to prohibit such modernizing amendments to the General Agreement as defining eligibility requirements in Part IV and permitting selective safeguard action in response to injurious targeting, the United States should use the powerful leverage of access to its market to make possible a shift to weighted voting in the GATT. Should the United States cease to support the GATT as it presently exists, there would be no world trading order. It is in the best interest of the United States and the world that rules of proper trading procedure be honored by all trading countries. If the United States guaranteed MFN treatment only to those willing to support trade-weighted voting in the GATT, the amended GATT would attract a large number of adherents.

Trade-weighted voting would mean control of GATT decisions by those countries that are the large traders. The United States and the EC would have about equal weight; Japan would have about two-thirds the voting power of each of the leaders. Together the three would control nearly 40 percent of all votes. It is the large traders who have most interest in making the world trading system work. Their will should not be frustrated by a numerous minority whose interests are totally parochial.

A GATT subject to trade-weighted voting would be a much more manageable organization than the current GATT. With such a voting system in place, modernizing amendments would be much more feasible of adoption. Hopefully all OECD members would willingly cooperate toward the goal of making the system work.

With weighted voting in place, one correlative initiative to the modernizations suggested above that the United States also should pursue would be that of outlawing all quantitative controls on imports. Where import controls are necessary—for safeguard actions or to protect infant industries, for example—only tariff increases should be allowed. Tariffs can be equally protective, are more equitable and far more visible, and can be negotiated down much more easily than quantitative restraints.

Although the threat of limited market access lies behind all of the bilaterally negotiated VERs, aggregate access to its market is an instrument of persuasion that the United States has never used. It should be used only with great prudence, only very rarely, and only in support of principles of the most basic importance. Using the leverage of access to its market to make the world trading order work is precisely the kind of principle in support of which this leverage should be employed. Only the United States possesses so persuasive an instrument. The time to use it has arrived.

NOTES

1. *Exchange Arrangements and Exchange Restrictions, Annual Report, 1986* (Washington, D.C.: International Monetary Fund, 1986), p. 168. In addition, the lead article of the *Wall Street Journal* of July 17, 1986 discusses at length the frustrations of Western businessmen currently trying to deal with China. The frustrations are all traceable to government and bureaucratic controls.
2. Literature on Soviet-type economies indicates the existence of price insensitivity in foreign trade; see Thomas A. Wolf, "Optimal Foreign Trade for the Price Insensitive Soviet-Type Economy," *Journal of Comparative Economics* 6 (1982): 37; Michael Marrese, "Unconventional Gains from Trade," *Journal of Comparative Economics* 7 (1983): 382; Harry C. Durham, Jr.,

"Comparative Economies and International Trade," Association for Comparative Economic Studies, *Bulletin* 18, no. 2-3 (Winter 1975): 47; and David Conn, "Economic Theory and Comparative Economic Systems: A Partial Literature Survey," *Journal of Comparative Economics* 2 (1978): 355.

3. During the 1960s average annual GNP growth rates were USSR, 5.2%; Eastern Europe (net national product), 3.75%; U.S., 3.9%; EC, 4.75 (CIA, *Handbook of Economic Statistics* [Washington, D.C.: National Technical Information Service 1980], p. 28). For the period 1950–1981 average annual GNP growth in the USSR was 4.6%, in the U.S., 3.4%.

4. Estimates of China's foreign borrowing vary considerably; the data in the text are from the Department of Commerce by telephone. See also A. Doak Barnett, "Ten Years After Mao," *Foreign Affairs* (Fall 1986): 54.

5. The summary discussion of precedents in the following sections on Reciprocity, Discrimination, and Subsidies and Safeguards draws considerably on Kostecki, *East-West Trade and the Gatt System*, 65–109.

6. As of September 1986 U.S. International Trade Commission records show a total of twenty-two trade cases brought in the United States against China of which fourteen involved dumping, four the escape clause, and four market disruption. Of the total, twelve cases resulted in an affirmative finding, eight negative, one termination, and one pending.

7. *Financial Times*, August 12, 1986, p. 4 on Taiwan's recalcitrance.

8. Economic argument for outlaying injurious export targeting lies in the fact that comparative advantage is determined by demand as well as supply. If a country's domestic market is too small to absorb the capacity output of an industry subject to large economies of scale, then the small country can establish and maintain such an industry only by securing an export market. In the course of establishing such an industry the small country must either subsidize exports as its domestic output expands to capacity or it must "dump"—that is, export below domestic cost or selling price in order to obtain a lower average cost on its entire output. If the domestic market is not sufficiently large to absorb capacity output, that industry could not be profitable in that country, regardless of its low wages, raw material prices, or other costs. If the industry already exists profitably in the larger targeted market and if that market is not large enough to absorb the domestic industry's output *plus* the targeted imports, that industry would be injured, at least until its market had grown sufficiently to absorb the imports as well as domestic output at a profit, or until it had lowered its cost to the level of its competitor. If after a period of two or three years, it is still not able to meet the competition, the safeguard action should be removed or compensation given, on the presumptive evidence that the newcomer is the more efficient producer.

REFERENCES

Asian Wall Street Journal. 1981. March 2.
Economist. 1986. August 2.

Ellis, James L. 1986. "Eastern Europe: Changing Trade Patterns and Perspectives." *Foreign Trade and International Finance*, Vol. 2, *East European Economies: Slow Growth in the 1980s: Selected Papers*, Joint Economic Committee, 99th Cong., 2d sess., March 28.

Financial Times. 1981. September 15.

———. 1983. February 3.

———. 1984. May 4.

Frank, Issaiah. 1979. "The Graduation Issue in Trade Policy Toward the LDCs." World Bank Staff Working Paper No. 334. Washington, D.C.

Gadbow, R. M. 1982. "Reciprocity and Its Implications for U.S. Trade Policy." *Law and Policy in International Business* 14, no. 3.

Hudec, Norbert. 1978. *Adjudication of International Trade Disputes*. Thames Essay No. 16. London: The Trade Policy Research Center.

Jackson, John H. 1969. *World Trade and the Law of GATT*. New York: Bobbs-Merrill Company.

Journal of Commerce. 1986a. April 4.

———. 1986b. July 25.

Kostecki, M. M. 1978. *East-West Trade and the GATT System*. New York: St. Martin's Press for the Trade Policy Research Center, London.

OECD. 1983. *Generalized System of Preferences: Review of the First Decade.* Report by the Secretary-General. Paris: OECD.

U.S. International Trade Commission. 1985. *Emerging Textile Exporting Countries*. Publication 1716. July.

U.S. Trade Representative. 1986. Telephone interview with author.

Wall Street Journal. 1986. July 17.

Washington Post. 1984. January 6.

World Business Weekly. 1980. December 22.

11 THE UNITED STATES AND THE NICs IN THE URUGUAY ROUND
Bargaining Barriers

Henry R. Nau

Although the OPEC revolution received most of the attention in the 1970s, the real revolution in the Third World occurred through the trade of manufactures and associated development and transfer of industrial technology. From 1960–80, a small group of developing countries emerged from the pack of poor countries to achieve per capita income levels of $2,000 and above. Aside from the lightly populated, oil surplus countries—Saudi Arabia, Kuwait, and Abu Dhabi—the key members of this new group of middle-income developing countries are the newly industrialized countries (NICs), principally Korea, Brazil, Taiwan, Hong Kong, and Singapore. Each of these countries relies significantly on manufactured exports for economic growth and development. In 1985, Brazil exported $26 billion worth of merchandise, about two-thirds being manufactured goods. Korea exported $30 billion, 95 percent being manufactured goods.

NICs also include a second level of middle-income countries whose growth depends more on domestic markets and commodity trade but whose manufactured exports began to grow rapidly in the late 1970s and early 1980s. These countries, sometimes referred to as the NECs (newly exporting countries), include Argentina, Mexico, India, Yugoslavia, Chile, Colombia, Malaysia, Thailand, and Peru. Growing on a smaller base, their manufactured exports actually increased more rapidly in the 1970s than those of the principal NICs.

Ironically, despite this dependence and successful development through trade, many of these middle-income countries are skeptical participants in the new round of comprehensive trade negotiations launched by the GATT in 1986. Brazil and India oppose liberalization of trade in areas such as services, investment, and intellectual property. They also demand as preconditions of early progress in the new round unilateral steps on the part of industrial countries to remove existing restrictions on trade in goods. While a few NICs or NECs such as Korea, Colombia, and Chile are more favorably disposed to the new round, they are reluctant to confront the more hostile leadership of Brazil, India, Argentina, and Yugoslavia.

What accounts for this apparent paradox between the real interests of developing countries in trade and their resistance to an improvement and expansion of the trading system? And how might this divergence be overcome to achieve a more meaningful participation of the developing countries in the upcoming trade round? Part of the answer lies in a better understanding of patterns of trade and technology transfer between developing and developed countries though various phases of the postwar period. These patterns reflect the relationship of the trading system to other important aspects of the world economy including the domestic policies of both industrial and developing countries, exchange-rate policies, foreign investment and technology flows, and balance-of-payments lending. They also suggest the legacies that contribute to the current suspicions and in some cases misunderstandings that developing countries harbor toward their multilateral trading system today.

HALCYON DAYS OF THE TRADING SYSTEM:
1950s AND 1960s

When the trading system functioned most successfully in the 1950s and 1960s, few developing countries participated. Despite the membership of many Latin American countries in GATT, the immediate postwar period was marked by the prevalence of export pessimism and import substitution strategies in the developing world. Development strategists, led by the U.N. Economic Commission for Latin America (ECLA) and its Secretary-General Raul Prebisch, foresaw poor prospects for the traditional raw material and agricultural exports of developing countries and urged these countries instead to develop their own manufacturing capabilities through import substitution. While this approach was not entirely inappropriate, given the absence of significant industrial facilities in many developing countries, it was carried to the extreme and adhered to longer in most developing countries than was appropriate, especially in Latin American countries, which started the period with more industrial capacity. From the late 1940s to 1960, for example, Brazil's exports did not grow at all, reflecting the total preoccupation with import substitution and the domestic market. The only NIC during this period that opened its markets was Hong Kong, and its situation was in most respects unique.

Import substitution encouraged some foreign investment where this was permitted. It tended, however, to direct this investment and associated technology transfer into markets defined by elite consumption and previous import patterns. These markets were often characterized by high capital and relatively sophisticated technological requirements, rather than the low-cost labor and smaller, artisan-type manufacturing capabilities that represented the comparative advantage of these countries. Moreover, in this period, only U.S. companies operated on any scale internationally. Thus, both the misdirected allocation of foreign capital and technology, caused largely by local policies themselves, and the relative monopoly of U.S. multinationals built up a legacy in developing countries of distrust and alleged exploitation by multinationals. This distrust reinforced the reluctance to open markets to foreign trade because trade was seen as a precursor to foreign investment.

In the mid-1960s, a number of NICs, including Brazil, Korea, Singapore, and Taiwan, shifted course and began to liberalize imports, unify and decontrol exchange rates, and promote exports. These countries realized unprecedented growth rates. From 1960–73, Korea's exports expanded at a real annual rate of 14 percent, while its GNP grew at an annual rate of 8.9 percent. From 1968–73, Brazil's exports and GNP grew in real terms by 13.6 percent and 11.2 percent per year, respectively, while from 1965–73 real annual growth of Singapore's exports and production was 12.6 percent and 12.7 percent, respectively (Preeg, 1985). By contrast, countries that continued to pursue import substitution policies grew much less rapidly—Argentina by 4 percent per year in both exports and GNP, India by 3 percent per year, and Chile by roughly 4 percent.

Brazil, Korea, and the other early NICs entered the trading system when other aspects of the world economy were most supportive of trade. Inflation was low and predictable in the key industrial countries. From 1950–67, inflation in the United States averaged about 1 percent per year. Growth was moderate and steady. The United States experienced its longest period to date of economic expansion in the 1960s. Exchange rates were relatively stable because of the underlying conditions of low inflation, moderate growth, and the fixed exchange-rate system established at Bretton Woods in 1944. Finally, the world financial system was relatively small and stable compared to later years. Many countries, especially in Europe and Japan, imposed capital controls on international financial flows. Where capital exports expanded, they took the form largely of equity investments. The multinational corporation spread, especially among industrial countries (the period of the "American challenge" in Europe). Foreign investment was also attracted to the liberalizing NICs, but regulation and screening of foreign investment continued and even intensified.

Also in the 1960s trade stood at the top of the agenda of the international economic dialogue. The Kennedy Round from 1963-67 reduced tariffs by an average of 50 percent across the board of internationally traded manufacturing goods. The world community focused on the real goods economy rather than the financial economy that came to dominate the international dialogue in the 1970s.

As Table 11-1 shows, the net result of these factors for the period from 1963-73 was unprecedented growth in the volume of world exports and production. Overall rates reached 9 percent and 6 percent per year, respectively, while manufacturing trade and output grew even more rapidly at 11.5 percent and 7.5 percent per year, respectively.

Thus, the earliest NICs and also Japan, which some analysts regard as the first NIC, shifted into manufacturing at the most favorable time in terms of the expansion of the world production and trading system. The relative ease of their entry into the international trading system made it all seem quite natural and automatic. Without participating in or contributing to the liberalization of trade (no LDC participated significantly in Kennedy Round tariff reductions), they

Table 11-1. Growth of World Merchandise Trade and Production (*average annual percentage change in volume*).

	1963-73	1973-79	1979-84	1984	1985
Exports					
All merchandise	9	4	2	9	3
Agriculture	4	3	3	4	-2.5
Mining	7.5	1	-4	3	-3
Manufacturing	11.5	5.5	4.5	12	5
Production					
All merchandise	6	3	1.5	5.5	3
Agriculture	2.5	2.5	2.5	5	2
Mining	5	2.5	-3	2	-2
Manufacturing	7.5	3.5	2	7.5	3.5

Source: GATT Secretariat estimates.

were able to benefit from it. This experience may be a factor affecting the attitude of these countries today. While they know the benefits of trade, they do not recognize its obligations.

TROUBLED DECADE FOR TRADE: 1970s

Two economic shocks in the 1970s, one internal and one external,
ended the halcyon era of the trading system. The internal one, relatively underemphasized in the subsequent analysis of this period, was
the erosion of price stability in the key industrial countries, particularly in the United States. From 1967–73, before the oil shock, the
average annual inflation rate in the United States tripled from the
previous six-year period. Through an overvalued dollar, the United
States exported its inflation. The external shock—the oil price increases—added to domestic distortions and shifted the focus to
finance and recycle of petrodollars. Trade receded from the international dialogue; commodity and financial issues ascended. Foreign
investment came under attack (for example, the various international
codes and national regulations), even as it took a back seat to balance-
of-payments lending. In conjunction multinationals from Europe,
Japan, and even some of the developing countries reduced the dominance of U.S. firms on world markets. Developing countries once
again shunned the trade liberalizing negotiations under the Tokyo
Round and advocated an aid approach to trade in the form of special and differential treatment for developing countries (preferences in effect shifting tariff revenues from developed to developing
countries).

   The unprecedented expansion of international financial flows, particularly through commercial balance-of-payments lending, fueled
the continued expansion of international trade, especially for the oil
surplus and newly industrializing countries. But this expansion now
occurred increasingly on a foundation of weaker and less stable
domestic conditions. As a result, exchange-rate volatility increased
and international debt obligations mounted. Table 11–1 shows that
from 1973–79 growth of world exports and production slowed
dramatically to one-half or less of the annual growth rates of the
1960s.

   The original NICs—Brazil and Korea—reacted to these shocks in
contradictory ways. On the one hand, they accelerated their emphasis on manufactured exports to sustain growth and pay for higher-
priced oil imports. On the other hand, however, they reversed their
earlier policies of liberalizing imports and decontrolling exchange
rates. Korea and Brazil extended import substitution policies to

heavy and capital goods industries, justifying such policies by the need to diversify exports and reduce import requirements (particularly capital goods requirements that had grown substantially as a result of the first wave of import substitution policies). The net result was to raise dramatically the costs of export-led development and to exacerbate domestic distortions already created by the higher costs of energy.

Belatedly, subsequent NICs or NECs—Mexico, Argentina, and Chile—shifted to export-led growth in this period. Their policies, however, were even more compromised by legacies of import substitution and greater historical reliance on commodity as opposed to manufacturing trade. Their experiments in outward-oriented growth were short-lived and relatively unsuccessful.

Thus, the energy crisis of the 1970s affected the trading system in two important ways. It necessitated overnight a massive expansion of international financial, especially commercial bank, lending. International lending, in turn, drove the expansion of trade and, to a lesser extent, foreign investment, especially between developed and oil surplus and newly industrializing developing countries. At the same time, the energy crisis compounded inflation and encouraged trade restrictions, both of which substantially increased the misallocation of domestic resources in industrial as well as developing economies. The easy availability of finance diverted attention from the need to restore more efficient domestic policies and to emphasize market-opening trade negotiations. Finance came to be regarded as the solution to energy problems. Yet finance, arguably, drove trade in the 1970s, especially between developed and developing countries, into some inefficient sectors, beyond the point justified by existing domestic market conditions and comparative advantage.

ADJUSTMENT EXACERBATES TRADE
PROBLEMS: EARLY 1980s

The policy directions of the 1970s in both industrial and developing countries were unsustainable. Pressure for adjustment came after the second oil crisis in the form of contractionary monetary policies in the key industrial countries and spiraling interest rates and debt burdens in the developing countries. External finance, which had driven trade and growth in the late 1970s, dried up and world trade and growth slumped. As Table 11-1 shows, annual rates for both slowed to 2 percent or less.

Reactions to these developments in both industrial and developing countries have put enormous stress on the trading system. Adjustment policies have shifted costs to the external sector, severely restricting trade flows.

In the United States, initially tight money and continuing loose fiscal policy produced a historically unprecedented high dollar, which made foreign imports more competitive and U.S. exports less competitive. Traded goods sectors in the United States underwent severe contraction.

Developing country policies exacerbated these developments. Reacting to the interest-rate shock, heavily indebted developing countries, which include most of the key NICs, drastically cut imports. Average import growth in these countries dropped from a plus 30 percent per year in 1978-81 to a negative 7 percent per year in 1981-84. From 1981-84, these countries cut imports by a total of $43 billion, 40 percent of this amount or $16 billion with the United States alone. U.S. exports to Brazil dropped by $1.2 billion, to Argentina by $2.1 billion, and to Mexico by $9.6 billion. U.S. exports to Korea stagnated even though Korea increased overall exports by 10 percent (IMF, 1987).

Recovery in the United States after 1982 restored growth to developing country exports. From 1981–84, exports of the high-debt developing countries to the United States rose by $15 billion, increasing the U.S. share of exports from these countries from 25 percent to 32 percent. Exports from Brazil increased by $3.5 billion or 85 percent, from Korea by $5 billion or 90 percent, and from Chile by $450 million of 75 percent.

The slower pace of recovery in the other industrial countries put the primary burden of absorbing developing country exports on the United States. Today the United States takes in 68 percent of all manufacturing exports of developing countries, up from 52 percent in 1981. Meanwhile, Europe accounts for only 24 percent down from 40 percent in 1981, while Japan's share remains unchanged at 7 percent. This imbalance among industrial countries has exacerbated the protectionist pressures in the United States, further straining the stability of the international trading system.

These abnormal pressures on the trading system may have been worth the price if they had been accompanied by improvements in domestic policies and conditions, the foundation for sound international trade as evidenced in the 1950s and 1960s. Some improvements have been achieved, most impressively in the inflation rate among industrialized countries. Inflation in the OECD countries was less than 3 percent in 1986, helped along during the year by unexpected oil price declines. Investment and growth in the OECD countries have also been revived. Real growth in the five major industrial countries averaged approximately 3 percent in 1983, 4 percent in 1984, 3 percent in 1985, and 2.5 percent in 1986.

Nevertheless, serious distortions and rigidities remain in OECD economies. The U.S. fiscal deficit persists, while fiscal conservatism continues in Europe and Japan. Under these circumstances, sustained growth relies increasingly on rapid money growth and political pressures to lower official discount rates. Inflation has been accelerating for a couple of years in the service sector, and food and energy prices cannot be expected to sustain the declines of recent months.

If domestic conditions in the industrial world are still troublesome, inflation and inefficiency in the developing countries remain alarming. Despite the emphasis on adjustment and IMF programs of recent years, the newly industrializing countries, with the exception perhaps of Korea, have made few improvements in the flexibility and efficiency of their home markets. The weighted average annual inflation rate of consumer prices in the fifteen most heavily indebted countries increased from 57.7 percent in 1982 to 126.9 percent in 1985 before falling again to 76.2 percent in 1986 (IMF, 1987). Instead of adjusting to meet fiscal and monetary targets of IMF agreements, indebted countries have negotiated a series of adjustments to the IMF agreements. Brazil alone has signed seven letters of intent with the IMF since 1982, and since 1986 has refused to sign any IMF agreement at all. The adjustments that occurred have come primarily through trade rather than domestic policy. In 1985 as the GATT Secretariat notes, the heavily indebted countries, again including the principal NICs—Brazil, Korea, Argentina, Mexico, Yugoslavia, Chile, Colombia, and so forth—"returned to the import-contracting adjustment that characterized their performance in 1982 and 1983" (GATT 1986). Exports in only five of these countries increased, while imports in thirteen of them declined. As growth slows and protectionism increases in industrial markets, the NICs restrict imports even more, thereby magnifying further their own domestic distortions and inefficiencies while also fanning additional protectionist sentiment in industrial markets.

U.S. POLICY OPTIONS

The incomplete adjustment in both industrial and developing countries presents the United States with new choices:

Should the United States give priority to further macroeconomic adjustment in both groups of countries? This would imply renewed efforts to reduce the U.S. budget deficit, stimulate growth in Europe and Japan, and press stabilization and structural reform programs in the developing world.

Should the United States shift policy priorities to international financial and monetary reforms, as it appears to have done since 1985? This implies continuing concern to maintain a low dollar, coordinate international economic and exchange-rate policies, and mobilize new financial resources (Baker Plan) to alleviate debt-servicing constraints or perhaps even, as Senator Bradley has suggested, to write down some portion of the outstanding long-term debt of developing countries.

Should the United States pursue more aggressively the multilateral liberalization of trade policy as the central priority of international economic strategy in the last half of the 1980s? This would imply both a willingness to bargain with Congress for new flexibility and authority to negotiate in the upcoming multilateral trade round and a readiness to subordinate bilateral and plurilateral trade actions and negotiations to multilateral objectives in the new round.

These directions for U.S. policy are by no means exclusive of one another. Yet the priority accorded among them is critical. In its first term, the administration clearly gave priority to domestic macroeconomic adjustment, even at the expense of a considerable shock to the world's financial and trading system. Since 1985 the administration has given more emphasis to international financial and monetary reforms. Throughout this period, the United States has been generally defensive toward trade policy, resisting rhetorically protectionist pressures but conceding to these pressures increasingly in practice and since 1985 pursuing a more aggressive bilateral and plurilateral policy toward both trade liberalization (Israel, now Canada, maybe ASEAN) and threatened trade retaliation. The less aggressive support for multilateral trade liberalization has been not only understandable but probably inevitable given the earlier preoccupation with domestic adjustment and lingering problems with the high dollar and debt constraints.

Today, however, the opportunity to give multilateral trade policy a higher priority in U.S. economic strategy may be greater. On the surface at least, the world's financial and monetary situation is considerably improved. The dollar is down, and the world community has finally reached the point, in the absence of short-term emergencies, where it can consider the longer-term management of the debt crisis. If U.S. initiatives over the past year toward exchange rates and debt financing have helped to achieve this outcome, they have been well targeted. On the other hand, these initiatives may have run their course. A further decline of the dollar is now resisted by both Germany and Japan, and the dollar's decline thus far has not helped the United States a great deal with some of its major trading partners, especially the key NICs whose currencies are tied to the dollar. Moreover, it is not yet clear whether underlying economic conditions have improved as much as the financial indicators. There are few signs that further fiscal policy adjustment is being achieved in the United States or in other industrial countries. The emphasis on more financing for indebted countries may have turned their attention away from further adjustment just when its continuation was most needed, judging at least from the growing resistance among these countries to IMF agreements and the slow development of an acceptable and effective role for the World Bank in structural policy reform. In these circumstances, giving new priority to multilateral trade liberalization may be helpful both to sustain the emphasis on adjustment, which is necessary albeit politically difficult, and to open up new opportunities for renewed capital flows to developing countries.

Adjustment thus far has been pursued primarily in a bilateral context under the aegis of IMF surveillance and adjustment programs. In this context, it has become increasingly politicized and in any case has not been particularly conducive to trade liberalization. In the winter of 1984–85, for example, the IMF director approached the United States and other industrial countries worried about the reluctance of developing countries to liberalize trade in the context of IMF programs. He asked if the industrialized countries would be willing to reciprocate for trade liberalization measures that the developing countries might adopt unilaterally, thereby encouraging the latter to take such measures. For various reasons, including institutional difficulties between the GATT and IMF, the proposal could not be implemented.

Similarly, the World Bank has sought to encourage greater trade liberalization, but its efforts too have fallen short. The Development Committee, as its session in April 1985, featured trade issues for the first time. In the absence of an appropriate bargaining framework, however, the United States opposed any reference in the communiqué to textile trade. Developing country interest in the new round declined accordingly, and the Development Committee shifted its focus in April 1986, in the wake of the Baker Initiative, back to the familiar ground of development finance. The communiqué in 1986 did affirm the concept of a "trade credit" whereby developing countries would receive credit in the GATT round for unilateral steps they might take to liberalize trade on their own. Nevertheless, it is hard to conceive how such a trade credit might be implemented, especially when the World Bank, which would monitor such measures, has no country dialogue with industrial countries.

The new GATT round offers a way to move an important element of adjustment policy—namely, trade policy—out of the bilateral context, where it has languished, into a new multilateral arena where countries exchange real concessions in trade and do so without the adversarial monitoring of international bureaucrats. The Fund and Bank could then reinforce the participation of developing countries in the new round by offering financing in support of trade liberalization where it may be expected that imports of developing countries will expand more quickly than exports. In the end, trade liberalization itself may become the biggest factor catalyzing once again new flows of financial resources to developing countries. As the World Bank emphasized in its background report for the 1985 Development Committee meeting, "trade liberalization would improve the prospects of indebted countries by encouraging the supply of direct investment and commercial bank funds to export-oriented industries" (World Bank 1985). Thus, a more aggressive U.S. policy toward the trade round fits in well with the administration's financial objectives toward the indebted countries and sustains an emphasis on policy adjustment, particularly in trade policy where developing countries' attitudes remain most difficult to change.

NIC POLICY CHOICES

The strategic policy choices for the NICs are twofold:

To persist in the trade restricting policies of the past four decades and extend them into new areas of information and communications technologies;

To alter fundamental attitudes toward the trading system and progressively liberalize imports in exchange for enlarged and more secure access to industrial country markets.

The first choice assumes that the international trading system will continue to accommodate NIC exports and that the international financial system will continue to finance the higher costs of protected domestic development. Neither assumption is likely. But even if they were, the NICs would derive less benefit from this approach in the future than they have in the past because of the increasing incompatibility of restrictive trade policies and integrated world markets for production, technology, and trade.

Trade has become increasingly linked with international production. GATT estimates that some 40 percent of world trade is now intrafirm trade. Trade in services, it is argued (though the statistics are still missing), is also closely linked with investment. While this fact raises old fears of multinational and restrictive business practices in some developing countries, it actually reflects the increasing competition among multinationals and the growing prevalence of joint ventures and decentralized management of multinational networks of affiliated firms and subsidiaries. Multinational expansion today involves a more significant sharing of technology and financing with foreign partners than was the case before.

More equitable international arrangements among firms from different countries are a direct consequence of the accelerating pace and diffusion of technological change in world markets and resulting in the collapse of the product life cycle. National firms can no longer hold a competitive technological advantage long enough to export products from the home to foreign markets; they must immediately seek joint arrangements to produce and market the product abroad, even in some cases to design and develop the product initially in collaboration with foreign partners.

These developments create an entirely different world market for trade, investment, and technology transfer. Under the old product life cycle concept, products were designed primarily for home markets and then sold and produced abroad as nontechnological factors, such as transportation costs and wage rates. Today products are designed with foreign markets in mind. Chances are considerably greater therefore that products designed by foreign firms will reflect local factor endowments and demand requirements in host countries. Second, multinationals are now more numerous and competitive than before. They are forced to sell and produce abroad more quickly, or lose their markets not just to local producers as in the past, but also now to third country multinationals. Host countries enjoy enviable bargaining leverage. Third, access to foreign markets is increasingly critical not only to sell and produce products but also to keep pace with technological change and to acquire or share technology in these markets as needed.

The range of technological change in world markets is also broadening. Today new production technologies are as important as, if not more important than, product technologies. Flexible automated manufacturing systems reduce production costs for labor-intensive products such as apparel and footwear, while permitting more efficient production of capital-intensive products for smaller markets or niches in larger markets, such as the luxury end of the automobile market. These developments alter in some ways the traditional comparative advantage of less developed countries in labor-intensive products and of industrial countries in capital-intensive manufacturing sectors. They make it less likely that developing countries will produce only lower-end technology items or that industrial countries will lose their manufacturing sectors altogether.

There are two schools of thought as to how a country exploits these new features of world markets. One is to manipulate domestic and trade policy to target technology, investment, and trade in specific products. The other is to open markets and let the greater forces of competition determine comparative advantage, trade, and investment flows.

The first is possible in a country that has a reasonably coherent policymaking process or large domestic savings, the latter being necessary because mistakes in this more centrally steered approach are costlier. Japan is considered to have both, Korea also to a lesser extent. Even then the sustainability of this approach is limited by the tolerance of trading partners. The second is more congenial to a country with a competitive policymaking process or lower domestic savings. The United States reflects these characteristics as do many developing countries, especially those undergoing recent democratic changes.

Nevertheless, developing countries hesitate to open their markets to greater competition, fearing that they lack sufficient entrepreneurial capabilities to hold their own in domestic, let alone world, markets and determined to protect their natural resources, industrial assets, and national sovereignty. In rapidly changing world markets, these attitudes are a prescription for falling farther and farther behind. Import substitution or, as they are now called, market reserve policies condemn the home country to accelerating technological backwardness as technological change in world markets moves faster than technological catch-up in protected home markets. What is more, such policies raise costs to domestic users of protected products and thus impair the competitiveness of a wide range of manufacturing and export activities. This makes it unlikely that the country can ever attain competitiveness in world markets even if it succeeds in reserving a large share of the home market for its own industries. Countries with small home markets are at an even greater disadvantage.

In many ways, the lead-in to the growing integration of world production and technology is freer trade. Countries that do not trade with one another also do not invest or transfer technology with one another. The United States and Japan, which import more manufactured goods from developing countries than Europe, have closer manufacturing and technology relations with these countries than Europe. The NICs need to consider whether they can remain a part of an increasingly integrated world market if they restrict trade and in turn cut themselves off from global technological change.

BARGAINING IN THE NEW ROUND

World market developments therefore offer both the United States and the NICs a new opportunity to emphasize international trade liberalization talks. In September 1986, the GATT Contracting Parties met in Punta del Este, Uruguay, to launch the eighth postwar round of multilateral trade negotiations. A Trade Negotiations Committee was established under which both a Group for Negotiations on Goods (GNG) and a Group for Negotiations on Services (GNS) operate. In early 1987, the GNG set up fourteen subgroups dealing with specific issues—tariffs, agriculture, tropical products, and so forth. In addition, a surveillance body to implement standstill and rollback provisions was established. All the groups have begun meeting in Geneva. The Punta Declaration calls for the new round to be completed in four years, but the negotiations are off to a slow start and, with French and U.S. elections in 1988, are unlikely to make significant progress before 1989 at the earliest. Many observers expect this round to last the better part of the next decade.

Two aspects of the new round stand out. The agenda is longer and more complex than for previous rounds. The issues include traditional industrial tariff and institutional matters (such as safeguards and dispute settlements) more recent concern with nontariff measures including standstill and rollback of existing quota restrictions, and largely new issues such as agriculture, services, intellectual property, and trade-related investment measures. Second, the active participants are more numerous and now include many developing countries. Unlike the pattern of previous rounds, developing countries played a key role in launching the new round, acting through various groupings some of which cut across traditional North–South lines (for example, Cairns group on agriculture or G-48).

The longer agenda and larger number of active participants make the Uruguay Round significantly different from earlier ones. The round begins with no single, overriding issue or objective, such as the across-the-board tariff-cutting formulas of the previous two rounds. Nor is there any agreement on the priority of the many issues on the agenda. Positions of the GATT members vary—from hard-line developing countries that seek immediate implementation of standstill and rollback commitments to the United States, which seeks priority treatment for agriculture and new issues, such as services. Agreement at Punta was possible only because everyone's issue was included.

Several large questions have plagued the launching and now the early bargaining of the new round:

Can the GATT expand beyond manufacturing goods and develop effective rules for new sectors such as services, investment, and intellectual property?

If not, can the GATT strengthen existing rules for goods, especially provisions covering controversial nontariff barriers such as subsidies, and possibly extend these rules to agriculture?

If GATT can do neither, is the alternative world of bilateral and regional trading agreements a viable alternative for either industrial or developing countries?

To resolve any of these questions, the two sides must be ready to bargain. Thus far, the developing countries have given no hint that they understand the GATT process of reciprocal bargaining. Historically unused to assuming obligations, they demand concessions rather than offer propositions. The United States, too, has been reluctant to bargain. Trade liberalization has never had top priority in the international economic policy of the Reagan administration (Nau 1984-85). One clear indication of this fact is that the administration for the first time is seeking new authority to participate in this round on the basis of legislation drafted by Congress rather than initiated by the president. The administration demands that GATT be expanded but it holds a weak bargaining position vis-à-vis Congress, which is reluctant to make any concessions to strengthen GATT, particularly in products of special interest to the NICs—such as steel and textiles.

The new round thus exhibits a painful irony. Without expanding the GATT, it is doubtful that GATT can be significantly strengthened. And if the new round drags on too long, trade talks would devolve to bilateral and plurilateral arrangements where substantive trade-offs will be made in any case. So the issue is not whether to bargain, but where and when. The NICs can strike a better deal in GATT than outside GATT. And the United States is better off bargaining now to ensure early progress in the new round.

Expanding the GATT

Brazil, India, Argentina, Egypt, and Yugoslavia currently lead a group of developing countries strongly opposed to progress on new issues in the GATT round—services, investment, and intellectual property. They argue instead for immediate implementation of the standstill and rollback commitments in the Punta Declaration on all trade-restricting measures affecting manufactured goods (textiles, steel, footwear, and so forth) and agriculture—sectors that are clearly within the existing jurisdiction of GATT. They argue further for a tightening of the safeguard rules in GATT to prevent future derogations from GATT.

The United States accepts the standstill and rollback provisions drafted at Punta but interprets these commitments in such a way that they would not apply to most measures that offend the developing countries. The problem for the United States is that a meaningful standstill and rollback commitment would apply to existing U.S. restrictions in sugar, meat imports, textiles, steel, automobiles, and so forth as well as the use of future 301 actions in both goods and services trade. The United States insists, however, that the Punta commitment applies only to new measures, not existing restrictions or extensions of existing programs (such as another voluntary restraint agreement [VRA] in steel or tightening sugar quotas under existing programs) and does not apply at all to trade legislation consistent with GATT (Section 201 escape clause actions, countervailing duty and antidumping provisions, and national security). Moreover, while the United States has in the past and conceivably in the future would again submit 301 cases to GATT in goods, it retains the right in new areas, such as services, to retaliate under 301, including retaliation that restricts U.S. imports of goods, without submitting to GATT rules.

What needs to be done in this situation? Ideally, the NICs should recognize that developing rules for new issues is a bargaining, not a theological, matter. They should use their services "card" to secure the clearest possible commitment from the United States to standstill and rollback. At the moment, they continue to do just the opposite—that is, refuse to link services and goods for fear that they will have to give up something in services. The United States, in turn, should consider the broad framework compromises it must make now with both Congress and the developing countries to facilitate early success in the new round. It might accept a firm commitment against any new bilateral or plurilateral trade action in goods and agree to negotiate a rollback of existing restrictions by a certain date (for example, by 1989 when both the current steel agreements and possibly the new Multifiber Agreement [MFA] will expire). If it could secure a date for completion of service negotiations, it might even accept a standstill on 301 actions in service sectors, at least in those sectors given priority in the trade round. This commitment could be made for one year, renewable if the services negotiations warranted it.

The more the developing countries give in services and other new sectors, particularly intellectual property, the more carrots the United States should offer by way of restraining its actions outside the GATT. In this way, the United States makes compromises that Congress has a better chance to accept. Services exporters and many traditional industries, which have a stake in intellectual property rights, will support such a compromise. And even within a traditional sector such as textiles, an agreement to negotiate on counterfeiting and intellectual property rights may offset to some extent the commitment to negotiate a long-term phaseout of quantitative restrictions in textiles.

In retrospect, the prospects for mutual compromises by the United States and the NICs are hardly bright. The trade bill currently in conference between the U.S. House of Representatives and the U.S. Senate contains negotiating authority for the United States in the new round, but numerous provisions that are likely to be viewed abroad as protectionist. Indeed, the bill may well precipitate retaliation abroad and a retrogression in the negotiations in Geneva. With U.S. elections in 1988, the chance of expanding the GATT would seem to be on hold, at least until 1989.

Strengthening the GATT

If the GATT round could achieve broad commitments such as those outlined above, strengthening the GATT becomes easier. On the other hand, without such commitments, there may not be a sufficient balance of benefits within the GATT issues themselves to warrant compromise.

The key issues involved in strengthening the GATT are safeguards, tariffs, nontariff barriers, agriculture, and dispute settlements. All of these issues require some give and take on both sides, but the benefits are insufficiently balanced in order to encourage compromise either individually or collectively.

On safeguards, for example, the NICs ask for strict adherence to a nondiscriminatory and strengthened Article XIX. In return, the United States asks for greater discipline by developing countries under Article XVIII, which gives developing countries broad discretion to impose quantitative restrictions for balance of payments and infant industry purposes. The European Community seeks to amend Article XIX to allow discrimination or selective application of relief against offending exporters only. It is doubtful that firmer adherence to Article XVIII by developing countries offers enough either to the United States to rollback quantitative restrictions on goods such as textiles, or to the EC to drop its demands for selectivity, especially when developing countries retain high existing levels of protection on most of their imports.

Thus, the safeguard issue blends with the issue of tariff reductions. In this area, the industrial countries are not likely to have much to offer, since their tariffs are already low. To secure the basis for compromise, therefore, the industrial countries would have to throw in nontariff measures or quantitative restrictions. They might convert quantitative restrictions to tariffs in such sectors as textiles, steel, and leather goods and then proceed to bargain reciprocally to lower tariffs in developing countries.

As high as they are, however, tariffs are not the only or even main restraint on imports in developing countries. Subsidies, licensing policies, and other administrative measures are frequently more important. The United States has long sought to bring the NICs under the provisions of the subsidy code, offering in return the injury test for U.S. imports from developing countries. In many cases this incentive was not enough. If, however, export subsidies for agriculture as well as industrial products are included, the developing countries acquire a much broader incentive.

Subsidy issues are at the heart of the larger and very controversial agricultural issue. But now the European Community is put on the spot. Within the export subsidy area, the EC does not have sufficient incentive to reach a compromise. So it argues for negotiations on all aspects of agricultural policy, not just subsidies; yet its flexibility to modify significantly the price support system for agriculture is limited, even under severe budget pressures.

Finally, the issue of dispute settlement reflects overall willingness of GATT members to submit to GATT disciplines. This willingness, in turn, is a function of the overall benefits of GATT participation. If those benefits are inadequate, countries will circumvent GATT. This, it may be argued, has become the biggest reason for expanding the GATT and also for liberalizing agriculture.

Bilateral and Plurilateral Alternatives

If the basis for broadening of GATT membership cannot be found, trade disputes and solutions will devolve to a bilateral or plurilateral context. Trade-offs will be made in more constrained and possibly more coercive circumstances. The issue for the United States and the NICs, therefore, is whether they prefer to negotiate these disputes in the multilateral trade round or in bilateral and regional relations. To this point, the NICs have shown a decided preference for negotiating bilaterally. That explains their acceptance of the MFA in practice even while they denounce it in theory. They like the economic rents they gain from these restraint arrangements and the political assets they can turn to their advantage in bilateral situations (such as Korea's security value to the United States).

Under pressure from Congress the administration is beginning to push its weight around in bilateral trade relations. For individual trading partners that are ready to negotiate services, such as Israel and Canada, the United States is offering broad free trade area negotiations. With those partners unwilling to negotiate services or reciprocate in goods trade, the United States is using the big stick. Through Section 301 actions against Brazil, Taiwan, and Korea, discretionary graduation of these same countries from the generalized system of preferences (GSP) in specific product areas, and more restrictive bilateral arrangements under the current MFA renewal, the U.S. bargaining power in the bilateral context is being used more aggressively and with fewer residual benefits from the NICs.

Japan, although not a NIC in the terms of this chapter, has already recognized the need to seek refuge from U.S. bilateral badgering in the more diffuse setting of multilateral negotiations. Will the NICs follow suit? They do not have an unlimited amount of time to make their decision. While, for some U.S. policymakers, the aggressive use of bilateral and regional arrangements has always been a tactic to compel greater interest in multilateral negotiations, the longer the tactic persists and multilateral negotiations stall, the more likely the trading system will devolve into a set of individual, albeit overlapping, trading arrangements in which reciprocity with the NICs will be negotiated bilaterally rather than multilaterally. The choice for the NICs therefore is not between retaining special and differential treatment or giving it up but whether they will negotiate their assumption of reciprocal obligations in the new trade round bilaterally. They are very likely to secure better terms in the GATT where they can coordinate their interests where appropriate with other developing countries and where commitments will be exposed to multilateral surveillance (and thus less subject to abuse than bilateral arrangements).

CONCLUSION

The opportunities for mutually beneficial bargains in the new round are numerous. But the NICs' historical attitudes toward the trading system and severe political constraints in the United States create an enormous reluctance to bargain. Who should take the initiative to break this deadlock?

A good part of the responsibility rests with the United States. To make gains in negotiations on services and intellectual property, it should be ready to take firm commitments on standstill and rollback to include not only European VCR restraints or Japanese agricultural quotas but also the long-term phasing out of textile, steel, and other restrictions of primary interest to the NICs. Such an offer could smoke out the NIC hard-liners and inject a hopeful spirit of concession and compromise in the early phases of the new round. If necessary these commitments could be time bound and renewed each year or so, depending on mutual satisfaction of all parties with progress in the negotiations of special interest to them.

Once this level of bargain is struck, the way would be clear for reciprocal bargaining in all other areas. In each of these areas, whether it be a specific service sector or tariff negotiations of nontariff barriers (NTBs), special and differential treatment (SDT) for developing countries might be preserved. Numerous possibilities arise:

SDT might be more generous in service sectors than in traded goods and in high technology than in other manufactured goods, on the grounds that there is greater justification for infant industry protection at the upper end of the technology spectrum.

Bargains in individual negotiations might reflect unequal substantive concessions by industrial and developing countries. This is the way developing countries have participated in previous GATT rounds. These bargains are made best in specific negotiating situations rather than on the basis of general principles.

Substantively equal concessions in individual negotiations might be implemented differentially with developing countries being given more time to implement reduction of tariff or nontariff measures.

Concessions by industrial countries might be implemented on a non-MFN or preferential basis with respect to developing country imports. This is the basis of GSP. Caution should be exercised here however. It is not at all clear that preferences have worked in favor of developing countries, certainly not the later industrializers. If the industrial countries eventually give up non-MFN action in the area of safeguards, the developing countries should think about doing so in the area of preferences.

The tactical features of bargaining are less important than the strategy constraints that make both the United States and the NICs reluctant to bargain. These constraints can be overcome only by new vision and statesmanship. The NICs should see the opportunity, after forty years of abstention from the reciprocal trading system, to try a new and proven path of higher growth through measured trade liberalization. And the United States should finally give trade the priority it had in earlier postwar periods when the United States led the world toward unprecedented prosperity.

REFERENCES

Commonwealth Secretariat. 1986. *The Uruguay Round Multilateral Trade Negotiations: Commonwealth Interests and Opportunities.* London.

Destler, I. M. 1986. *American Trade Policies: System under Stress, Institute for International Economics*, Washington, D.C.

General Agreement on Tariffs and Trade. 1986. "International Trade in 1985 and Current Prospects." Press release. Geneva, Switzerland: GATT.

Glick, Leslie Alan. 1984. *Multilateral Trade Negotiations: World Trade after the Tokyo Round.* Totowa, N.J.: Rowman and Allanheld.

International Monetary Fund. 1987. *World Economic Outlook.* Washington, D.C.: IMF.

Nau, Henry R. 1984-85. "Where Reaganomics Works." *Foreign Policy* 53 (Winter): pp. 14-47.

_____ . 1985. "The NICs in a New Trade Round." *Hard Bargaining Ahead: U.S. Trade Policy and Developing Countries*, edited by Ernest H. Preeg, New Brunswick, N.J.: Transaction Books.

Preeg, Ernest H. 1970. *Traders and Diplomats.* Washington, D.C.: The Brookings Institution.

World Bank. 1985. "Trade, Protection and Development." Background paper for Development Committee Meeting, Washington, D.C., April 18-19.

12 IMPROVING U.S. TRADE PERFORMANCE
The Outlook to 1990

Gary C. Hufbauer and
Jeffrey J. Schott

By 1990, President Reagan, Chancellor Kohl, and Prime Minister Nakasone will be part of history. In the United States by 1990 there will have been two administrations and two Congresses. Yet new leaders will necessarily face old problems, one of which is trade, which promises to create friction for many years.

In September 1986, the ninety-two members of the General Agreement on Tariffs and Trade (GATT) met in Punta del Este, Uruguay, to launch a new round of multilateral trade negotiations. The Uruguay Round holds the potential for reinvigorating the GATT and strengthening the framework of the world trading system. But the GATT talks will only begin the process of addressing trade problems in such vexing areas as agriculture, services, and safeguards. Talks among trade ministers will not address the overriding problems of macroeconomic imbalance and inadequate world growth. Thus, even as GATT members earnestly negotiate in Geneva, trade disputes will proliferate for four key reasons.

First, the U.S. trade deficit is unlikely to drop much below $100 billion before 1990, despite the 1985–87 depreciation of the dollar by some 25 percent on a trade-weighted basis. The adjustments needed to restore the U.S. trade account to a sustainable equilibrium level (say, a deficit of $50 billion or 1 percent of projected GNP by the end of the decade) will either require greater global growth and more cooperative macroeconomic policies than recently exhibited by the Group of Five (G-5) countries[1] or, alternatively, still more depreciation of the dollar.[2] In any event, it seems likely that the U.S. trade deficit will continue to generate political pressures for protection for the rest of the 1980s.

Second, the protectionist pressure will be heightened as Japan continues to run staggeringly large trade and current account surpluses and outstrips the United States in high-technology industries (helped, in some instances, by industrial promotion practices that range from unorthodox to unfair). The trade backlash emanating from Japanese success will overtake Europe as well as the United States.

Third, agricultural surpluses will continue to flood world markets, depressing prices, and prompting acute competition between exporters. "Subsidy wars" may continue to feed bilateral trade tensions, especially between the United States and Europe.

Fourth, the newly industrializing countries (NICs) will change the shape of comparative advantage across a wide range of manufactured goods. East Asian NICs, for example, will replace Japan as an export platform for such products as steel, autos, and semiconductors. Barriers to exports by one OECD area will result in trade diversion to other OECD areas, complicating trade ties between industrial countries and increasing pressure to "manage" trade.

THE U.S. TRADE DEFICIT AND MACROECONOMIC POLICY

The infamous J-curve effect promises to delay the start of any significant improvement in the U.S. trade and current account deficits until 1988.[3] In 1987, the current account surpluses of Japan and Germany reached $85 billion and $45 billion, respectively, while the U.S. deficit on current account exceeded $160 billion. Three factors point to extended weakness in the U.S. external accounts:

Sluggish growth in Japan and Europe continues to deprive the United States of vital export markets despite the sharp fall of the dollar against the yen and the mark since February 1985.

Latin America no longer provides the strong market for U.S. exports that it did in the late 1970s. Most Latin nations are mired in debt, and barriers to their own exports (especially of tropical products and manufactured goods) add to Latin difficulties.

U.S. farm exports are unlikely to recover to their previous levels. The global agricultural outlook has a dismal cast for years to come. Moreover, since the Plaza Hotel accord, the U.S. dollar has appreciated or held steady against the currencies of Australia, Argentina, and Canada—competitors against the United States for foreign agricultural markets.

Protectionist pressures generated by the U.S. deficit have already resulted in a more restrictive Multifiber Arrangement (MFA), a further tightening of bilateral restraints on textile and apparel trade, a system of steel trade restraints that is fast coming to resemble the MFA, new U.S. farm export subsidies, and a receptivity to managed trade in products ranging from semiconductors to machine tools. Both to ease these protectionist pressures and to provide an inviting climate for the conclusion of trade agreements, the U.S. trade deficit must fall. If the United States reduces its trade deficit in the early 1990s by, say, $100 billion, other countries will have to reduce their surpluses or increase their deficits by a like amount. Much of the burden would have to be absorbed by trade surplus countries such as Japan, Germany, and a few NICs such as Taiwan. There are three ways the United States and its partners can work together—or at odds—to curb the trade imbalance.

First, and most responsibly, the United States could take meaningful action (not Gramm-Rudman rhetoric) to reduce its budget deficit substantially.[4] At the same time, the major U.S. trading partners—especially Germany and Japan—could stimulate their economies through a combination of tax cuts and liberal monetary growth. The Reagan administration has rightly championed this approach as the proper way to grow out of the trade deficit.

Second, and less responsibly, the United States could overshoot the depreciation of the dollar in the exchange markets. Indeed, the failure of the growth option could provoke the overshooting option. In a true panic, the dollar could drop another 30 percent from its August 1987 levels. A sufficiently large drop in the dollar would eventually ensure that U.S. firms attract business from their German and Japanese competitors. A panic drop in the dollar, however, could disrupt the world financial system, ignite inflation, and intensify trade protection in Europe and Japan.

Third, and least desirable, the United States could adopt a policy of protection—subsidizing exports and restricting imports. Mercantilist policies used to recapture traditional markets and to win new sales would surely prove contentious. Unfortunately, the trade legislation of 1988 has a somewhat mercantilist flavor, while the Textile Act of 1987 represents protectionism at its worst. Retaliation is often cited as a major risk of such legislation. Imitation is an equal danger. Indeed, the foreign reaction to U.S. protectionism could well offset any potential U.S. trade gains and leave the U.S. trade balance unchanged.

Faced with these broad alternatives, it is natural to focus on the Reagan administration program, which calls for domestic stimulus in Europe and Japan. The success of the G-5 initiative at the Plaza Hotel in September 1985 conferred new respect on the concept of macroeconomic policy coordination. The goal then was to bring the dollar down. But that was only the first step—the more important and more difficult task lies ahead. To achieve a sustainable macroeconomic balance, the G-5 nations need to now implement a new mix of income policies, emphasizing greater domestic stimulation in Europe and Japan and lesser domestic stimulation in the United States.

Unfortunately, at this juncture no one wants to take the initiative. The wave of macroeconomic cooperation crested in early 1986 and the G-5 consensus has now broken down to bilateral squabbling. Japan and Germany blame U.S. policies, especially the budget deficit, and argue that the United States must get its house in order. The United States responds that a sudden decrease in the federal budget deficit would throw the U.S. and world economies into recession. The world economy calls for monetary and fiscal stimulus, not restraint. The stimulus should properly come from nations enjoying comfortable current account positions.

Can Japan and Germany do more? Bonn is often asked to pump the Germany economy. For some time now, prominent Germans have argued that their policy is just about right and that, in any event, "the West German economy is simply too small and its interdependency with the U.S. economy insufficient" to make much of a difference in the U.S. deficit (Lambsdorff 1986: 20). But German unemployment is high and capacity utilization relatively low. Germany should be able to enhance its modest growth by 1 to 2 percent of GNP annually for the next several years.

Meanwhile, two initiatives have been proposed to curb Japan's external surpluses—remove nontariff barriers and stimulate domestic demand. In 1986, two-way trade between Japan and the United States totaled more than $110 billion; 39 percent of Japanese exports went to the United States, while only 23 percent of Japanese imports came from the United States. As a result, the bilateral U.S. trade deficit soared to almost $60 billion in 1986 and stayed at that level through 1987. Trade reform could take a modest but politically significant bite out of the bilateral deficit. One recent study estimates that the total liberalization of Japanese nontariff barriers (NTBs) would increase U.S. exports to Japan by up to $10 billion, a sum that includes sensitive items such as rice (Hufbauer and Schott 1985). Japanese NTBs are a cancer on the world trading system and should be removed; but even their total removal would leave a very large bilateral trade deficit.

Attention has therefore focused on stimulating Japanese domestic demand to spur growth and to increase demand for imports. In the context of bilateral discussions with the United States (the G-2 talks), the Japanese government has adopted a demand stimulus program that would boost GNP by about $20 to $25 billion, equivalent to about 1 percent of GNP. A much larger stimulus program—encompassing major tax and regulatory reforms—would be required to significantly reduce Japan's trade surplus.

To summarize: As of early 1988, neither Germany nor Japan appears willing to play the role of locomotive for the world economy. As a consequence, it seems likely that the U.S. trade deficit will be "solved" by a combination of further dollar depreciation and mercantilistic trade policies.

BILATERAL AND SECTORAL TRADE ISSUES

To help deflect protectionist pressures, the U.S. president will have to pursue both bilateral and multilateral trade initiatives. This needs to be done, however, with the recognition that it will be hard to bring home results from trade talks until the macroeconomic picture is corrected.

If the macroeconomic picture is corrected, attention will shift to the multilateral trade talks. But if, as seems likely, the macroeconomic picture remains as is, trade ministers will likely focus their attention on bilateral and sectoral trade issues.

Some bilateral and sectoral agreements could serve as precedents for broader multilateral arrangements in new areas such as services, investment, and high-technology trade. For example, the United States–Israel declaration on trade in services has been heralded as a framework for future negotiations both bilaterally between the United States and Canada, and multilaterally among the like-minded members of GATT. But there is a distinct risk that trade-restricting bilateral agreements will also serve as precedents for multilateral talks. With the conclusion of the 1986 United States–Japan bilateral negotiations, semiconductor trade has begun the slide towards cartelized world markets in the same manner as steel in the late 1970s, and textiles in the early 1960s. Machine tools are not far behind, with the conclusion of a series of restraint arrangements in late 1986 and early 1987.

Bilateral and sectoral trade talks thus provide both an opportunity to advance trade liberalization and a threat to the post–World War II system of open markets. The following sections highlight the key issues that are likely to dominate the U.S. bilateral agendas with the European Community, Japan, and Canada.

The United States, Europe, and Agriculture

The United States and Europe share a common problem largely caused by their own domestic policies: The overproduction of agricultural commodities such as wheat and feedgrains, dairy products, and sugar has led to a rash of trade disputes concentrated on export subsidies, but extending more broadly to a range of agricultural programs. A closer look at the wheat market is instructive. In many ways, the wheat market is analogous to the oil market. The United States has become the world's swing producer, much like Saudi Arabia in oil. Like the Saudis, the United States does not want to cede traditional export markets to its competitors. On the other hand, Europe must find an outlet on world markets for excess wheat production stimulated by high internal prices. The United States and the European Community will thus dig deep into their budgets to bolster farm incomes at home. In doing so they will force other producing countries—Australia, Argentina, and Canada—to suffer miserable earnings on their agricultural exports.

The cost of such profligate policies is staggering. One might think that budgetary constraint would bring sense to Washington and Brussels. But the immediate response has been to feed the monster instead of starving it. The European Community has raised the value added tax (VAT) contribution to farm programs, buying time (at a steep price) to resolve the farm budget crisis. President Reagan has increased export subsidies on wheat, rice, and sugar and supplemented direct payments to farmers for grain storage without regard to the mounting costs of the farm programs (which totaled $26 to $30 billion in fiscal year 1986).

The latest round of subsidized competition has not changed market shares to any great extent; it has merely driven down prices to the immense benefit of importing countries such as the Soviet Union, Japan, China, and Egypt—and at a huge cost to U.S. and EC taxpayers, and to Argentinian, Australian, and Canadian exporters.

So far, trade negotiators seem incapable of stopping this madness—they have argued agricultural trade in the GATT for twenty-five years without success. Even worse, finance ministers have lacked the clout to take on the farm lobby—as shown by recent events in Washington and Brussels.

Agricultural overproduction in the United States and Europe will have to be addressed squarely by political leaders. The right note was struck at the Venice Summit in May 1987. The United States decided to seek political agreement that agricultural subsidies, broadly defined, will be reduced gradually. By the early twenty-first century, the United States would like world market prices to prevail both for production for home markets and production for export. At the very least, world market prices should govern the amount and location of incremental production. Meanwhile, the link between farm subsidies and farm output should be broken—"decoupling" in the jargon of trade negotiators.

United States, Japan, and High Technology

Japan crept up on U.S. industrial leadership in the 1960s and 1970s and is now gaining at an alarming pace. With a yen of 140 to 150 per dollar, Japan has surpassed the United States in apparent per capita income. The trade policy fallout is hard to predict, but one area likely to receive close scrutiny is high-technology trade and investment.

Gone are the days when Japan was known for exports of children's toys and "copycat products." Japan today controls a large segment of the international consumer electronics market and plays a major role in advanced high-technology products such as personal computers, semiconductors, robots, and advanced manufacturing tools.

On the one hand, the United States applauds the drive and determination behind Japan's breakthrough. On the other hand, this breakthrough threatens the dominant U.S. position in electronics, computers, and biogenetics. The threat is just as real whether Japan's success is built on patent infringements, subsidies, dumping, and government procurement or whether the success is the result of sheer brilliance and hard work unaided by "unfair" practices.

U.S. industry has often responded to the Japanese threat by appealing to the federal government for relief against unfair practices. So far the executive branch has typically responded by negotiating "voluntary" export restraint arrangements with Japan or by initiating sector talks to open Japan's economy to U.S. exports of high-technology products (such as the Market-Oriented Sector-Selective [MOSS] talks on telecommunications). In short, the United States has used the threat of countervailing and antidumping duties, and Section 301 retaliation, to negotiate market-sharing arrangements with Japan. Recent disputes over semiconductor trade, machine tools, and access to Nippon Telephone and Telegraph (NTT) procurement are only the start. In the next few years, tensions are likely to rise over the research and development subsidies provided to manufacturers of fifth-generation computers, airplanes and satellite launchers, and telecommunications hardware and software.

U.S. companies will continue to resort to the countervailing and antidumping duty statutes to coerce the Japanese government into opening up its market to U.S. goods and services. Where injurious subsidization or dumping occurs, penalty duties should be levied. These cases should not be used as an excuse to institute quantitative trade controls.

Instead, U.S. policymakers should strive to meet the high-technology challenge from Japan in a way that preserves a free-market approach to trade policy. Market-sharing arrangements are fundamentally distasteful; more preferable would be regulatory reforms and other measures that foster joint ventures between U.S. and Japanese firms in production and research. This may be the best possible way of keeping the United States on the leading edge of high technology. Unfortunately, the U.S. government took the opposite tack when it barred Fujitsu from acquiring an ownership interest in Fairchild Semiconductor Corporation in 1987.

The United States, Canada, and Free Trade

The United States and Canada have completed negotiations to establish a free-trade area. Notification of the pact has been sent to Congress for consideration under the "fast track" implementing procedures. The talks have covered a broad range of issues in four key areas: the development of a bilateral accord on services, investment, and intellectual property; special accommodation for Canadian firms under U.S. contingent protection laws (the escape clause, retaliation under Section 301, and the antidumping and countervailing duty statutes); reciprocal accommodation for U.S. firms selling in the Canadian market; corresponding discipline on domestic subsidies, especially those granted by the states and the provinces; and finally, a satisfactory dispute settlement mechanism.

U.S.–Canadian agreements in the "new issues"—services, investment, and intellectual property—could serve as building blocks for broader GATT arrangements. The United States and Canada should attempt to design a model code that requires transparency in barriers to services trade, establishment rights, nondiscrimination between domestic and foreign firms, and surveillance of regulatory bodies at the federal and subfederal levels. Sectoral agreements could follow—proposals have already surfaced for liberalization of traded computer services; similar efforts could be made in financial services and telecommunications.

International investment issues invariably come to the surface as trade barriers are liberalized. A U.S.-Canada agreement on investment needs to be an integral part of the bilateral talks. As in services, a model code should be negotiated. The agreement could provide a framework both for addressing U.S. concerns about discrimination and the distortion entailed by investment incentives and performance requirements and for addressing Canadian concerns about U.S. domination of major sectors of the Canadian economy.

Domestic subsidies—regional aids, research and development grants, preferential loans, and farm price supports—provide the bread and butter of politics and are extremely sensitive to negotiate. But subsidies distort trade, especially between countries as interdependent as the United States and Canada. If the countervailing duty component of contingent protection is to be disciplined, some regime will have to be negotiated to give transparency to national, state, and provincial incentive programs, and to cap those programs when they provoke trade disputes or subsidy wars.

This said, the Canadian attempt to negotiate special treatment under the U.S. apparatus of contingent protection flies in the face of congressional efforts in the trade legislation of 1988 to limit presidential discretion and to extend the reach of existing provisions to cover a wider range of trade measures. Yet contingent protection statutes do not apply between the states, or between Canadian provinces, or between the members of the European Community. It should be possible to find politically acceptable means of limiting contingent protection in the context of a North American trade agreement. For example, agreement might be reached to harmonize U.S. and Canadian contingent protection legislation over a period of several years.

MULTILATERAL TRADE NEGOTIATIONS

The GATT meeting of trade ministers in September 1986 at Punta del Este was a great procedural success. The ministers agreed to launch a new round of multilateral trade negotiations, the Uruguay Round. The agenda for these talks is comprehensive and the terms of reference were crafted to include difficult issues such as farm subsidies and services.

The Punta declaration sets a four-year time limit for negotiations on both goods and services. Although such deadlines are notoriously "soft" and frequently extended, the declaration sets a feasible time period to complete the substantive agenda—and, more significant, indicates the first "political window" to conclude negotiations. Much attention will be given to the "new issues" such as services, investment, and intellectual property rights, but the focus of the next GATT round will be on "traditional" trade problems such as subsidies and import safeguards.

Subsidies

Subsidies lie at the root of most disputes over unfair trade practices and export targeting. They distort the pattern of trade and waste resources. Moreover, the years since the Tokyo Round have demonstrated—in semiconductors, steel, and other products—that subsidy and dumping practices can all too easily provide a platform for erecting regimes of managed trade.

GATT rules limiting export subsidies on industrial products were strengthened in the Subsidies Code negotiated during the Tokyo Round. Yet significant loopholes remain, for example, in the definition of domestic subsidies and mixed export credits (official export credits that "mix" trade finance and development assistance). More important, the Code did not address antisubsidy provisions on agricultural trade, and it made little effort at designing a regime of GATT discipline on domestic subsidies.

Further progress must be made. At Venice, the economic summit nations struck at the heart of subsidized trade and, simultaneously, boosted the GATT negotiating process with their declaration to bring better economic sense to agricultural production and trade. The task now is to reach agreement, both domestically and internationally, on measures to limit domestic subsidies and export subsidies.

Import Safeguards

Political support for liberal trade depends on the existence of a viable "escape clause" that allows distressed industries to receive temporary import protection while they adjust to changing market conditions. This bargain was recognized in GATT Article XIX. But the GATT safeguards system has now fallen into disuse; instead, countries have relied on extra-GATT arrangements of indefinite duration such as the Multifiber Arrangement, quotas on dairy products, and "voluntary" export restraints on autos and steel to protect domestic industries from import competition. Such measures create incentives among both export and import-competing industries for the continuation of trade restraints and provide little reason to adjust. But it is just these protected sectors where trade could expand most sharply both among the industrial countries and between the industrial north and the developing south.

A new GATT safeguard code that restricts extra-GATT protective measures must receive priority attention in the new round. To discourage the spread of extra-GATT protection, adjustment requirements must be an essential component of safeguard measures.

Incentives both to workers and firms would facilitate adjustment out of uncompetitive sectors and the downsizing of troubled industries to a viable core. Such incentives are costly, but new revenues to finance adjustment are potentially available from auctioning existing quotas or converting quotas to tariffs (Hufbauer and Rosen 1986; Bergsten, Elliott, Schott, and Takacs 1987). In an era of fiscal restraint, any new program arouses suspicion, but imaginatively designed adjustment programs can very quickly repay their costs.

U.S. OBJECTIVES: 1988–90

To manage protectionist pressures, the United States should adopt a two-track approach for the duration of the 1980s. First, U.S. trade negotiators need to restore a bipartisan domestic consensus on trade policy. To that end, the Reagan administration needs to reach an accord with Congress on the trade legislation of 1988. Second, U.S. trade negotiators should seek preliminary agreements in multilateral trade negotiations to provide credibility for the negotiating process and to complement the accord that could be reached with Canada.

The prospect of a continuing string of U.S. trade deficits means that protectionist pressures will be with us for many years. That in turn will impose strains on the entire world trading system. In fact, a deficit above $100 billion almost guarantees that trade will remain a hot political issue. Trade will become all the hotter if the United States experiences a growth recession. Although the 1988 trade legislation may prove irrelevant to the macroeconomic climate that broadly determines the path of the U.S. trade deficit, the Trade Act could well set the tone of trade negotiations for years to come.

What does the trade bill imply for the future direction of U.S. trade policy? More specifically, will it lead to a greater focus on unilateralism and less reliance on the multilateral trading system?

Such questions unfortunately demand the economist's standard response because the Congress, as usual, is sending mixed signals. On the one hand, the bill is highly supportive of the GATT system. It contains new negotiating authority for both tariffs and nontariff barriers and authorizes adherence to the new harmonized system of tariff nomenclature. On the other hand, the bill flaunts GATT disciplines by promoting unilateral retaliation in Section 301 cases and in the telecommunications sector and by incorporating into U.S. law other provisions that violate either the spirit or the letter of the GATT.

The main value of the trade bill is the provision of trade negotiating authorities. The bill provides new tariff reduction authority and extends "fast-track" procedures to implement trade agreements, which would otherwise expire on January 3, 1988. As a practical matter, both are prerequisites for the United States to engage in the final stage of negotiations: U.S. trading partners will not be willing to commit to significant concessions to conclude a trade agreement without the assurance that Congress will not renegotiate trade agreements. As such, fast-track procedures have become de facto negotiating authority.

By contrast, most of the troublesome provisions in the bill involve technical revisions that broaden the scope and coverage of U.S. trade statutes and redesign standards so that U.S. industries are more likely to qualify for import relief in Sections 201 and 301 and in antidumping and countervailing duty cases. Many of these changes accommodate specific industries that have had problems gaining relief in the past and are not consistent with the spirit and/or the letter of U.S. obligations under the GATT. Is it worth trading off such increased protectionism for the new trade negotiating authorities?

The United States does not need the fast-track authority to conduct negotiations, but it needs such provisions to conclude negotiations. If the fast-track authority expires, U.S. trading partners— especially the EC—would have a ready excuse to pull back from the negotiating table. Talks would probably still continue in a perfunctory fashion but no real bargaining would take place.

As a practical matter, the trade legislation of 1988 will have little immediate impact on the GATT trade negotiations. Multilateral trade talks will soon be bogged down with 1988 election campaigns in the United States, France, and possibly in Canada. The real impetus for the next GATT round will come—if at all—from the president who takes office in 1989.

NOTES

1. The G-5 consists of France, Germany, Japan, the United Kingdom, and the United States. Canada and Italy are added to make the seven industrial nations at the annual economic summits.

2. In a revision of his earlier study, Stephen Marris (1987) now forecasts a further 20 percent decline in the trade-weighted value of the dollar from levels reached in August 1987.
3. While the trade deficit has not improved in value terms through September 1987, there has been a noticeable improvement in volume terms. The volume of U.S. exports has rebounded significantly since late 1986, while the growth in the volume of imports has moderated in response to sharply higher import prices.
4. Even then, it must be remembered that a $90 billion cut in the federal budget deficit may improve the trade balance by only about $30 billion after several years (IMF 1986: 128).

REFERENCES

Bergsten, C. Fred, Kimberly Ann Elliott, Jeffrey J. Schott, and Wendy E. Takacs. 1987. *Auction Quotas and United States Trade Policy.* Policy Analyses in International Economics 19. Washington, D.C.: Institute for International Economics.

Hufbauer, Gary Clyde, and Howard Rosen. 1986. *Trade Policy for Troubled Industries.* Policy Analyses in International Economics 19. Washington, D.C.: Institute for International Economics.

Hufbauer, Gary Clyde, and Jeffrey J. Schott. 1985. *Trading for Growth: The Next Round of Trade Negotiations.* Policy Analyses in International Economics 11. Washington, D.C.: Institute for International Economics.

International Monetary Fund. 1986. *Staff Studies for the World Economic Outlook.* Washington, D.C.: IMF.

_____ . 1987. *Deficits and the Dollar Revisited.* Washington, D.C.: IMF.

Lambsdorff, Otto. 1986. "Don't Blame Bonn." *Wall Street Journal*, August 18, p. 20.

13 U.S. INTERESTS IN INTERNATIONAL AGRICULTURAL POLICY

Robert L. Paarlberg

U.S. commercial, diplomatic, and humanitarian interests in world agriculture have become more difficult to secure in recent years. The costly 1982–86 collapse of U.S. farm exports is only one recent manifestation of this trend. Pursuing a consistent set of U.S. interests in world agriculture became more difficult with the onset of disruptive international economic conditions and stop-and-go East–West diplomatic detente early in the 1970s.

During the 1970s, which were marked by rapid inflationary growth and heavy international borrowing, commodity markets boomed and U.S. agriculture received an enormous commercial windfall from international trade. World grain trade doubled, and U.S. exporters captured 75 percent of the increased business. The United States multiplied its net farm trade surplus from less than $2 billion in 1971 to more than $25 billion by the end of the decade. Anticipating that this export growth would continue, U.S. farmers borrowed heavily—with encouragement from their government—to expand their production capacity. The share of total U.S. harvested cropland producing for export increased from 25 percent to nearly 40 percent, and total U.S. farm indebtedness increased by roughly 60 percent.

Just as U.S. farmers were adjusting to this sudden change, the world commodity boom went bust. In 1981 U.S. farm exports suddenly stopped growing and entered a sustained decline, falling 40 percent by 1986. As exports fell, so did prices and farm income. It was painfully clear that the international trade boom of the 1970s had been an insecure basis on which to rest U.S. farm investments.

In fact, both the world farm trade boom of the 1970s and the world farm trade collapse of the early 1980s were symptomatic of the same disturbing trend toward global macroeconomic instability. Following the move away from a fixed exchange-rate system in 1971, real interest rates and dollar exchange rates both fell sharply. These were conditions of enormous temporary benefit to U.S. agriculture. Income growth worldwide was temporarily sustained by record borrowing at negative real interest rates, and the larger foreign food purchases driven by this income growth were disproportionately made in the United States because dollars were cheap abroad.

These conditions were dramatically reversed when new leadership came to the U.S. Federal Reserve Board in 1979 and resolved to tighten the U.S. money supply to bring inflation under control. Record high interest rates, a world recession, and surging dollar exchange rates resulted. This proved, again temporarily, to be the worst possible combination of global macroeconomic circumstances for U.S. agriculture. Exports fell, commodity prices fell, farmland values fell, and farm debts became unserviceable. At the low point of this cycle, in the summer of 1986, the U.S. farm trade balance actually went into deficit for the first time in more than twenty-five years. Added public spending on export subsidies did little to reverse this collapse.

The exposure of U.S. agriculture to this unstable world marketplace since the 1970s has also brought on adverse diplomatic effects. In 1973 when surging foreign demand began pushing U.S. consumer food prices up too quickly (at a 30 percent annual rate during the first half of that year), panicky officials responded by suddenly suspending all U.S. soybean exports. Japan, an important soybean customer as well as an important ally, was badly shocked. In similar fashion, both in 1974 and 1975, the United States temporarily suspended grain sales to the Soviet Union, interfering with the prevailing policy of detente.

Food trade policy and U.S. foreign policy were again badly out of phase at the end of the decade. Detente was collapsing precisely at the moment the U.S. agriculture was becoming more dependent on exports. In September 1979, only three months before the Soviet invasion of Afghanistan, the United States made an official offer to sell a record 25 million tons of grain to the Soviet Union. After the Soviet invasion, most of these sales were canceled by President Jimmy Carter, who went on to impose a leaky embargo that received little or no support from grain exporting allies. Farm lobby pressures obliged President Ronald Reagan to reverse gears once more and to lift this embargo early in 1981 just when a new East-West crisis was heating up in Poland.

The Reagan administration, which generally tried to toughen U.S. policy toward the Soviet Union, lost credibility with its allies by doing the opposite in the arena of agriculture. Following the imposition of martial law in Poland in December 1981, when sanctions of every other kind were being imposed on the Soviet Union, the United States allowed grain sales to continue and even pushed for their expansion. By 1986 the United States was offering to subsidize grain sales to the Soviet Union at a rate of $15 a ton. Secretary of State George Shultz, who had bitterly but unsuccessfully opposed this policy, commented that the Soviets must be "chortling and scratching their heads about a system that says we're going to fix it up so that American taxpayers make it possible for a Soviet housewife to buy American-produced food at prices lower than an American housewife" (*Journal of Commerce* 1986: 16B). The Soviet Union, to make matters worse, turned down this first U.S. subsidy offer. They did not buy until the spring of 1987, by which time the U.S. subsidies had increased to more than $40 a ton. This recent spectacle of offering lavish subsidies to a foreign policy adversary—angering, in the process, important allies such as Canada, Australia, and the EC—illustrates how difficult it can be to operate a food policy and a foreign policy in harmony with each other.

U.S. humanitarian interests in world agriculture have also become more difficult to pursue recently. In response to the agricultural crisis in Africa and elsewhere in the developing world, the United States should be playing a lead role not only in providing emergency famine relief but also in encouraging local agricultural development. The former task, unfortunately, has sometimes been complicated by commercial considerations and diplomatic constraints. U.S. food aid levels fell during the commodity price boom of the 1970s, when food aid was most needed in poor countries. Meanwhile Egypt, hardly the hungriest of African nations in recent years, but one of the most strategic, has been getting roughly four times as much U.S. food aid as the next largest recipient. And the latter task of supporting agricultural development in poor countries has increasingly been blocked by U.S. domestic farm interests, which have come to see Third World farm production as a threat to future U.S. farm export expansion.

THE ROLE OF DOMESTIC FARM
POLICY REFORM

Because so many of the recent disruptions and dislocations in world agricultural trade have been a direct consequence of unstable global macroeconomic conditions, the best remedy for U.S. agirucultural policy would be a restoration of stability and balance in macroeconomic policy, encouraged in the first instance by much greater U.S. fiscal policy discipline plus improved international fiscal and monetary policy coordination. Without these fundamental macroeconomic improvements, there will be a limit to the gains that can come from any policy steps prescribed within the narrow farm sector.

It is nonetheless possible to outline a farm-sector strategy that will improve the prospect for securing U.S. commercial, diplomatic, and humanitarian interests abroad, even in the currently unstable macroeconomic environment. This is a strategy that begins by recognizing the influential role that U.S. domestic farm policy plays in shaping the structure and condition of world agricultural markets. As the world's largest efficient producer and exporter of so many tradable farm products, and also as a large consumer and importer of farm commodities from abroad, the United States can affect world farm trade simply through the way it manages its own domestic food and farm sector. One of the best ways to pursue U.S. farm trade interests abroad, as a consequence, is to undertake farm policy change at home.[1]

U.S. farm and farm trade policies have traditionally been crafted with inward-looking commodity price support objectives uppermost in mind. These price support objectives have often been pursued through the use of unilateral U.S. supply constraints and unilateral public stock accumulations, both of which have tended to prop up prices not only in the United States but also worldwide.[2] The consequences of U.S. international farm trade have been mostly unfortunate. In farm markets such as corn, soybeans, and wheat, where the United States is a relatively low-cost producer, propping up world prices with unilateral production cutbacks is a strategy that gives less efficient foreign competitors more leeway to expand production and exports.

A significant part of the U.S. farm export collapse since 1981 has grown out of this tendency to respond too quickly to falling world prices by unilaterally taking land out of production and by unilaterally carrying larger stocks. It should not be the United States that always plays this disadvantageous role of residual supplier in world wheat and coarse grain markets. It should be less efficient, high-cost foreign producers who are under pressure to cut back first when prices go down. The United States unfortunately relieves others of this pressure whenever it defends its own high domestic price supports with unilateral production cutbacks.

This tendency showed itself most clearly in the Payment In Kind (PIK) acreage reduction program of 1982–83. Through this program, which was designed to halt the costly accumulation of government-owned surplus stocks, U.S. farmers were paid in kind with surplus stocks to take their farmland out of production. U.S. wheat producers cut their harvested acreage by roughly 22 percent. U.S. corn production was cut by a massive 49 percent, in part due to drought as well as to the PIK program. The price-firming effects of these unilateral U.S. production cutbacks were nullified by the opportunistic response of most foreign competitors. While the United States was setting aside 77 million acres of land in 1983, other countries responded by increasing their plantings by 63 million acres. The EC, which had originally been expecting to run out of money for agricultural subsidy programs in 1983, was given some financial breathing space by higher prices and kept its full production policies in place. Canada, Australia, and Argentina all boosted their wheat output, and their share of world wheat trade expanded while the U.S. share continued in steep decline. Total U.S. wheat and coarse grain production fell by 38 percent under the PIK program, while the production of major export competitors such as Canada, Australia, Argentina, South Africa, and Thailand increased by 11 percent (*Cargill Bulletin* 1984: 5).

Because U.S. domestic commodity price and income support levels remained high after the PIK program, it did not take long for surplus stocks to mount up again. Between 1983 and 1985, the U.S. share of total world stocks increased from 44 percent to 60 percent. By accumulating this disproportionate share of world stocks, the United States was once again firming up international prices for its less disciplined foreign competitors, who, in response, increased their share of world wheat and coarse grain exports still more, from 46 percent to 64 percent between 1981 and 1985 (USDA 1985, 1986b).

The foundation of this recent U.S. tendency to prop up international prices for less efficient foreign competitors has been the high federal budget exposure contained in U.S. domestic farm price support programs. These domestic programs have long been built around an option given to U.S. farmers to loan (in effect, sell) their various commodities to the government at legislated support prices called loan rates. If these legislated commodity loan rates are inflexibly set above market-clearing levels, disadvantageous things start to happen. The cost to taxpayers of purchasing and holding surplus stocks can rapidly increase. To contain these costs, the U.S. government is tempted to offer farmers incentives to take land out of production. This saves some budget costs in the short run, but it destroys the competitiveness of U.S. farming in the long run.

Unrealistic price expectations, generated by the inflationary commodity boom of the 1970s, helped lure U.S. agricultural policy into this trap. The political courtship of farm votes also played a role, especially in 1976 and 1980 when incumbent administrations agreed to higher commodity loan rates just prior to closely contested presidential elections. These higher loan rates together with an inflexible schedule for still higher target prices were then written into the new four-year farm bill that Congress enacted in 1981. By 1982–85, as a consequence, real support price levels for U.S. wheat were back up to 20 percent above the levels of 1968–72 (Johnson 1986).

When world markets suddenly went slack after 1981, these high domestic price support guarantees could not easily be moved downward.[3] The predictable results were larger U.S. government purchases of surplus products and much higher farm program costs, leading in turn to the self-defeating 1982–83 PIK acreage reduction program.

Some important progress was made in the 1985 farm bill to correct this unfortunate tendency for U.S. domestic commodity loan levels to undermine the competitive trade position of U.S. agriculture. It was finally accepted that loan rates should come down and should be linked in the future to a moving average of market prices, with the Secretary of Agriculture given explicit authority in any given year to reduce these loan rates by an additional 20 percent if necessary to regain a competitive trading posture. The Secretary of Agriculture immediately began to use this authority in 1986, and loan rates suddenly fell sharply—for wheat from $3.30 a bushel down to $2.40. With such market-oriented loan rates in place, and with dollar exchange rates also falling sharply in 1986, the United States was at last on its way to regaining a competitive position in international farm export markets.

Unfortunately, a second feature in the 1985 farm bill has now threatened to reverse some of this progress. While agreeing to lower loan rates in 1985, farm interests in Congress insisted on no immediate reduction in target prices. These target prices, which are set above loan rates, are used to calculate the cash deficiency payment that farmers get from the government. Because loan rates and market prices would rapidly fall under the new legislation, these high, frozen target prices meant that the budget costs of making deficiency payments to farmers were almost certain to get out of hand. When the new farm bill was enacted in December 1985, USDA economists predicted that its farm support programs might cost as much as $17.5 billion in fiscal year 1986. This seemed expensive at the time because these programs had already cost $12 billion a year during the first five years of the Reagan administration, compared to only $3.4 billion a year for the previous five years. But these initial cost estimates were actually much too low. The first-year cost of the new legislation eventually proved to be $25.8 billion.

These high budget costs associated with record deficiency payments threatened to undermine support for the market-oriented loan rates in the 1985 farm bill. Some farm interest groups believed that producing for world market prices would never be an affordable income generating strategy and began to promote what they considered to be a cheaper alternative—boosting prices through mandatory production controls. The so-called Harkin–Gephardt farm bill, as introduced in 1986, envisioned a mandatory set-aside of up to 35 percent of every farm's acreage, the intent being to roughly double commodity prices.

There is little doubt that mandatory production controls could raise U.S. farm prices while lowering direct farm program costs. But this approach would cause further damage to U.S. farm trade. The sharp reduction in U.S. output would prop up prices mostly for the benefit of competitors abroad, who would expand their own production and exports accordingly. The kind of damage that was done to U.S. farm trade by the PIK acreage reduction program would become permanent and cumulative under mandatory production controls.

Damage would be done at home as well. With production controls, a highly regressive tax would fall on U.S. consumers, who would have to pay more for food. Also, those sectors of the U.S. economy that supply inputs to farmers and that transport and process U.S. farm products downstream would also have to shrink in size. By one Department of Agriculture estimate, a supply cutback on the scale envisioned by the Harkin–Gephardt bill might destroy almost as many jobs, upstream and downstream from farms, as there are farmers (USDA 1986a).

Rather than down-sizing the U.S. agricultural sector by reverting to a noncompetitive farm pricing posture, policymakers might consider solving their farm budget problems by other means. Adjusting target prices downward in a market-oriented fashion, to make them more nearly parallel with loan rates, is a logical approach, but one that will probably remain blocked by farm interest objections. Improved targeting of farm program benefits, away from the largest and wealthiest farmers, might be a more acceptable way to proceed. At present, almost one-quarter of all commodity program outlays go to large farms with annual sales above $225,000.

In addition to targeting, the decoupling of program benefits from production incentives would also be desirable. Decoupling would free less efficient farmers from the current need to keep producing surplus commodities in order to qualify for income support. It would also free efficient farmers from the need to take land out of production. Decoupled cash payments of this kind would allow market prices to move more freely, making U.S. agriculture more efficient at home and even more competitive abroad. So as to ensure affordability to taxpayers, these payments might be scaled down in size over time.

During the 1985 farm bill debate, one comprehensive plan was put forward that managed to incorporate most of these useful concepts. The Boschwitz–Boren bill was a bipartisan measure introduced too late to figure strongly in the compromise package that was finally enacted. It was praised for its targeted and decoupled transition payment approach to farm income support yet criticized by those who thought it would be too expensive. If it could have been compared to a more realistic estimate of what the 1985 farm bill would actually cost, it probably would have received more support. Continued movement of U.S. domestic farm legislation in a more market-oriented direction would have beneficial consequences for U.S. commercial, diplomatic, and humanitarian interests abroad.

COMMERCIAL GAINS FROM MARKET-ORIENTED FARM POLICIES

The international commercial gains from market-oriented domestic farm policies are obvious enough. Instead of propping up world prices for competitors abroad through disproportionate stocks and unilateral production restraints, the United States would once again be giving its own producers and exporters a chance to compete. The U.S. share of world farm exports, which fell from 19.3 percent to 16.6 percent between 1981 and 1985 due to noncompetitive pricing, could start expanding again.

Even among those who recognize the commercial benefits that would accompany competitive export pricing, doubts will be raised about any U.S. plan to liberalize its own domestic farm programs unilaterally. Some will argue that commercial objectives will be better served by using trade subsidies more heavily. The United

States could decide to fight fire with fire—by waging and winning an international farm trade war.

In fact, there are at least three reasons why the United States cannot expect to prevail in a farm trade war. First, the United States enters that competition at a relative disadvantage because it has the largest existing foreign markets to defend. Simply to protect its existing market share, the United States would have to be ready to offer export subsidies in every foreign market where it is currently making sales. Because its current sales are still much larger than those of its rivals (the United States still exports 50 percent more wheat than the EC), it would have to outspend its rivals by a wide margin simply to stay even.

Second, the United States also has to spend more in an escalating export subsidy war because of the way it operates its domestic farm programs. A subsidy war lowers world prices, which in turn lowers U.S. domestic farm prices, leading to an increase in the size of U.S. target price deficiency payments. The EC protects its budget from this added internal cost by using variable levies that prevent lower world farm prices from crossing its borders.

Third, the United States would also be at a disadvantage because of the likelihood that an all-out export subsidy war would eventually spill over to include tit-for-tat import restrictions as well. Because the United States exports much more than it imports, it would stand to lose from such a spillover. In the case of its bilateral trade with the EC, the United States would stand to lose roughly 50 percent more because it sells roughly $5.3 billion worth of farm products to the EC every year while importing only $3.6 billion worth of EC farm products in return. Duty-free U.S. soybean and corn gluten feed sales to the Community would be one particularly inviting target for retaliation. Until now the EC has been willing to honor its GATT obligation not to alter (without compensation) the duty-free entry status of these nongrain livestock feed ingredients. In the more highly charged context of an escalating farm trade war, this inclination toward restraint might disappear.

Many of these unattractive aspects of an export subsidy competition have already been revealed in the performance of the Export Enhancement Program (EEP), a $1.5 billion three-year export subsidy program originally written into the 1985 farm bill. The EEP has shown a tendency to produce large additional U.S. sales in some individual markets, but little increase in U.S. sales overall. Shipments of U.S. wheat and wheat products went up sharply to markets in North Africa and the Middle East, where most early EEP sales were concentrated beginning in late 1985. Total U.S. sales in these markets increased by 73 percent during the first fiscal year the program was in effect, and EC sales to these targeted markets momentarily declined (USDA 1986c: 7). However, total U.S. wheat exports to markets did not increase during this period. The United States managed temporarily to displace some EC exports that had been going to markets in North Africa and the Middle East, but those exports only shifted to other markets such as China, Brazil, and the Soviet Union—where U.S. sales were displaced.

By one calculation, the EEP actually decreased the total volume of U.S. exports by giving the Soviet Union, originally excluded from the program, an excuse to purchase less U.S. wheat than would have otherwise been required under the terms of its bilateral long-term agreement with the United States. The Soviets argued that their exclusion from the EEP violated a term of this agreement that they be offered wheat at a nondiscriminatory price, so in 1985 they purchased less than the minimum quantity of U.S. wheat required and in 1986 purchased almost no U.S. wheat at all. This damaging boycott forced the administration to reverse itself and to announce that a limited quantity of U.S. wheat sold to the Soviet Union would henceforth be eligible for a $15 a ton EEP bonus bushel subsidy. The diplomatic embarrassment that accompanied this announcement was made worse by the Soviet refusal of the offer. Not until early 1987, when the United States finally agreed to offer a far more generous subsidy rate of $40 a ton, did the Soviet Union resume buying U.S. wheat.

In addition to advocates of a farm trade war, a U.S. plan to liberalize its own domestic farm programs faces opposition from those who want GATT negotiations to be the starting point for U.S. commercial farm trade policy. Proponents of this view point out that the final benefit to U.S. agriculture would be considerably larger if other nations could be persuaded to liberalize along with the United States. Therefore, the United States should consider additional steps toward farm policy liberalization only in the context of a larger multilateral agreement. To continue the domestic policy reform process without such an agreement would be like embracing unilateral disarmament.

This well-meaning view unfortunately overstates the prospect of reaching a negotiated agreement on farm trade reform within GATT. It also understates the gains to be made from starting the reform process, if necessary, outside of GATT.

Numerous efforts have been made in the past to use the rules and procedures of GATT to liberalize international farm trade. As yet, none of these efforts has been successful. During the Dillon Round

of negotiations, customs tariffs on manufactured trade were successfully brought down, but agricultural trade barriers were left largely
untouched. This lack of progress on agriculture continued during the
1963–67 Kennedy Round, in which the EC was so busy increasing its
internal farm support levels with the newly established Common
Agricultural Policy (CAP) that it took no interest in any effort to
negotiate coordinated international reductions. During the subsequent 1973–79 Tokyo Round, all that the United States could secure
on agriculture was a loosely constructed Subsidies Code, which eventually proved to be of little value. In the first case initiated by the
United States concerning EC wheat flour export subsidies, a GATT
panel procrastinated for six years before finally issuing what was
essentially a nonverdict. The panel acknowledged that the EC wheat
flour export share had increased considerably; that this increase
would not have been possible without export subsidies; and that
these EC export subsidies may have resulted in reduced sales opportunities for the United States. The panel nonetheless refused to conclude that the EC had used its subsidies to gain a more than equitable
market share on the grounds that the terms of the Subsidy Code
were not sufficiently "operational, stringent, and effective" (Sanderson 1986: 13).[4]

There are good reasons why GATT has never been able to extend
its healthy liberalizing influence very far into the agricultural sector.
GATT has been able to bring down tariff barriers to manufactured
trade in large part because those barriers have not usually been linked
to elaborate and politically sacrosanct domestic pricing and production policies. Unfortunately, the nontariff barriers that predominate
in the farm policy arena are all intimately tied to such domestic
policy mechanisms. For this reason, GATT negotiations on agriculture cannot be restricted to a simple bargained reduction of trade
interventions at the border. All of the domestic farm policies that
these interventions are designed to protect must also, at least implicitly, be placed on the negotiating table. And this is something the
powerful domestic political authorities who author these farm policies have never been willing to allow.

In tacit recognition of these political realities, the fundamental
trade-liberalizing rules of GATT were written from the very beginning to make huge exceptions for agriculture. As foreigners never fail
to point out, this was done primarily at the insistence of the United
States. It was the United States that originally called for an allow-
ance in Article XI for quantitative restrictions on agricultural imports
in some circumstances. The United States also insisted on making the
conditional use of export subsidies for primary products legal under

GATT. Without these original exceptions for agriculture, some U.S. domestic farm programs would not have been able to function, and Congress would never have been willing to approve U.S. participation in GATT. To make matters worse, in 1955 the United States asked for a permanent waiver from the lenient rules on import restrictions that it had authored, in order to accommodate its increasingly protectionist dairy and sugar programs.

There is no evidence that the current Uruguay Round of GATT negotiations has yet found a way to overcome these domestic policy barriers to a liberalizing international farm trade agreement. U.S. negotiators in Geneva have bravely claimed that "everything is on the table" but so far there has been no embrace of this assertion by U.S. farm groups or by those in Congress who hold the final power to decide. Some U.S. farm interests are supporting the current GATT round, but mostly out of a mistaken belief that it will be used to force other nations, especially the EC, to undertake unilateral farm policy reforms or trade concessions. This is a vain hope because concessions in GATT must always be reciprocal. U.S. agriculturalists must be prepared to give in order to get, and even then they will probably be disappointed by GATT. EC negotiators have never expressed any interest in trading away the fundamental mechanisms of the CAP, whatever the United States might wish to offer in return. Being on balance more heavily subsidized than U.S. farmers, EC farmers correctly see themselves as the relative losers in any multilateral GATT liberalization scheme. If the pace of agricultural policy reform is left up to GATT, the EC will be in a position to drag its heels indefinitely.

Prospects for achieving a timely multilateral reform in GATT were probably not brightened by the U.S. decision, in July 1987, to place before the Uruguay Round a plan for ending all trade and production distorting subsidies in ten years. This grandiose objective goes beyond the terms of the carefully negotiated ministerial declaration that launched the Round and beyond what the EC and Japan can ever be expected to accept. Realistically, it also goes beyond what U.S. agriculture can accept. For these reasons, it will most likely not be taken seriously. The current administration will leave office having talked for years about what GATT can do to help reform agricultural policy but with nothing in the end to show for it.

Rather than trying to launch the domestic reform process in GATT, the United States might consider proceeding with some kind of reforms entirely on its own. Taking the first step unilaterally might, in the end, prove the best way to get the sticky multilateral GATT process moving.

If a unilateral cereals policy reform were to end the periodic U.S. practice of propping up world market prices through massive acreage reduction programs, indirect pressure would be brought to bear on the EC through market and budget mechanisms to move more swiftly toward reform as well. With lower world prices, EC budget spending on export restitution payments would have to increase. Internal budget pressures have been, until now, the only mechanism strong enough to push EC farm policymakers to consider price and production reforms. If unilateral U.S. liberalization measures can be used to increase these already severe budget pressures even a little, then the chances of moving toward reform, and the chances of finally codifying these reforms in a GATT agreement, would increase as well.

Unilateral U.S. farm policy liberalization could also be good for the GATT if it reduced some of the existing inconsistencies between U.S. domestic farm programs and important GATT rules. If U.S. sugar and dairy programs were in the process of being liberalized at home, then the United States could more easily offer to give up its 1955 waiver on Article XI import quota rules. This would make it easier to negotiate refinements of Article XI and also to hold foreign competitors, including the EC, to their existing obligations under Article XI. A unilateral decoupling of U.S. farm program payments would also help the GATT process because it would allow the United States to pursue a tightening of the Subsidies Code without having to place its own domestic income support payments to farmers on the bargaining table. Far from being incompatible with GATT, therefore, unilateral U.S. domestic farm policy reforms could eventually make strong contributions to the GATT process.

For the purpose of advancing U.S. commercial trade interests, market-oriented domestic farm policy reforms therefore seem better than either of the two most popular alternatives. The coercive alternative of trying to use ever larger export subsidies to wage and win a farm trade war is both costly and dangerous. And the cooperative option of trying to advance U.S. commercial farm trade interests exclusively through GATT negotiations should be used as an adjunct to a strategy of price competition, driven where possible by liberal domestic policy reform.

DIPLOMATIC GAINS FROM MARKET-ORIENTED FARM POLICIES

If the United States were to continue moving its domestic farm policies in a market-oriented direction, some of the diplomatic disadvantages recently associated with international farm trade activities might also be remedied. Most important, diplomatic tensions with farm trading allies could substantially be reduced. If the United States were to rely more on liberal competitive pricing to clear its agricultural markets and less on direct trade interventions such as export subsidies or import quotas, its international farm trade relations could be substantially depoliticized. Foreign farm interests would feel pressure through the marketplace, but diplomatic and trade officials in rival states would find fewer opportunities to accuse the United States of a GATT violation and would be under less pressure to create a diplomatic crisis or to threaten retaliation.

Because the United States is such a large and conspicuous farm product exporter, the trade policies of the U.S. government tend to be held to a higher political and diplomatic standard. For example, the U.S. decision in 1986 to offer wheat export subsidies to the Soviet Union brought howls of protest from both Canada and Australia even though both practice a highly illiberal form of state trading in wheat, both had recently been enjoying a rising share of world markets at the expense of the United States, and the Soviets did not take up the U.S. offer. Nonetheless, stiff formal complaints were registered by Canadian Prime Minister Brian Mulroney and by Australian Prime Minister Robert Hawke. Argentine President Raul Alfonsin went so far as to issue instructions on the possible halt of Argentine foreign debt repayments in protest over the U.S. subsidy initiative (*Journal of Commerce* 1986: 3A). Because U.S. farm trade policy is bound to be measured in the international arena by such high standards, the United States would reap political and diplomatic gains from reducing as much as possible its reliance on illiberal public sector farm trade interventions.

Moving the official hand of the U.S. government farther away from the conduct of international farm trade might also provide diplomatic advantages in relations with adversaries such as the Soviet Union. The United States learned, while trying to implement the ineffectual 1980-81 grain embargo, that manipulating the flow of U.S. farm products to the Soviet Union was a source of almost no perceptible foreign policy gain and much domestic political distress. Because so many non-U.S. suppliers were willing to replace embargoed U.S. grain sales, the total volume of Soviet grain imports actually continued to increase at a 5 percent annual rate during the first year that this so-called embargo was in effect. U.S. efforts to halt these non-U.S. sales to the Soviet Union only led to more squabbles with allies, which redoubled the diplomatic disadvantage (Paarlberg 1985: 170-212).[5] Because farm sales cannot be used effectively as a foreign policy weapon, perhaps they should be allowed to serve their primary commercial purpose unhindered by diplomatic complications or appearances. The best way to do this is to remove the official hand of the U.S. government from their day-to-day management.

As a first step in this direction, the United States should consider not renewing the current U.S.-Soviet bilateral agreement on wheat, corn, and soybean trade when that agreement expires in 1988. The negotiation of these periodic five-year minimum purchase and minimum access agreements was, to begin with, a Soviet idea. If the United States had followed its original instinct, which was to let such things be handled through private trade, U.S. diplomatic and commercial interests in the years since probably would have been better served.

The first of these official U.S.-Soviet grain trade agreements, signed in 1975, never produced any certifiable increase in Soviet purchases of U.S. grain. Total Soviet import needs remained so large throughout the life of that agreement—averaging 28 million tons a year—that the minimum annual purchase stipulation in the agreement of just 6 million tons never constrained Soviet behavior. The only real constraint later fell on the United States, which was inconveniently obliged during the 1980-81 embargo to continue honoring the 8 million ton annual minimum-access provision. By continuing to sell the Soviets an annual 8 million tons of U.S. grain during the embargo, the United States embarrassed itself abroad and practically ensured that rival exporters would not cooperate.

Following the embargo, it was U.S. domestic farm interest pressures rather than foreign policy considerations that eventually led to a renegotiation of the original agreement. This renegotiation, built on a generous 50 percent increase in the annual Soviet minimum access guarantee, was badly timed, taking place just a few weeks before the 1983 shooting of an unarmed Korean commercial jet airliner by the Soviet Union. Worst of all, this generous new agreement was eventually not honored by the Soviet Union. In 1985 the Soviet Union used the convenient excuse of some relatively small U.S. export subsidy payments to other customers as a reason to fall 1.1 million tons short of its 4 million ton minimum wheat purchase obligation. Then in 1986 on the strength of an improved grain harvest at home, the Soviets used this same flimsy excuse to fall 3.85 million tons short.[6]

There will never be an easy way to keep U.S.-Soviet commercial farm trade relations from complicating the highly volatile conduct of U.S.-Soviet foreign policy relations, or vice versa. The recent practice of allowing official bilateral agreements and direct farm export subsidy policies to dominate the commercial side, however, has so politicized trade as to turn every little discrepancy between U.S. commercial and diplomatic interests into a source of needless political controversy and diplomatic pain. Moving away from both official bilateral agreements and from official export subsidies—a course of action compatible with moving U.S. domestic farm policy in a more market-oriented direction—could help remedy some of these needless difficulties.

HUMANITARIAN GAINS FROM MARKET-ORIENTED FARM POLICIES

All of the world's citizens depend on the healthy state of agriculture for their daily nourishment. Most of the world's poorest citizens— those living in rural Asia, Africa, and Latin America—also depend on agriculture for their employment and daily income as well. It is therefore important, for humanitarian reasons, that the conduct of U.S. international agricultural policy be undertaken with these larger nourishment, employment, and income effects constantly in mind.

The U.S. record on this score has been mixed. Whenever U.S. policy has been relatively liberal, important global humanitarian interests have been tolerably well served. In cereals markets the United States has at times performed an important service by allowing international price fluctuations to be felt directly within the large U.S. domestic market. This has permitted large, internationally helpful U.S. production and consumption adjustments to occur. Too many other rich nations such as Japan, the EC, and the Soviet Union have resisted such cyclical production and consumption adjustments. These other nations prefer to make only trade adjustments, with an eye toward stabilizing their own food and farm prices at home. This of course causes greater price instability abroad.

If the United States were not so willing to absorb instability by keeping its borders relatively open to world price fluctuations, the less wealthy and more vulnerable users of the world's all-important cereals markets would find themselves at greater risk. This is particularly true during times of tightening world supplies such as the food crisis years of the mid-1970s. If the United States had not allowed higher food prices to enter its own domestic market, thus forcing consumers to cut back sharply (especially on meat consumption, which released large quantities of grain for export and for direct human consumption), and if the United States had not allowed those same high prices to reach producers, signaling a need for expanded output, then the price of internationally traded cereals would have gone even higher than it did. This would have forced an even larger adjustment burden onto poorly fed consumers in the developing world, with tragic social consequences.

Conversely, in times of relative supply abundance like the 1980s, if the United States were not willing to allow falling world price signals to cross its borders, the appropriate production and consumption adjustments would not be made in the large U.S. market, and international prices would have to fall that much farther. This would pinch the incomes of highly vulnerable farm producers in the developing world. Because of the large size of the U.S. cereals market, and because of the large and highly adjustable share of U.S. cereals production that is fed to livestock, this cyclical "shock absorbing" role in world markets is one that the United States can well enough afford to play.[7]

When U.S. cereals policies start to stray from this commendable sort of market sensitivity—for example, when U.S. price-support rigidities lead to surplus accumulation and when export subsidies are then used to dump U.S. surplus stocks into the world market abroad at low prices—the interests of agricultural producers in the developing world are not so well served. U.S. farm export subsidies can be helpful, in the short run, to some officials in poor countries who have allowed themselves to become dependent on artificially cheap imports. But the long-run effect in those same countries can be a further postponement of indigenous agricultural policy reform and development essential for improving the circumstances of the rural poor. And the impact on agricultural exporting poor countries is disadvantageous as well.[8]

In import markets such as sugar, where U.S. agricultural policy is even more highly protective, humanitarian interests are currently not being well served. U.S. sugar policy protects relatively well-to-do and inefficient U.S. producers by imposing quota restrictions on imports from poor countries in the developing world. The damage done to agricultural production in the developing world is particularly lamentable because so much of it is absorbed by diplomatically significant allied countries including the Philippines and already impoverished and now heavily indebted states in Central and South America. Prior to the most recent renewal of this highly protectionist U.S. domestic sugar program, Secretary of State Shultz warned Congress that further reductions in access to the U.S. sugar market will exacerbate foreign exchange and unemployment problems in the Caribbean Basin and other important countries and could even lead to political instability. The agricultural committees of the Congress, deferring to the U.S. domestic sugar lobby, ignored these warnings.

Those who make U.S. agricultural trade policy should realize that they have a large and growing interest in the economic success of the developing world. Agricultural markets in the well-fed industrial world are mature. Population growth is slow and trade barriers abound. An increasing share of U.S. commercial farm exports are thus being purchased by the developing world—up from 30 percent in 1976 to roughly 40 percent by 1986. It is the most rapidly developing Third World countries such as South Korea and Taiwan that make the largest purchases. Wherever incomes have gone up rapidly in the developing world, demand for a better diet has increased, and imports of U.S. farm products have increased as well. South Korea and Taiwan import more wheat and coarse grains every year—much of it for animal feed needed to increase meat production—than all of the larger and more numerous "hungry" nations of sub-Saharan Africa combined. Rapid and broad-based income growth in the developing world is the engine that now must be relied on to drive farm export growth. Without such income growth in the populous nations of the developing world, U.S. exports will remain stalled.

Regrettably, some U.S. farm interests do not want any of this needed income to come from success in the farm sector. They perceive any increase in agricultural production within the poor countries as a threat to their own export prospects. For several reasons this fear is misguided.

First, the poor countries as a whole have not yet shown any conclusive signs of suddenly increasing their own agricultural production. Between 1980 and 1985, according to the Food and Agriculture Organization of the UN, the volume index of agricultural production for all of the developing market economies (excluding China) increased less than 3 percent annually. This represents no significant change from their annual growth rate during the previous decade, the so-called food crisis decade from 1970–80 (United Nations Food and Agriculture Organization 1980: 78; 1985: 80).

It is true that the developing market economies did slow the growth of their farm imports at the start of the 1980s, but a local production surge was not the reason. The farm imports of the developing countries were being pulled down in the 1980s by a larger macroeconomic change, the sudden onset of a world recession, and a world debt crisis.[9]

It is often noted that both India and China made considerable farm production progress early in the 1980s and, as a consequence, were able to transform themselves from net importers (of wheat and corn, respectively) into small net exporters. Fortunately for the

United States, these two highly visible transformations were neither particularly significant in terms of the total trade involved nor were they representative of what was going on in the rest of the developing world. Among all the developing importing countries excluding China, self-sufficiency in wheat and coarse grains was continuing to decline, from a level of 86 percent in 1960 to 75 percent in 1985 (U.S. Department of Agriculture 1986).

Food self-sufficiency has been increasing mostly among the rich countries, where agriculture is subsidized instead of taxed, where populations have stopped growing rapidly, and where diets have little room to improve. In poor countries, and even in agriculturally successful poor countries, self-sufficiency continues to decline because diets have such vast room to improve.

In fact, when developing countries do learn to improve their own agricultural performance, one of the first things they do with the resulting income growth is to upgrade their diet—which can actually make them better customers for U.S. farm exports. This somewhat paradoxical tendency, for farm success in poor countries to be accompanied by larger rather than smaller farm imports, has recently been documented in a half dozen separate studies.[10]

CREATING THE PROPER ENVIRONMENT TO ENCOURAGE DOMESTIC FARM POLICY CHANGE

With so many international advantages—commercial, diplomatic, and humanitarian—to be gained from moving U.S. domestic agricultural policy in a more market-oriented direction, why has this movement been so difficult? Frustrated liberal reformers like to blame politically powerful domestic farm interests that naturally prefer their current commodity program benefits to the disciplines of the marketplace. Much more must be included in an explanation. Domestic political resistance to reform, which would be strong under the best of circumstances, has needlessly been strengthened in recent years by a sequence of macroeconomic fluctuations that were highly disruptive to the U.S. farm sector. Recall that loose U.S. monetary and fiscal policies in the 1970s first helped to send commodity prices and land values soaring. Then, just when the farm sector had gone heavily into debt in the expectation that these conditions would continue, the worst possible reversal occurred. Fiscal policy became even less disciplined—with the huge supply-side tax cuts of 1981—while monetary policy was simultaneously being tightened. Interest rates and dollar exchange rates soared and economic growth rates, exports, commodity prices, and farmland values suddenly fell.

It will be hard to persuade U.S. farmers to trust their future to the market as long as they see such poorly disciplined and poorly coordinated macroeconomic policies distorting and disrupting that market. Without improved macroeconomic policy discipline, it is understandable that liberal farm policy reform will be viewed suspiciously by farm interests. Out of necessity, we have focused here primarily on the helpful policy steps that might be taken within the relatively narrow farm sector, and especially on the advantages that can be gained from making U.S. farm policy more sensitive to market forces. In order to maximize those advantages, and in order to persuade suspicious U.S. domestic farm interests to take the risks needed to seize those advantages, important policy reforms will also have to be undertaken in the larger and increasingly important macroeconomic realm.

NOTES

1. For a statement of the general view that U.S. international economic interests are best pursued through domestic reform policies, see Nau (1984–85: 14–37).

2. For estimates of the precise magnitude of this price-firming influence of U.S. cereals policy, see IBRD (1986: Table 6.7, p. 129).

3. There was a provision in the 1981 farm bill that authorized the Secretary of Agriculture to lower loan levels by as much as 10 percent if prices during the preceding year averaged less than a fixed percentage of the loan rate. But this discretionary provision proved politically difficult for the Secretary to invoke in the "farm crisis" atmosphere of the early 1980s.

4. Sanderson argues that a bolder panel might have found enough negotiating history to support the selection of a three-year period immediately prior to the adoption of the Code as a basis for defining the EC's equitable share.

5. For a review of the equally dubious impact of this embargo on U.S. farm interests, see U.S. Department of Agriculture (1986).

6. The Soviet Union is not alone among the centrally planned economies in its failure to live up to the terms of bilateral farm trade agreements with the United States. In 1983, using as its excuse some admittedly protectionist U.S. textile trade restrictions, the People's Republic of China backed out of fulfilling its own minimum wheat purchase obligations under a 1980 U.S.–PRC bilateral agreement.

7. However, the United States plays this role to its own disadvantage when it acts (as in the early 1980s) to stabilize world prices at too high a level, a level that allows high-cost foreign producers to survive as competitors for U.S. agriculture over the long run.

8. In April 1986, through the use of a radical new marketing loan subsidy program, the United States suddenly and sharply reduced—by more than 20 percent—the price at which it was prepared to export rice. The resulting drop in world rice prices brought immediate and understandable complaints from more efficient developing country exporters, such as Thailand, which lost markets simply because they could not outspend the U.S. international cotton markets, where once again the most important competing producers are found among the poor countries of the developing world.

9. In fact, these same adverse macroeconomic conditions were pulling down the farm exports of the developing countries by even more than developed countries, so that the net farm trade balance of these countries actually diminished early in the 1980s, and fell into a rare deficit in 1981 and 1982.

10. See Robert L. Paarlberg, "United States Agriculture and the Developing World: Partners or Competitors?" Curry Foundation, Washington, D.C., 1986.

REFERENCES

Cargill Bulletin. 1984. (May): 5.

IBRD. 1986. *World Development Report 1986.* New York: Oxford University Press.

Johnson, D. Gale. 1986. "Broadening the Horizon." In *U.S. Agricultural Exports and Third World Development: The Critical Linkage.* An Agricultural Policy Study of the Curry Foundation, Conference Papers and Materials, Washington, D.C., July 14 and 15.

Journal of Commerce. 1986a. (August 7): 3A.

_____ . 1986b. (September 5): 16B.

Nau, Henry R. 1984-85. "Where Reaganomics Works." *Foreign Policy* 57 (Winter): 14-37.

Paarlberg, Robert L. 1985. *Food Trade and Foreign Policy.* Ithaca, N.Y.: Cornell University Press.

Sanderson, Fred H. 1986. "Statement to the Senate Subcommittee on Foreign Agriculture of the Committee on Agriculture." 99th Cong., 2nd Sess. (August 5).

United Nations Food and Agriculture Organization. 1980. *FAO Production Yearbook 1980.* New York: United Nations.

_____ . 1985. *FAO Production Yearbook 1985.* New York: United Nations.

U.S. Department of Agriculture. 1985. Foreign Agriculture Circular, FG-7-85. Washington, D.C.: Foreign Agricultural Service.

_____ . 1986. Foreign Agriculture Circular, FG-1-86. Washington, D.C.: Foreign Agricultural Service.

_____ . 1986a. "Agriculture Links to the National Economy." Washington, D.C.: Economic Research Service, Agriculture Information Bulletin No. 504.

_____ . 1986b. Foreign Agriculture Circular, FG-10-86. Washington, D.C.: Foreign Agricultural Service.

_____ . 1986c. Foreign Agriculture Circular, Grains, FG-12-86. Washington, D.C.: Foreign Agricultural Service.

_____ . 1986d. "Embargoes, Surplus Disposal, and U.S. Agriculture: A Summary." Washington, D.C.: Economic Research Service, Agricultural Information Bulletin No. 503.

INDEX

ABOUT THE EDITOR

John Yochelson is vice president for corporate affairs at the Center for Strategic and International Studies where, he directs programs on international trade, investment, and finance, including a policy research component and an international CEO group. Before joining CSIS, Mr. Yochelson served with the State Department's Bureau of Politico-Military Affairs. He has been a research fellow at Harvard University's Center for International Affairs and at The Brookings Institution. He has also been a consultant to the Joint Economic Committee of the U.S. Congress and has lectured at the French Council on Foreign Relations. His most recent publications include *Under Pressure: U.S. Industry and the World Economy* (Westview 1985) and *Breaking the Economic Impasse: An Urgent Quadrangular Agenda* (CSIS Significant Issues Series, 1987). Mr. Yochelson holds an M.P.A. degree from the Woodrow Wilson School, Princeton University.

ABOUT THE CONTRIBUTORS

Robert R. Bruce is a partner in the Washington, D.C. office of Debevoise & Plimpton. He was General Counsel of the Federal Communications Commission from 1977 to 1981. Mr. Bruce is the director of a study of telecommunications structures and is coauthor of a report on the first phase of that study: *From Telecommunications to Electronic Services: A Global Spectrum of Definitions, Boundary Lines and Structures* (International Institute of Communications, London, 1985).

Pat Choate is vice president for policy analysis at TRW Inc. He has been a fellow at the Battelle Memorial Institute's public policy arm, the Academy for Contemporary Problems. He has held a number of positions with the U.S. Department of Commerce and the state governments of Tennessee and Oklahoma. He is chairman of the Congressional Economic Leadership Institute and a board member of several public policy organizations. Mr. Choate's most recent book is *The High-Flex Society: Shaping America's Economic Future* (Alfred A. Knopf, 1986). He holds a Ph.D. in economics from the University of Oklahoma.

Irving S. Friedman has had over forty years of wide experience in international economics and finance. He has served in senior positions in the U.S. Treasury, International Monetary Fund, World Bank, Citibank, First Boston Corporation, and as a senior adviser to the African, Asian, and Inter-American Development Banks. He has

271

also been author, professor, lecturer, and leader in public affairs. Most recent among his books is *Toward World Prosperity: Reshaping the Global Money System* (Lexington Books, 1987). Dr. Friedman earned his Ph.D. from Columbia University.

Penelope Hartland-Thunberg is the William M. Scholl fellow in international business at the Center for Strategic and International Studies and has long been active in the field of international economics and foreign trade. She served on the senior staff of the Council of Economic Advisers, was a member of the Board of National Estimates, and was appointed by President Lyndon B. Johnson to the U.S. Tariff Commission, now the International Trade Commission. She has taught at Wells College, Mount Holyoke College, Brown University, and Georgetown University. She holds a Ph.D. from Radcliffe College. She is the author of numerous books, articles, and monographs, including: *Banks, Petrodollars, Sovereign Debtors: Blood from a Stone* (Lexington Books, 1985).

Gary C. Hufbauer is the Marcus Wallenberg Professor of International Financial Diplomacy at Georgetown University. A graduate of Harvard University, Dr. Hufbauer received his Ph.D. in economics from King's College in 1963 and his J.D. from Georgetown University Law School in 1980. Professor Hufbauer has had a distinguished career in academia, government, and the practice of law. From 1977 to 1980, he served as deputy assistant secretary of treasury. He has published eight books and numerous articles on subjects ranging from international finance and investment to international trade and tax policy.

Juyne Linger is a policy consultant specializing in economic development and demographic issues. She was formerly a policy analyst with TRW Inc., where she worked in the area of international trade and U.S. competitiveness. She has written numerous articles and is coauthor, with Pat Choate, of *The High-Flex Society: Shaping America's Economic Future.* A graduate of the Pennsylvania State University, Ms. Linger has held research positions with the National Council for Urban Economic Development, the American Institute of Planners, and Harvard University's Kennedy Institute of Politics.

Harald B. Malmgren, of Malmgren, Inc., is director of Malmgren, Golt, Kingston, & Co. He is also adjunct professor at Georgetown University, director of the Trade Policy Research Centre in London, editor of *The World Economy*, and author of the monthly *World*

Trade Outlook. In the 1960s and 1970s, Dr. Malmgren served in various official capacities in the Office of the U.S. Trade Representative and the Senate staff, becoming the deputy special representative for trade negotiations in 1972. He has a B.A. summa cum laude from Yale University and a Ph.D. in economics from Oxford University.

Stephen A. Merrill directs the Office of Government Affairs at the National Academy of Sciences/National Research Council and is an adjunct professor of international affairs at Georgetown University. He was principal consultant to the Academy's panel on international technology transfer, whose report, *Balancing the National Interest: National Security Export Controls and Global Economic Competition*, was released in January 1987. From 1982 to 1985, Mr. Merrill was a fellow in international business at CSIS, where he specialized in technology trade areas. He holds a Ph.D. in political science from Yale University.

Henry R. Nau is associate dean and professor of Political Science and International Affairs at the School of International Affairs, George Washington University. He was a senior staff member of the National Security Council and has taught at Williams College, The Johns Hopkins School of Advanced International Studies, Stanford University, and Columbia University. He holds a B.S. degree in economics, politics, and science from the Massachusetts Institute of Technology and M.A. and Ph.D. degrees in International Relations from The Johns Hopkins University's School of Advanced International Studies. He has written *Technology Transfer and U.S. Foreign Policy* (Praeger, 1976), as well as several articles and books.

Robert L. Paarlberg is associate professor of political science at Wellesley College and an associate at the Harvard Center for International Affairs. He received his B.A. from Carlton College and his Ph.D. in international relations from Harvard University. He has conducted research on international food and agricultural policy and has written several books on the subject. His most recent book is *Fixing Farm Trade: Policy Options for the United States* (Ballinger, 1988).

Ernest H. Preeg is chief economist and deputy assistant administrator of the Agency for International Development (AID). He has held various posts during his long tenure as a State Department foreign service officer including senior economic adviser for the Philippines, ambassador to Haiti, and deputy assistant secretary for international finance and development. He holds a Ph.D. degree in economics from the New School for Social Research. He is author of *Hard Bargaining Ahead: U.S. Trade Policy and Developing Countries* (Overseas Development Council, 1985) and other publications on foreign policy and international economics.

Jeffrey J. Schott is a research associate at the Institute of International Economics. He was formerly a senior associate at the Carnegie Endowment for International Peace. He is coauthor with Gary Hufbauer of *Economic Sanctions Reconsidered* (Institute of International Economics, 1985).

Alan Stoga is senior associate with Kissinger Associates. He was formerly vice president and head of the Country Risk Management Division at the First National Bank of Chicago. He has recently served as a consultant to the Agency for International Development. Mr. Stoga received an M.A. degree in international relations from Yale University. His articles have appeared in major newspapers and he has contributed to many essay collections on international economic and financial issues.

Lawrence Veit is manager and international economist of Brown Brothers, Harriman and Co. He has served in the U.S. Treasury and the State Department. Mr. Veit received an M.A. degree from the New School for Social Research. He has written extensively on the world economy, the international financial system, and economic development. His books include: *Economic Adjustment to an Energy Short World* (Atlantic Institute for International Affairs, 1979).

Cynthia Day Wallace is a senior fellow at the Center for Strategic and International Studies. She was formerly a fellow at the Mac-Planck Institute of International Law in Heidelberg specializing in foreign direct investment and has held U.N. posts in Vienna, Geneva, and New York. Dr. Wallace chairs the American Bar Association Subcommittee on International Codes and Guidelines for Multinational Corporations. She holds a Ph.D. in international law from Cambridge University. Her latest book is *Foreign Direct Investment and the Multinational Enterprise: A Topical Bibliography* (Nijhoff, 1988). Her articles have appeared in publications dealing with international law and investment.